The Phenoı
of Modern Art

Also available from Continuum:

Deleuze and the Schizoanalysis of Cinema
Edited by Patricia MacCormack and Ian Buchanan

Gilles Deleuze: Image and Text
Edited by Daniel W. Smith, Charles J. Stivale and
    Eugene W. Holland

Foucault's Philosophy of Art
Joseph J. Tanke

Seeing the Invisible
Michel Henry, Translated by Scott Davidson

Forthcoming:

Deleuze and Art
Anne Sauvagnargues, Translated by Samantha Bankston and
    Robert King

The Phenomenology of Modern Art
Exploding Deleuze, Illuminating Style

Paul Crowther

continuum

Continuum International Publishing Group
The Tower Building   80 Maiden Lane
11 York Road   Suite 704
London SE1 7NX   New York NY 10038

www.continuumbooks.com

British Library Cataloguing-in-Publication Data
A catalogue record for this book is available from the British Library.

ISBN: HB: 978-1-4411-3091-4
     PB: 978-1-4411-4258-0

Library of Congress Cataloguing-in-Publication Data
  Crowther, Paul.
  The phenomenology of modern art : exploding Deleuze, illuminating style / Paul Crowther. – First [edition].
    pages cm
  Includes bibliographical references and index.
  ISBN 978-1-4411-4258-0 (pbk. : alk. paper) – ISBN 978-1-4411-3091-4 (hardcover : alk. paper) – ISBN 978-1-4411-3607-7 (ebook epub : alk. paper) – ISBN 978-1-4411-1506-5 (ebook pdf : alk. paper)
  1. Art, Modern–20th century. 2. Deleuze, Gilles, 1925-1995. 3. Phenomenology. I. Title.
  N6490.C765 2012
  709.04001–dc23

                   2011050251

Typeset by Newgen Imaging Systems Pvt Ltd, Chennai, India
Printed and bound in India

Contents

vi   *Contents*

List of Illustrations

Colour versions of illustrations 1, 4, 10, 17 and 18 can be found on the plate section in the centre of this book.

Acknowledgements

Chapter Seven was published under the same title in the *British Journal of Aesthetics*, Vol. 25, 1985, pp. 317–25. It is the only chapter which is presented with few modifications from the original publication. The remaining chapters are either dedicated new material, or contain some extracts from previous publications (deployed within much larger structures of argument written for this book, expressly). More specifically, Chapter Two is a revised and extended version of 'Origins of Modernism, Destinies of the Avant-Garde' published in *Perspectives on Aesthetics, Art, and Culture*: Essays in Honour of Las-Olof Ahlberg, Thales, Stockholm, 2005, pp. 81–92; Chapter Three is a heavily revised and much extended version of 'Nietzsche to Neo-Expressionism; the Case of Baselitz', published in *Art and Design*, March 1990, pp. 77–83; Chapter Four incorporates material from Part One of 'Post-Analytic Phenomenology of Painting and Beyond', *Aesthetic Pathways*, Vol. 1, No. 1, 2010, pp. 77–96; Chapter Five incorporates significantly revised and extended versions of Parts One and Two of 'Cubism, Kant and Ideology', from *Word and Image*, Vol. 3, No. 2, 1987, pp. 195–201. Part Two of Chapter Six is a revised version of my short review of Thierry de Duve's *Kant After Duchamp*, published in the *British Journal of Aesthetics*, Vol. 37, No. 4, pp. 410–12, 1997; Chapter Nine contains an extract from 'Meaning in Abstract Art: From *Ur*-Nature to the Transperceptual' included in P. Crowther and I. Wunsche (eds), *Meanings of Abstract Art: Between Nature and Theory*, Routledge Advances in Visual Studies, 2012. Thanks are due to Desislava Parashkevova for her assistance in preparing this book.

Introduction

The Interpretation of Modern Art

The age of modern art is generally accepted as beginning, mainly, with Manet and the impressionist painters of the late nineteenth century. Thereafter its figurative idioms develop in complex ways – most notably in various forms of expressionism distributed across the entire twentieth century.

Other main trajectories lead from Cezanne's figuration to cubism (with complex offshoots from the latter), and to Duchampian conceptualism. The final major trajectory is that of abstraction – whose origins and development relate importantly to all the other idioms I have mentioned. And while one can reasonably talk of 'postmodern' developments, these often involve refinements of, or critical reflections upon, modernist innovations.

The present work addresses these basic features of modern art on the basis of *style* as a bearer of aesthetic meaning. An approach of this kind may arouse immediate suspicion – insofar as 'style' is a term much associated with an elitist connoisseurship. But this association is empirical rather than conceptual. In fact, it is possible to offer a conceptual recovery of style – as the individual way in which an artist represents the world. This centres on such things as his or her way of handling paint, choice of colours and kinds of subject matter, and overall compositional strategies.

What is at issue, here, is more than questions of harmonies of shape and colour, or purely technical issues. Rather, *style is a way of visually disclosing attitudes towards aspects of the world (including social factors) and which engages, indeed, with some of the deepest aspects of human experience.* Style in this sense, in other words, is not just the way a picture looks. It embodies a way of acting upon the world, through painting or sculpture, that changes the character of the subject matter being addressed. This brings about a change (however slight) in the scope of the medium involved.

To attend to style on these terms, is, to investigate the way in which it brings about *fundamental changes between subject and object of experience at the level of visible things.* There is a philosophical meaning inherent to style, that is given a distinctive aesthetic character by virtue of being inseparable from the visual idioms through which it is realized.

The conceptual content of a philosophical text can be grasped in basic terms through reading it, through someone else's exposition of it, or through an edited version of a text. In painting, however, a style can favour a way of looking at the world and privilege certain kinds of spatio-temporal structures and values. *But it does not say these, it shows them – through what is distinctive about the way the artist's style presents itself to the senses.*

This means that it is *aesthetic disclosure* rather than discursive exposition. The meaning of style emerges only through direct visual perception of the work. It is an invitation to 'see like this'. And whether the disclosure is worthwhile or not depends not only on how a painting's style reveals its character and content to immediate perception, but also on how its relation to other styles and cultural expectations accentuates or inhibits the disclosure.

Of course, while artists have their individual distinctive styles these are never created ex nihilo. The artist inherits idioms opened up by others and works within them or transforms them. There will be many shared characteristics – characteristics that enable us to talk of style in the more general sense of a *tendency*.

If our approach to this is qualified carefully enough, it will be possible to decide what is at issue in the basic stylistic tendencies of modern art without treating them in essentialist terms. Indeed, it is the more general notion of style that allows us to identify important philosophical shifts in how such art discloses the world – shifts that range beyond mere individual distinctiveness. In this work, accordingly, I shall investigate individual style in the context of more general stylistic tendency. The question arises, then, as to what philosophical method will best facilitate such an investigation.

Analytic approaches have paid little sustained attention to the historical forms of visual art except as a source of examples for more general theories of pictorial representation.[1] An exception to this is the late Richard Wollheim's work. He is one of the few philosophers to address painting's visible character in systematic terms. Unfortunately, as I will show at length elsewhere, his treatment of the topic is much too narrow in focus, and places the burden of aesthetic disclosure on a problematic treatment of 'expression'.[2]

In terms of continental philosophy, much interest has been shown in visual images by the likes of Jacques Ranciere, Jean-Luc Nancy, Jean-Francois Lyotard, and Gilles Deleuze.[3] However, with the magnificent exception of Deleuze (who is a major focus of the present work) their interest in the image is mainly in terms of broader societal and cultural implications, rather than what style (expressed through specific basic tendencies and individuals) discloses in relation to more concrete human experience.

Indeed, these thinkers offer surprisingly few sustained discussions of specific paintings in terms of their detailed phenomenal structure. As far as I can see, the only philosophical approach that can do justice to painting in terms of visuality and style is *phenomenology*.

A phenomenological approach addresses the artwork *as* a stylistic phenomenon, that is, *as created and experienced visually*, rather than reduced to some 'position' within bodies of aesthetic belief, or broader sociocultural discourses. Of course, this does not amount to a raw, unmediated perception. All our experience – even when based on intuitive recognition – is orientated by established expectations and practices. A phenomenological investigation might – in Husserlian vein – strive for some supposedly unmediated description of the essence of our experience of modern art, but such a method would not, on its own, get us very far.

In order to negotiate the work *as* art, and as a particular kind of art, *knowledge of how visual art transforms experience* must guide our phenomenology, otherwise – while engaging with aesthetic form – it would not be able to negotiate the deeper, and specifically artistic and historical dimensions of style. The problem is exacerbated in the case of modern art – whose tendencies often have a visual complexity that requires a very different cognitive orientation than those which are standard to conventional figuration.

Given these considerations, the question arises as to which phenomenological approaches are suited best to the demands of modern art? In this, it is important that the method is both adapted to the object, and able to elucidate its nature in detailed ways.

Now, whatever else modern painting might involve, discussions of it often emphasize one or other of a group of four prominent stylistic tendencies. These are so broad individually (and, of course, collectively) that to regard them as an 'essence' of modern art is to say nothing very useful. Their real interest lies in how they apply in specific artistic cases, and in the broader aesthetic and/or societal significance that they embody.

The tendencies in question are as follows:

(1) The overcoming or abandonment of traditional academic notions of ideal form, 'finish', and skill in terms of the application of paint, and compositional criteria. This overcoming is intended, often, to achieve some perceptually more direct or emotionally more authentic communication with the viewer. A radical variation on this is the willingness

to compose and create works of art (or criticize art) using artefacts of non-artistic origin, that were made by persons other than the artist.

(2) An emphasis on subject matter that is not constrained by traditional criteria of artistic and moral propriety. In terms of overcoming artistic propriety, this involves mainly the abandonment of such things as classical or biblical subject matter, and its replacement with scenes from everyday domestic and public life – especially scenes based on the dynamics of city living, and/or images based on the machines and mechanical power of modern society's technological infrastructure. In terms of overcoming moral propriety, subjects adopted are often provocative and/or explicit in their treatment of sexual material, or emotionally disturbing content. They can also challenge through extreme methods of handling the medium, or through using controversial physical materials.

(3) The embodiment of new pictorial codes that represent through partially, or entirely, adopting non-figurative means, and which extend, correspondingly, the kinds of perceptual relation that can be expressed directly through visual art.

(4) An insistently *planar* emphasis (with a correlated diminution or elimination of perspectival accents). Even when modern works have a strong figurative content, they tend, nevertheless, to *look* flatter than works which present such content through conventional perspectival means. *All* visual representation can be argued to involve planar structure to some degree, but modernist works declare it more directly – as a feature of style. (With some artists, this may arise only as a by-product of features (1), (2), and (3); with others, it may be an effect explicitly intended.)

It should be emphasized that there are obvious areas of overlap between these four features, and how they apply can be determined only by direct reference to the visual appearance of the specific work under consideration.

Indeed, a work does not have to be describable in terms of *all* these aspects in order to count as modern (though there are instances of such overlaps). But, if it was produced after about 1860, and can be described in terms of one of, or some combination of, these general stylistic features, then it is either a work of modern art or one created within the stylistic institutions established by such art.

In the broadest terms, points (1) and (2) are especially appropriate to impressionism, the various 'Post-Impressionists' and the fauves, various expressionist artists, and Duchamp and Dadaism, and surrealism. Indeed, it is in the varieties of expressionism, and through Duchamp and his legacy, that features (1) and (2) are explored in the most unqualified terms. The present work, accordingly, will pay special attention to these.

Features (3) and (4) are emphasized with particular strength in Cezanne, cubism, and the various idioms of partially or wholly *abstract art*. However, the character of this emphasis is extremely complex and variable, so it is necessary to address Cezanne, Braque, and Picasso's cubism, and the meaning of abstract art, in close individual terms, in order to understand the ramifications of how features (3) and (4) are embodied in them.

Given these main stylistic features of modern art, and a selection of their exemplars, I would suggest that they are most amenable to phenomenological investigation on the basis of ideas from Deleuze, Nietzsche, and Merleau-Ponty. This selection needs to be explained in terms of its omissions and inclusions.

First, I omit Heidegger – even though he does discuss some modern artists, such as Van Gogh. The problem with Heidegger is that his treatment of that artist's work, and other moderns, tends to negotiate them in the same broad terms as Greek temples – as a disclosure of the truth of Being. But while Van Gogh may, indeed, be describable in such terms, the *distinctively modern* aspects of his style – especially the four major features that I have identified – need to be done justice to. Heidegger, however, provides no clear means to this.[4]

I omit, also, discussion of Michel Henry's study of Kandinsky[5] and Jean-Luc Marion's *Crossing the Visible*.[6] Henry's book addresses a pivotal modern artist in detail, but in a discussion that is orientated mainly towards the spiritual implications of Kandinsky's *writings* about art, and which touches on how these theories are embodied in specific works by the artist only in passing. Marion's short book, in contrast, offers some very interesting discussions of individual modern artworks, but his central conceptual-pairing – between the visible and the unseen – is dealt with in far more comprehensive terms by Merleau-Ponty (who I shall come to a little further on).

Oddly enough, it is Gilles Deleuze who can provide us with a more useful contemporary phenomenological orientation. He did not describe himself as a phenomenologist, and is, at times, extremely wary of phenomenology as a philosophical method.[7] Indeed, Deleuze has found a wide audience attracted by the anarchical and, at time, extremely oracular character of his writings.

It is, perhaps, the *penchant* for this that has deflected Deleuze's readers from some extraordinary reversals that take place in his discussion of Francis Bacon and modern painting. Here his thinking is constrained by attentiveness to the *demands* of his object of study. In fact, his is by far the most original, searching, and ambitious *phenomenology* of painting to be formulated since Merleau-Ponty's decisive essay 'Eye and Mind', of 1961.

In particular, Deleuze is the only theorist to pay sustained phenomenological attention to all four of the commonly accepted criteria of modern artistic style described earlier. His explorations of these, accordingly, make him a logical starting point for the present investigation.

However, I shall not merely apply Deleuze's insights. There is an already well-established tendency to apply his ideas to the visual arts in a way that is largely uncritical of the ideas themselves.[8] He tends to be treated as an *authority*. This has the effect of deflecting the reader not only from Deleuze's phenomenological turn, but also from an *astonishingly* rigid set of hierarchies and essentializing factors that distort the brilliant aspects of this turn (and which are found in both his discussion of Bacon and his more general theory of painting).

These features have not been identified previously because we have no reason to look for such things in a thinker like Deleuze. Our attention tends to be absorbed, rather, by his work's anarchical and oracular aspects. To do justice to the phenomenological dimension, accordingly, a sustained and critical analysis of Deleuze's arguments is demanded.

My initial strategy, therefore, will be to explain Deleuze's position in great detail, and then explode the unwarranted rigidities in it, so that his worthwhile insights are scattered free, and made available for non-hierarchical phenomenological use throughout this book. Indeed, by challenging the Deleuzian hierarchies, I will indicate further trajectories – based on the meaning of style – which require other phenomenological insights in order to be developed.

Nietzsche will be one source of these. Like Deleuze, he is attentive to art's phenomenal presence, in a way that few other thinkers are. His insights can be developed so as to illuminate the phenomenological sensuousness and directness of representation found in modern art – constellating, as it does, around the overcoming of 'finish' and constraints on subject matter (and, indeed, the idea of visual art as a basis for more authentic communication between humans).

And while Nietzsche himself may well have had the greatest reservations about art having this character in manifest terms, it is in the direction of the sensuously direct that his theory of art, and, indeed, *the very style of his own writing*, pushes. It has, in particular, a close kinship with the varieties of expressionism – both figurative and abstract.

Merleau-Ponty is even more decisive. His ideas are of particular relevance to modern art's development of new pictorial codes and ranges of perceptual effect – arising from the abandonment of conventional perspective. He tells us, in fact, that 'The entire history of painting in the modern period, with its efforts to detach itself from illusionism and acquire its own dimensions, has a metaphysical significance.'[9]

It is significant, also, that Merleau-Ponty (like Deleuze) assigns a special importance to Cezanne – who, as we shall see, is central to the consolidation of modern art through his planar emphasis, his challenging of accepted notions of finish, and his complex extension of painting's perceptual scope.

This being said, the critical development of ideas from Deleuze, Nietzsche, and Merleau-Ponty is not, in itself a sufficient basis for a phenomenology of modern art. It will provide us with starting points that must be developed more fully through concrete analyses of specific works.

Indeed, in the course of this, tensions within Nietzsche's and Merleau-Ponty's theories (as well as Deleuze's) will have to be dealt with. There is also a second important argumentative axis to my book. A phenomenology of modern art cannot be satisfied with a descriptive emphasis alone. For there have been other attempts to explain modern art's general stylistic features on the basis of philosophical models – most notably that of Kant's thought.

In many previous works,[10] I have defended and upgraded ideas from Kant in the aesthetic context, but in relation to understanding the stylistic features of modern art, Kantian references have been a source of persistent confusion. A phenomenological approach, in consequence, can *reinforce* itself by showing the limitations of such alternative philosophical models. And the reinforcement is all the more compelling, when the critique can makes use of the phenomenological investigation of specific works, or idioms of aesthetic experience.

I will, accordingly, in the middle chapters of my book, offer a sustained critique of supposed Kantian criteria of modern art, through arguments and examples based on my own general phenomenological method.[11]

This orientation has a quite specific character. It is a *post-analytic phenomenology*. An approach of this kind is not content to simply relate a few attractive insights from selected thinkers to selected modern works. Rather, it relates theory to modern artistic practice through a sustained *analysis* of the relevant thinker's ideas. Equally important, it is willing to engage critically with those ideas – to show their scope and limits – and, to *develop* them in a more viable form, or offer alternatives to them. It should be emphasized that a strategy of this kind, is not a mere lecture-room type introduction to the relevant thinker or topic. Phenomenology must acknowledge that thought itself requires its own phenomenology, based on how its discursive/ argumentative forms develop and articulate the object of thought.

In the age of global consumerism, it is all too easy to simply *consume* ideas – to pluck a few interesting notions which are obscure or problematic, and put them to use without reflecting upon their exact meaning and consistency. However, if one wishes to resist such easy consumerism, it is vital to subject the relevant ideas to critical reflection, so that the meaning of what is being said, and its philosophical viability, can be done justice to.

Without such reflection, the thinkers addressed are treated as mere authorities. Even worse, they are *abused*, insofar as what are, in many cases, carefully constructed progressions of thought, are *reduced* to a few putatively attractive salient features. Indeed, even if such thinkers are plundered for bits of apparent 'oppositional' content, the consumerist manner of the plundering is an idiom which actively contradicts such content.

There is another advantage to a post-analytic phenomenology. By thinking through the relevant thinkers' ideas in great detail, and testing them in relation to their chosen objects of investigation, those objects are kept more clearly in view. This is, of course, especially important when the object being addressed is visual art – with all its aesthetic and historical specificity. Through being attentive to post-analytic considerations, in other words, phenomenology can be *renewed* as a means of engaging philosophically with the structure of artistic phenomena.

Preliminaries aside, the book is organized, more specifically, as follows: Chapter One expounds the details of Deleuze's analysis of Francis Bacon and modern painting, at great length. It argues that Deleuze's essentialist and hierarchical approach, and 'grand narrative' of modern painting is extremely problematic, but points ahead in fruitful directions. Indeed, it is exemplary in its insistent attentiveness to painting as both visual phenomenon and physical medium.

In Chapter Two, an alternative account of the origins of modernism and the avant-garde in the visual arts is proposed. The analysis converges on the notion of *ontological reciprocity* (a concept I derive from Merleau-Ponty, mainly) as a factor whose historical transformation in visual art is profoundly implicated in the rise of visual modernism from impressionism onwards, and especially the four major stylistic features which I identified earlier.

Chapters Three and Four employ phenomenological insights to address the stylistic meaning of specific painters or artistic tendencies. In this respect, Chapter Three outlines Nietzsche's philosophy of art as found (primarily) in the notes contained in *The Will to Power*. It is argued that this philosophy is highly amenable to the ratification of such features as the overcoming of 'finish' and the constraints of aesthetic and moral propriety. I then consider how the theory illuminates those recurrent idioms of modern art called 'Expressionism'.

In Chapter Four Merleau-Ponty's general theory of painting is introduced and explained. The special importance that it assigns to Cezanne is then investigated. I show, however, that the perceptual effects he ascribes to Cezanne can only be justified as a development of one of the four stylistic features of modern art that his account does not do justice to – namely the emphasis on planarity.

The arguments in Chapter Five centre on the interpretation of cubism. Here, I introduce a discussion of Kantian criteria for understanding this tendency, and, on the basis of both analysis, and a phenomenology of specific cubist works (by Braque and Picasso) show the general inappropriateness of such criteria.

I go on to consider why the Kantian approach has been so influential, and then to broach some more general principles for the interpretation of visual art.

Chapter Six continues the critique of Kantianism, but in an unusual way. I begin by noting the significance of Duchamp – an artist whose importance is conceptual – as the creator of works whose main elements were not physically created by himself. This seems either to eliminate the notion of style, or to displace it to the realm of choice and conceptualization, alone. The meaning of Duchamp's choices, and the relevance of Kantian ideas in this context, are then explored through Deleuze's distinction between analogical and digital coding, and a critique of Thierry de Duve's book *Kant after Duchamp*.

In Chapter Seven, I continue my critique of Kantian analyses of modern art by offering a detailed analysis of Clement Greenberg's attempts to explain the planar emphasis of modern art, on the basis of a supposed Kantian 'infra-logic'. I argue that, among other factors, Greenberg does not do justice to the significance of individual style.

Having negotiated, critically, the alternative Kantian approach to modern art, I return in my last chapters to the phenomenology of style, as such. Specifically, I address a complex tendency that arises from all the tendencies and individuals considered earlier, and which is unique to modern art, namely abstraction.

As a starting point for this, in Chapter Eight, I look again at Deleuze's theory of painting, and the ontological basis of the distinction between 'abstraction' and '*art informel*' which, for him, is fundamental to abstract art. I criticize Deleuze's continuing unwarranted hierarchies and essentialism, but extract from these, an important clue to the meaning of abstract art, as such.

This clue is explored in Chapter Nine, through a very extensive development of ideas from Hans Hofmann and Merleau-Ponty. The theory of modern art so developed, is one that does justice to what is distinctive about the meaning of abstract works, *qua* abstract. I end with a few remarks concerning the trajectory of this book, as a whole.

It should be emphasized, that I am not attempting to offer a comprehensive survey account of all modern art. Rather, I am addressing those general tendencies and individuals whose innovations have had the most radical structural repercussions.

Chapter One

Releasing Style from Sensation: Deleuze, Francis Bacon and Modern Painting

Introduction

The great merit of Deleuze's approach is that it is phenomenological in an important fourfold sense. It attempts to integrate closely, the ontological structures of painting *qua* painting, perception of these structures, our affective response to them, and the way in which painting focuses these aspects in its historical development.

In his study of Bacon, Deleuze frequently notes phenomenology's explanatory restrictiveness.[1] However, the fourfold emphasis just described is one that gives his approach a phenomenological authority in relation to modern painting, irrespective of his reservations concerning phenomenology as a method.

Now, while Deleuze's interpretation of Bacon and theory of modern painting is extremely rich, it also contains a great deal of material that is used in an essentialist and hierarchical way, without the appropriate justification. Indeed, this relates to various other grey areas in his theory, and to suspicions concerning how far his general theory is, in effect, a disguised teleology designed to present the achievements of Cezanne and Bacon as its great outcome.

Generally speaking, Deleuze's philosophy of painting is a kind of phenomenology *in denial*. The real potential of his ideas emerges only if the denial is exploded, and his ideas developed more critically.

In this chapter, therefore, Part One will expound the key features of Deleuze's analysis of Francis Bacon. Part Two will consider the general theory of painting and the privileging of modern work that he formulates on the basis of his approach to Bacon. Part Three addresses in detail Deleuze's complex notion of sensation – a notion that is foregrounded, especially, in his advocacy of colourism. In Part Four, the essentialist and partial character of Deleuze's theories will be identified and criticized at length. The Conclusion will extract the very important and valid insights that would otherwise be lost in Deleuze's denial of phenomenology.

Part One

For Deleuze, 'The task of painting is defined as the attempt to render visible forces that are not themselves visible'.[2] In relation to Bacon, this takes a specific form: The human figure dominates his *oeuvre*, and is presented as a focus of physical forces that are made visible through their effects on the body. In his work, flesh appears 'shaken' – as something *descended* from the bones. The face gives way to the head.

It is argued by Deleuze that the apparent violence of Bacon's images is not due to their content, but rather, to considerations of 'sensation', that gravitate around issues of colour, line, and expression. Bacon's 'Figures', indeed, are not tortured and wracked bodies, but ordinary ones, presented under conditions of constraint and discomfort – as visible things subjected to the effects of different forces.

Deleuze capitalizes 'Figure' in relation to Bacon and other major artists, because it is the first key structural feature of painting. It should be emphasized, however, that it involves more than the factors just described. Of equal importance is the Figure's relation to a second pictorial structure, consisting of a ground from which the Figure appears to detach itself.

In Bacon's work, this 'material structure' (as Deleuze terms it, most frequently) consists of large fields of colour presented in a shallow, 'post-cubist' depth. These areas are themselves divided into sections, or traversed by tubes or thin rails, or sliced by a band or largish stripe. They form, in effect, an 'armature' or 'bone structure'.[3]

Figure and material structure in Bacon draw life from one another. As Deleuze puts it, 'But if these fields of color press toward the Figure, the Figure in turn presses outward, trying to pass and dissolve through the fields.'[4] For Deleuze, Bacon continues and develops a break with figuration that is actually based on elevating the Figure into prominence while maintaining a sense of the ground as the matrix from which the colour articulation of the Figure emerges. This is anticipated in Michelangelo, but is manifest, especially, in key moderns such as Van Gogh, and Gauguin, and more fully in Cezanne. Bacon, however, expresses the relation in a highly distinctive way that cannot be identified with any 'ism'.

In respect of this, we are told that,

It is the confrontation of the figure and the field, their solitary wrestling in *shallow depth*, that rips the painting away from all narrative but also from all symbolization. When narrative or symbolic, figuration obtains only the bogus violence of the represented or the signified; it expresses none of the violence of sensation – in other words, of the act of painting.[5]

This non-narrative aspect of painting is accompanied by a third pictorial structure that is extremely characteristic of Bacon. Deleuze calls it the 'contour'. It consists of round or oval areas – within the painting's edges, or even seeming to continue beyond it. These delimit the figure through an 'operative field' where the figure is explored 'upon itself' or even within this 'place'.[6] It is a zone of reciprocal visual exchange between the Figure and the material structure. These three key structural features are mediated and merged by two more specific formal devices of special significance to Bacon.

The first of these is what Deleuze calls the 'diagram' – a notion that is (as we shall see in much more detail later on) of great import for painting as such, but which Bacon uses, again, in a highly distinctive way. It consists of 'local scrubbing' – where paint is brushed or rubbed across an area, and 'asignifying traits' – free marks that appear to have no reference to figurative function (and which, of course, are one of the effects of local scrubbing).

The other merging device involves what Deleuze calls 'attendants'. The role of these forms – be they human or simulacra (such as photographs hung on a wall or railing) – is to not to be an internal spectator for the Figure, but to act as a reference point for the colour variations through which the Figure is achieved. The attendants help integrate Figure and field in strictly visual terms (and are important, especially, for the many Bacon triptychs).

It is the relation between the three structural features and the two key mediating factors which explains, further, why Deleuze capitalizes the term 'Figure' when discussing Bacon and other artists. The Figure is not some symbolic feature – a mere 'figure' represented against a ground. Rather it is a visual feature or 'trait' achieved through colour articulation of the ground – an articulation that suspends our simple narrative sense of what is represented, in favour of extreme attentiveness to *how* it is represented. As Deleuze puts it, 'Painting has to extract the Figure from the figurative.'[7]

Given these points, it is worth focusing, now, on Deleuze's more detailed consideration of Bacon's treatment of the body as Figure. A key concept used is that of 'deformation'. Deleuze claims that,

What makes deformation a destiny is that the body has a necessary relation with the material structure: not only does the material structure curl around it, but the body must return to

the material structure and dissipate into it, thereby passing
through or into . . . prostheses, instruments, [e.g. umbrellas]
which constitute passages and states that are real, physical,
and effective, and which are sensations and not imaginings.[8]

At the heart of this deformation is painting's attempt to make
the invisible forces that determine the body's character and
configuration, present to vision. These forces include time,
pressure, inertia, weight, attraction, gravitation, germination.[9]

Deleuze suggests that the expression of these involves deformation rather than transformation, because while the latter
can be dynamic, the former is always bodily and static and happens at one place. Examples of this are offered.

for both Bacon and Cezanne, the deformation is obtained
in the Form at rest; and at the same time, the whole material
environment, the structure, begins to stir: 'walls twitch and
slide, chairs bend or rear up a little, cloths curl like burning
paper. . .' [quoting D. H. Lawrence.] Everything is now related
to forces, everything is force. It is force that constitutes deformation as an act of painting: it lends itself neither to a transformation of form, nor to a decomposition of elements.[10]

In terms of this we might consider Bacon's *Four Studies for a Self-
Portrait* of 1967. Here any suggestion of movement or process
is derived not from motion itself, but from forces of dilation,
contraction, flattening, and elongation. This achieves a kind of
'dismantling' of the face (Deleuze's own term) through which
the character of the *head* is made visible. However, the dismantling is not a visual analysis, but one arising from the face
subjected to pressures. Indeed, (though Deleuze himself does
not say this, explicitly) the smeared areas of local scrubbing
around the mouths exemplify both a material deformation of
the painted surface and, through this action by the painter,
the suggestion of forces that would distend a face by impacting
upon it.

Of equal importance, is force exerted outwards by the body itself. This involves one of the most imaginative features of Deleuze's reading of Bacon. It interprets the painter as rendering visible the body's attempt to *escape* from itself – using one of its organs to rejoin the field or material structure. In the *Figure at a Washbasin* of 1976 (Museo de Arte Contemporaneo, Caracas), for example, 'the body-Figure exerts an intense motionless effort on itself in order to escape down the blackness of the drain'.[11] Here, Deleuze claims that the round shape of the washbasin bowl is a 'place' – a replication of the 'contour'. However, it is not the material structure of the painting that curls round the contour, so as to envelop the Figure, rather the visual thrust of the Figure is one that appears intent on pressing – mouth first – through the bowl into some darker, narrower depth, leading back into the material structure. And, in this, the figure's own shadow seems to be a co-conspirator, in that it too appears to be detaching itself from the body.

The body's striving to escape from itself is more than just a feature of how Bacon's Figures appear. It is an expression of something of more general significance, namely 'the body without organs'. This term is derived from Artaud, and is used in much of Deleuze's previous work (albeit with very different emphases).[12] In the present context, Deleuze stresses that it subverts the notion of 'organism' and characterizes the limit of the lived body. Here are some of his descriptions of it:

> The body without organs is opposed less to organs than to that organization of organs we call an organism. It is an intense and intensive body. It is traversed by a wave that traces waves or thresholds in the body according to the variation of amplitude.[13]

> the body without organs is flesh and nerve; a wave flows through it and traces levels upon it; a sensation is produced when the wave encounters the forces acting on the body . . .[14]

It is a whole nonorganic life, for the organism is not life, it is what imprisons life. The body is completely living, yet nonorganic.[15]

These extremely cryptic remarks might be made sense of as follows. The human animal has a body sense that hinges on sensations, potential acts, and states, which – even if they are based on the activity of a specific organ (such as the mouth) at a specific time – nevertheless give way, subsequently, to the acts of other organs, and their relevant sensation.

Indeed, what is at issue here is not the phenomenological unity of the body as a unified sensori-motor cognitive field, rather it is a sense of life that is immanent to the cognitive functions that grow around it. The body without organs is the flow, and projected flow of sensation, that can be known through the different levels of intensity, that its various shifts and motions occasion, or might occasion.

In this, sensation is registered through specific organs, but is not tied to any one of them except temporarily. It is this shifting, transitional nature of (as it were) organ assignment, that leads Deleuze to suggest that the body without organs is sometimes felt as an 'indeterminate polyvalent organ'.[16]

This provides the key link to painting. We are told that painting,

> invests the eye through color and line. But it does not treat the eye as a fixed organ. It liberates lines and colours from their representative function, but at the same time it also liberates the eye from its adherence to the organism, from its character as a fixed and qualified organ: the eye becomes virtually the polyvalent indeterminate organ that sees the body without organs (the Figure) as a pure presence.[17]

Deleuze is led, thus, to a 'double definition of painting'. Subjectively speaking, painting frees the eye to wander from its organic constraints so as to explore and capture invisible forces that determine the visible.

Objectively speaking, it presents the reality of a body, in lines and colours that are released from 'organic' representation (i.e. merely symbolic or narrative meaning). And the relation here is a reciprocal one. The polyvalent eye and reality of the body emerge through their action on one another.[18]

Deleuze also makes some difficult links between the body without organs, and the relation between Bacon's painting and time. He suggests that the fact that this body involves temporary organ assignment, allows Bacon's work to express time, indeed, to paint time itself.

The point is illustrated by reference to Bacon's *Three Studies of the Male Back*, 1970 (see Plate 1, Kunsthaus, Zurich).

In relation to this work, Deleuze tells us that,

The variation of texture and color on a body, a head, or a back . . . is actually a temporal variation regulated down to the tenth of a second. Hence the chromatic treatment of the body, which is very different from the treatment of the fields of color: the chronochromatism of the body is opposed to the monochromaticism of the flat fields. To put time inside the Figure – this is the force of bodies in Bacon . . .[19]

Plate 1 Francis Bacon, *Three Studies of the Male Back*, 1970, oil on canvas, 198 × 147.5 cm (78 × 57.5 in.), Kunsthaus, Zurich. © The estate of Francis Bacon/DACS, London 2011.
A colour version of this image can be found in the plate section in the centre on this book.

As I interpret these words, the polyvalent eye is able to discern invisible forces at work in the articulation of the body's visual appearance, because Bacon's treatment of the Figure involves great fluidity in how it is rendered. The intensity of chromatic detail and variation involved in this, presents *flesh* rather than an 'organic' focus on anatomy. Individual organs are recognizable in Bacon's painting, but they are not emphasized as anything other than terminals among mounds of flesh whose character is determined by physical forces at work in them. It is this fleshiness that engages the viewer. Through it, the intensity of chromatic detail in the delineation of the Figure exemplifies an intense sensation of time through the level of sustained attention that their exploration demands.

Now while the bulk of Deleuze's study of Bacon is an analysis of that artist's individual achievement, a substantial portion of the study is given over, also, to a more general theory of painting – that makes use of some of the key concepts broached, initially, in relation to Bacon. As we shall see, now, it has special significance for modern art.

Part Two

It will be recalled that, for Deleuze, 'The task of painting is defined as the attempt to render visible forces that are not themselves visible'. This is made into the basis of a historical 'grand narrative' by Deleuze whose more precise content I shall address later. However, in more immediate terms, Deleuze's theory of painting is a generalization of the significance of the Figure. As was shown earlier, Bacon creates 'Figure' rather than mere symbol or narrative, through liberating it from this 'figurative' level of meaning. This liberation involves rendering the figure as emergent from, and acting upon, the pictorial ground.

In Bacon's work, this involves treating the body in the ways described in Part One. Other painters achieve Figure in different ways. In some cases, for example, the capturing of forces is bound up with a 'less pure' problem such as the decomposition and recomposition of depth in Renaissance art, or the decomposition and recomposition of movement in cubism.[20]

To understand Deleuze's general theory of painting in more detail, it is worth considering what kind of signifying practice painting is. In respect of this, he distinguishes between 'analogue' and 'digital' codes of reference (a distinction that will be returned to on numerous occasions as this book progresses). At first sight, this might seem to be no more than a distinction between referential idioms (such as painting) that work through resemblance (or 'isomorphism') and sensuous immediacy, and those codes (such as language) whose referential rules are decided by convention.

However, Deleuze notes that some digital codes can be used to create 'isomorphic' messages or narratives (e.g. the literary use of language), and that some isomorphic codes are analogical in contrasting ways.

In traditional photography, for example, resemblance is based on the causal impact of light upon a negative, which is then reproduced as a print. For Deleuze, this means that the analogical basis of photography is 'figurative' and based on direct resemblance between the visual units of the coded image, and that which it is an image of. [21]

Painting, however, works on a different principle. As Deleuze puts it, 'resemblance is the product when it appears abruptly as the result of relations that are completely different from those it is supposed to reproduce: resemblance then emerges as the brutal product of non-resembling means.'[22]

On these terms, painting does not use or reproduce already existing codified elements, it creates these through its own means. Indeed, as Deleuze states,

> instead of being produced symbolically, through the detour of the code, it is produced 'sensually', through sensation. The name "aesthetic Analogy" must be reserved for this

last eminent type, in which there is neither primary resemblance nor prior code, and which is both figurative and noncodified.[23]

In this account Deleuze shows great phenomenological acuteness. Painting involves resemblance as a referential code, but has to create its referential resemblances through materials – paint, and gesture – that are not pre-codified to represent. This means that there is an *intrinsic* aesthetic character to painting. It is an idiom of representation that demands attentiveness to the fine gradations of painted details and passages, and the shift of sensations through which these are registered. These are the zones through which painting is actualized *qua* painting – through which it *creates* resemblance.

Deleuze continues,

> As an analogical language, painting has three dimensions: the planes, the connection or junction of planes (primarily of the vertical plane, and the horizontal plane), which replaces perspective; color, the modulation of color, which tends to suppress relations of value, chiaroscuro, and the contrast of shadow and light; and the body, the mass and declination of the body which exceeds the organism and destroys the form-background relationship.[24]

What is striking about Deleuze's position is its emphatically hierarchical emphasis. In the foregoing passage, he is describing an *essence* of painting that is far from neutral. It is one which privileges modern painting and those antecedents of it that emphasize colour and plane, rather than systematic illusionistic depth.

The question arises, then, as to how this essence of painting is liberated, how does Figure escape from mere figuration? In this task, the painter faces formidably difficult problems of orientation. Broader culture surrounds him or her with 'figurative givens' and 'psychic cliches' – images and narratives and narrative images, that, as it were, naturalize us to visual meaning *qua* figurative.

For painting to make its analogical essence active, something must happen. And the something in question is the introduction of 'catastrophe' – in the form of the 'diagram'. We have encountered the 'diagram' already in Deleuze's analysis of Bacon. In Bacon the diagram consists of a specific idiom – involving local scrubbing or wiping, and asignifying traits. Deleuze generalizes this as follows:

'The diagram is the operative set of asignifying and nonrepresentative lines and zones, line-strokes and color-patches'.[25] These serve to introduce 'possibilities of fact', without yet constituting a fully realized pictorial fact. In order to be so constituted, in order to evolve into Figure, they must be 'reinjected' into the visual whole.

Deleuze makes this position more concrete through reference to specific painters. We are told, for example, that,

The diagram is the operative set of traits and color-patches, of lines and zones. Van Gogh's diagram, for example, is the set of straight and curved hatch marks that raise and lower the ground, twist the trees, make the sky palpitate, and which assume a particular intensity from 1888 onwards.[26]

Indeed,

The diagram is . . . a chaos, a catastrophe, but it is also a germ of order or rhythm. It is a violent chaos to the figurative givens, but it is a germ of rhythm [a term which I will return to] in relation to the new order of the painting. The diagram ends the preparatory work and begins the act of painting.[27]

What Deleuze is describing here is the painter's generation of Figure out of those paintmarks and gestures whose character and emphases constitute an individual way of creating elements of resemblance. It is, in effect, the microfabric of colour and brushstroke from which Figure is generated in relation to ground.

Viewed from the appropriate distance they can be recognized as generating the overall Figure. Individually, however, at the level of the act of painting, itself, they are 'nonfigurative', or 'asignifying' because they are just brushstrokes and patches of colour. It is only as the painter juxtaposes them in a calibrated way, that they generate the Figure *as* that which is emergent from them and which relates back to them.

Of course, it is unusual for a painter to just start generating a painting from the diagram. He or she will often do preparatory sketches, either on the work's surface, or on accompanying ones. However, it is this initial figurative orientation that the diagram disrupts. As Deleuze puts it,

> *A probable visual whole (first figuration) has been disorganized and deformed by free manual traits which, by being reinjected into the whole, will produce the improbable visual Figure (second figuration).* The act of painting is the unity of these free manual traits and their effect upon and reinjection into the visual whole. By passing through these traits, figuration recovers and recreates, but does not resemble, the figuration from which it came.[28]

Deleuze makes it insistently clear that a rendered Figure in the sense just described, is, in effect, the body without organs.[29] This is because the Figure is presented *as* emergent. It is *not* a body or material thing or state of affairs that is represented in its natural 'organic' form. Rather, through its genesis from the diagram, it is a kind of flesh – rendered as a becoming of such and such a kind of thing, rather than as a thing of that kind, per se. *It exists through referring back* to the conditions that create the possibility of its emergence.

Concomitant with this, is the fact that all painting aspires to have the body escape from itself. Through escaping the body, painting's line-colour systems (and the eye as a polyvalent organ) serve to discover the 'materiality' of which the body is composed – the character of its 'pure presence'.[30]

As one might expect, Deleuze sees Bacon as an exemplar of the diagram. For this painter, the 'law of the diagram' is to start with a figurative form, and then to intervene upon it, and scramble it, so that Figure emerges from it.

We have already seen that one of the key means to this is a diagram based on local scrubbing and asignifying elements. Deleuze indicates another way in which Bacon uses the diagram. For example, in relation to *Painting*, 1946 (Museum of Modern Art, New York), we are told that the diagram works through creating aesthetic analogues of the starting form.

In his words,

> The diagram-accident has scrambled the intentional figurative form, the bird: it imposes nonformal color-patches and traits that function only as traits of birdness, of animality. It is from these 'nonfigurative' traits that the final whole emerges, as if from a pool; and it is they that raise it to the power of the pure Figure, beyond the figuration contained in the whole.[31]

On these terms, while Bacon starts with a bird form he recontextualizes this through diagrammatic marks. Through this, it becomes host to other kinds of shapes, and appears to turn into other kinds of thing. And, in turn, other features (such as the meat that seems to flow, and the umbrella that seems to seize) take on characteristics that are at odds with their usual appearances.

These visual ambiguities mean that between the founding bird shape and the other features, diagram injects a zone of objective indiscernibility, or indeterminacy, that deforms the figurative into Figure.

Now Deleuze holds that there are three major routes out of figuration each of which constitute a 'modern function' of painting. These are abstraction, action painting (or '*art informel*'), and a haptic/colouristic emphasis exemplified most emphatically by Cezanne, Bacon, Van Gogh, and Gauguin.

There is a strong hierarchical factor at work in Deleuze's position here that I will consider later in this book. For present purposes, it is worth looking at a broader – even more emphatic hierarchy – in which his account of modern painting is embedded.

We are told, for example, that, 'Modern painting begins when man no longer experiences himself as essence, but as an accident. There is always a fall, a risk of the fall; the form begins to express the accident and no longer the essence.'[32]

This was not always the case. Egyptian art has a special significance in this respect. Following Riegl, Deleuze claims that in Egyptian bas-reliefs (especially) there is an incisive use of contour that involves 'a geometry of the plane, of the line, and of essence'.[33] The importance of this essence is that it (supposedly) unites the tactile and the visual, the 'haptic' and the 'optic'.

However, 'Christianity subjected the form, or rather the Figure, to a fundamental deformation. As God was incarnated, painting is no longer linked to essence but to accident.'[34] Christianity is, indeed, not alone in its sinfulness in this respect. For, in its emphasis on the primacy of the foreground, Greek art,

> distinguished the planes, invented a perspective, and put into play light and shadow, hollows and reliefs. . . . Classical representation thus takes the accident as its object, but it incorporates the accident into an optical organization that makes it something well founded (a phenomenon) or a 'manifestation of essence'.[35]

On these terms, the pictorial contour ceases to be geometric, and becomes *organic* instead. The work is orientated to 'accident' in the sense that (one presumes) an organic painting is orientated towards visual effects and relations based on light (light being something that Deleuze associates with the temporal dimension).

In such painting, organic contour acts a mould in which tactile contact is a secondary – but necessary, and demanding – assistant in the individuation of optically perfect forms. As Deleuze puts it, 'What replaces haptic space is a tactile-optical space, in which what is expressed is no longer essence but connection; that is, the organic activity of man.'[36]

Deleuze sees the subsequent history of western painting as, in part, a dismantling of this space. On the one hand, in Byzantine art, and other later work there is a renewed optical emphasis, while in the 'Gothic line' there is a more emphatic emphasis on haptically charged contour.

Other artists still, maintain a reconciled tactile-optical space. Of special importance here, is Cezanne. For Deleuze, he makes the two aspects coexist in extremely positive way – using, on the one hand, local tone, shadow, and light, shaped by chiaroscuro, and, on the other hand (and more significantly) through a 'pure modulation' of colour that involves the sequential juxtaposition of tones in the order of the spectrum.

Deleuze suggests further that that this modulation of colour 'recreates a properly haptic function, in which the juxtaposition of pure tones arranged gradually on the flat surface forms a progression and a regression that culminates in a close vision'.[37] This leads to one of Deleuze's most important points. It is worth quoting at length:

colorism is the analogical language of painting: if there is still molding by color, it is no longer even an interior mold, but a temporal variable, and continuous mold, to which alone the name of modulation belongs, strictly speaking. There is neither an inside nor an outside, but only a continuous creation of space, the spatializing energy of color. By avoiding abstraction, colorism avoids both figuration and narration, and moves infinitely closer to the pure state of a pictorial 'fact' which has nothing left to narrate. This fact is the constitution or reconstitution of a haptic function of sight.[38]

These remarks present in the most unambiguous way, the arch-essentialist foundation of Deleuze's theory of painting. Painting is an analogical language based on the handling of colour. When it stays true to this essence it moves, at the same time, even closer to presenting that possibility of pictorial fact, which is declared in the fully realized Figure.

In relation to colourism, Deleuze goes on to say, defensively, that 'Certainly it is not a question of a better solution, but of a tendency that runs through painting and leaves behind characteristic masterpieces distinct from those that characterize other tendencies.'[39]

Such a qualification, however, blatantly contradicts the basic impulse of all his previous claims.

In this respect, for example, we will recall that by avoiding 'abstraction' (which, as we shall see later on in this book, Deleuze stigmatizes as 'digital'), he suggests that colouration avoids figuration and narrative and moves closer to the *possibility* of fact (i.e. the Figure) – a move which is the basis of everything on which he establishes the distinctiveness of painting as such. This means that – whatever official denials Deleuze may issue, or may be issued on his behalf – colourism is presented as painting's most authentic idiom, the most complete realization of painting's essence.

It is hardly surprising, also, that Bacon is assigned a duly heroic role in colourism's return to hapticity. Deleuze describes him as 'an Egyptian'[40] in that the form and ground of his work – connected to each other by the contour – lie on a single plane, and thence exemplify close haptic vision. However, because of the catastrophic function of the diagram, Bacon's forms have more the modern character of accident rather than essentiality of form.

Now it might seem that the essentialist position that sustains Deleuze's theory of painting and Bacon's privileged role in it, are, *qua* essentialist, to be rejected, on the basis of contemporary thought's general scepticism towards such positions. However, a rejection of this kind is no more than an appeal to the fashionable as dogmatic *authority*. If hierarchical and essentialist positions are to be criticized, then the critique must be a logical one that addresses the grounds which might justify such beliefs rather than the having of the beliefs as such.

In due course, I will subject Deleuze's entire strategy to a critical revision. Before that, however, we must address the remaining highly distinctive and complex feature of his analysis of Bacon and modern painting. It concerns the centrality of *sensation*. Since this notion intersects with just about all aspects of Deleuze's approach, it is worth extended consideration.

Part Three

As we have seen, for Deleuze, the task of painting is to capture the effects of invisible forces on visible bodies. For him, force is closely related to 'sensation'[41] insofar as sensation only exists through the effect of force on a body. However, while force is the condition of sensation, it is not the force itself that is sensed. Sensation 'gives' something completely different from the forces that condition it. Deleuze explores what is thus given by sensation in the greatest detail.

Of central importance is the notion of the Figure. We are told that,

> The Figure is the sensible form related to a sensation; it acts immediately on the nervous system, which is of the flesh, whereas abstract form is addressed to the head, and acts through the intermediary of the brain, which is closer to the bone.[42]

Indeed,

> Sensation has one face turned toward the subject (the nervous system, vital movement, 'instinct', 'temperament', . . . and one face turned toward the object (the 'fact', the place, the

event). Or rather it has no face at all, it is both things indis-
solubly, it is Being-in-the-World, as the phenomenologists say;
at one and the same time I become in the sensation and something happens through the sensation, one through the other,
one in the other.[43]

On these terms, the spectator experiences sensation only by
entering the painting and engaging with the unity of the sens-
ing and the sensed. Deleuze links this to Cezanne's critique
of impressionism, where the former paints not air, but bodies
experienced as sustaining sensation. He goes on to suggest that
despite differences between them, Bacon and Cezanne are both
orientated towards sensation. Sensation involves a passage from
one 'order' to another. The meaning of an 'order' is explained
by him as follows:

> It is each painting, each Figure that is itself a shifting sequence
> or series (and not simply a term in a series); it is each sen-
> sation that exists at diverse levels, in different orders, or in
> different domains. This means that there are not sensations
> of different orders, but different orders of one and the same
> sensation. It is the nature of sensation to envelop a constitu-
> tive difference of level, a plurality of constituting domains. . . .
> Hence the irreducibly synthetic character of sensation.[44]

As I interpret him, Deleuze is saying that our sensation of a
painting is an overall unity that emerges from different levels or aspects of the Figure's relation to the material ground.
It is a synthetic unity in that it is composed from the emergence of different aspects, and even – as we shall see – conflicts between them – and the way in which these engage us
perceptually.
        Deleuze is insistent that the synthetic unity of the sensation
is not that of the represented object, insofar as the Figure is
opposed to figuration. Any awareness of figurative content's
role in constituting the Figure, involves a 'secondary figuration'

that involves mere primary figuration being neutralized. And, in related terms, any violence in the sensation is not that of sensationalistic represented violence, because it is something inseparable from the Figure's multi-aspectual direct action on the nervous system.

A second interpretation of the synthetic unity of sensation is rejected, also, by Deleuze. The levels or valencies of sensation do not centre on mere *ambivalence* of feeling, rather 'Sensation is what determines instinct at a particular moment, just as instinct is the passage from one sensation to another.'[45]

A third 'more interesting' hypothesis also proves unacceptable to Deleuze. It is the claim that different levels of sensation are like arrests or snapshots of motion which recompose the movement synthetically, in all its continuity, speed, and violence. However, for Deleuze, such *represented* movement cannot explain sensation – 'on the contrary, it is explained by the elasticity of the sensation, its *vis elastica*'.[46]

He now considers a fourth hypothesis – a 'more phenomenological' one:

> The levels of sensation would really be domains of sensation that refer to the different sense organs; but precisely each level, each domain would have a way of referring to the others, independently of the represented object they have in common.[47]

Deleuze is here emphasizing the way in which sensation based on one sense is often informed and mediated through reference to other senses (e.g. when an apple looks juicy, or a piece of metal looks hard. However, while not denying the phenomenon, Deleuze claims that such synaesthestic operation is not a sufficient explanation for our sensation of the Figure. In painting,

> this operation is possible only if the sensation of a particular domain (here, the visual sensation) is in direct contact with a vital power that exceeds every domain and traverses them all.

This power is rhythm, which is more profound than vision, hearing, etc. . . .[48]

It is interesting that Deleuze does not characterize 'rhythm' in more concrete terms. Rather he continues in an arch-essentialist vein:

> Rhythm appears as music when it invests the auditory level, and as painting when it invests the visual level. This is a 'logic of the senses', as Cezanne said, which is neither rational nor cerebral. What is ultimate is thus the relation between sensation and rhythm, which places in each sensation the levels and domains through which it passes.[49]

Deleuze links 'rhythm' to the body without organs, insofar as it is the 'vibration' which animates that body, and makes the sensation pass from one level to another through the Figure. Rhythm unites the different orders.

As one might expect, Bacon is assigned a special role in relation to the synthetic unity of sensation. Deleuze sees him as giving a primacy to active descent, to the *fall*. This, however, is not taken to be a spatial descent, per se. 'It is the descent as the passage of sensation, as the difference in level contained in the sensation.'[50]

The key to this in Bacon is his orientation towards Figures based on deformation. In Deleuze's interpretation,[51] Bacon presents flesh as descending from the bones, and the body as descending from the arms and the raised thigh. Sensation develops, thereby, through falling from one level to another, and should be regarded as a positive and active 'reality'. The fall affirms such differences of level.

It is clear that, for Deleuze, this relation between sensation and falling, in painting, is a *general principle*, and not just one that applies to Bacon. In this, he appeals to the authority of Kant's theory of intensive magnitude set forth in the *Critique of Pure Reason*.[52] In Deleuze's reading of Kant, when sensation tends towards a higher level, it can only be experienced through relating this higher level to degree zero – that is, through a fall. 'Whatever the sensation may be, its intensive reality is a descent in depth that has a greater or lesser "magnitude," and not a rise.'[53]

Indeed, for Deleuze, the fall is both that which is most alive in sensation, and that through which sensation is experienced 'as living'. Such a fall of intensive magnitude can coincide with a spatial descent, but it can coincide, also, with a rise (though Deleuze does not clarify what enables this latter, surprising possibility).[54]

Now, as we saw earlier, for Deleuze, Figure acts 'directly' on the nervous system. He holds, also, that the 'colour system' itself involves direct action on the nervous system.[55] Colour, Figure, and sensation, are, therefore, inseparably bonded in the experience of painting.

Again, Cezanne and Bacon have special significance in this respect. We are told that sensation,

> is in the body, even the body of an apple. Color is in the body, sensation is in the body and not in the air. Sensation is what is painted. What is painted on the canvas is the body; not insofar as it is represented as an object, but insofar as it is experienced as sustaining *this* sensation (what Lawrence speaking of Cezanne called the 'appleyness of the apple').[56]

To paint the body as Figure, therefore, is to paint sensation, and the transition between 'orders' of sensation is embodied most purely in the modulation of colour. Deleuze claims, indeed, that Bacon's three key pictorial features – material structure, Figure, and contour, all converge on colour. As he puts it, 'it is modulation – that is, the relations between colours – which at the same time explains the unity of the whole, the distribution of each element, and the way each of them acts upon the others.'[57]

The upshot of all this, is that there is a 'creative taste' in colour which constitutes 'a properly visual sense of touch, or a haptic sense of sight'.[58] It is this haptic sight – exemplified in Cezanne and Bacon, especially – that Deleuze sees, in effect, as the great achievement of modern painting.

Part Four

It is quite clear that Deleuze's general theory of painting not only privileges modern art but appears designed to make Cezanne and Bacon its apotheosis. All the key concepts that Deleuze originally introduces in relation to Bacon – Figure, the diagram, the body escaping itself, the body without organs, and the primacy of colour modulation and sensation – are subsequently generalized as characteristics of all painting that exceeds figuration.

The question arises, then as to whether Deleuze is justified in both the specifics of his interpretations, and in his generalization of them.

I shall show that his account is beset by problems at all levels. However, before 'exploding' Deleuze, one point must be emphasized in the most unambiguous terms. This chapter has presented his position in great detail because of his attentiveness to the ontological structures of painting *qua* painting, the perception of these structures, our affective response to them, and the way in which painting focuses these aspects in its historical development.

I know of no other thinker who has maintained this level of philosophical engagement with painting. *Even if his position involves mistakes, its general orientation in terms of the factors just mentioned, makes it exemplary for the phenomenology of modern art – indeed for visual art in general.*

Now, it will be recalled that in the Introduction to this book, I indicated four commonly noted features of modernist painting: (1) the overcoming of conventional standards of finish and composition, (2) the embracing of subject matter, or treatments of it, that are at odds with conventional societal values and/or which are emotionally disturbing, (3) the development of new pictorial codes, and (4) the affirmation of the flatness or shallowness of the picture plane.

Deleuze's approach is strong, especially, in relation to these modern characteristics. For example, his notion of the diagram, his emphasis on colour modulation, and account of hapticity, are of the utmost value in clarifying factors (1) and (4). They address and stimulate ideas that take us to the heart of what is at issue in these root factors. And, as we shall see further on in this book, Deleuze's distinction between 'digital' and 'analogue' abstract art is of the greatest interest in relation to factor (3).

However, the problems inherent in his position mean that Deleuze's theory cannot be 'applied' in some pure state. It has to be exploded so as to scatter out his valid insights, and make them available on an *ad hoc* basis, rather than as a hierarchical system.

This means, of course, that in order to develop a more comprehensive account of the phenomenology of modern art, ideas from other thinkers will have to be introduced, as well as additional new connecting arguments and concepts.

A good starting point for critique is Deleuze's interpretation of Bacon. It should be noted that even the lengthy exposition of Deleuze's views that I have provided, does not even begin to do justice to his wealth of brilliant insights concerning the specifics of Bacon's work.

However, this being said, there is a significant fault line that crosses his understanding of both Bacon and painting in general. It centres on a problem related to an aspect of factor (2) noted above – namely, the emotionally disturbing treatment of subject matter.

We have seen how the emphases on Figure, diagram, the body escaping itself, and the body without organs, are most central to the analysis of Bacon. In the course of my text, indeed, I have tried to explain in more detail how these terms help us make sense of specific works.

To reiterate, Deleuze regards the 'task' of painting to be that of making invisible forces visible through their action on bodies (a claim that I shall return to). Bacon's Figures show this through the relation between the Figure's torsions as they relate to the painting's material structure. The body appears to be trying to escape from itself into this structure.

For Deleuze this is a formal relation. The body is not engaged in some narrative of escape rather the escape involves torsions integrated into a non-figurative feature of the painting. Indeed, it is the fact of their emergence from this ground, that makes them into Figure, and which allows us to explore the work with a roaming polyvalent eye – with a body without organs rather than an eye that reads a narrative.

This, according to Deleuze is why Bacon's figures are not monstrous. They involve torsions whose character is determined by a formal function, not a narrative one. Our response to them should be based accordingly on the modulation of colour, and the passage of sensations involved in this.

However, matters are by no means as clear cut as Deleuze imagines. If the body trying to escape itself amounts to no more than a formal device recognized through the appropriate sensations, then this is no more than formalism as such. In which case, it would raise the question of why the body treated in this way should be of the slightest interest to us.

As we saw earlier, Deleuze notes that 'figuration recovers and recreates, but does not resemble, the figuration from which it came'.[59] He is ambivalent, however, about what this amounts to in phenomenological terms.

His official position is that the modulations of colour, occasion a passage of sensations with special intensity, when we engage with the Figure. *But this amounts to no more than formalism*, and invites the question that blights all formalism – namely why should form be found significant at all?

Sensations of colour modulation may be pleasurable or intense, but what differentiates this from simply liking the look of a marvellous sunset, or deeply beautiful flowers, and the like? If it is the fact that the colours are painted, then this imports knowledge beyond mere sensation itself.

Colour sensations alone, cannot carry the burden of our aesthetic appreciation of Figure (a point, again, I shall return to, in detail), and this is especially the case in relation to Bacon's work. This means that some more positive role must be found for the symbolic dimension, for the figurative.

Interestingly, Deleuze himself notes the importance of Bacon's treatment of the body as *meat*. He tells, for example, in relation to *Three Figures and a Portrait* of 1975, that a 'pictorial tension' between flesh and bone is achieved insofar as the body is presented as 'meat', through the 'splendour' of the painting's colours:

> Meat is the state of the body in which flesh and bone confront each other locally rather than being composed structurally.[60] [Indeed,] Pity the meat! Meat is undoubtedly the the chief object of Bacon's pity, his only object of pity, his Anglo-Irish pity. On this point, he is like Soutine, with his immense pity for the Jew. Meat is not dead flesh; it retains all all the sufferings and assumes all the colours of living flesh.[61]

What Deleuze is emphasizing here is that – even if Bacon is not giving us some figurative narrative – elements of *symbolic meaning* bound up with emotionally disturbing general factors in our embodied condition, not only persist in his work but are factors *embedded* in the Figure. The sense of pity exemplifies this.

This means that the recovery and recreation of such symbolism, is not, primarily, in the direction of some experienced passage of sensations, but rather as an emotionally unsettling *aesthetic* symbolism that is more than mere figuration, but which does not reduce to formal relations alone.

However, Deleuze does no justice to the scope of this – either in relation to Bacon, or more generally. In terms of the former, there are many painters who treat the human body in terms of force exerted on it or from within it – Deleuze, indeed, cites Michelangelo as a key example. But Bacon's treatment of this is highly individual.

This is not just because of the particular way he relates the pressurized body to material structure and contour, but also because he renders it *as* meat. The fact that this, and the concomitant attempt to escape from the body is related to non-figurative structures rather than narrative space, makes the rendition all the more psychologically disturbing. It gives it a symbolic or narrative significance of an unorthodox kind.

On these terms, the body as meat is, indeed, *genuinely monstrous* and *emotionally disturbing* – despite Deleuze's strictures to the contrary – *precisely because it is 'happening' in a space where nothing is happening insofar as it is manifestly not a narratively determined one.*

Indeed, *the attempt to escape the body is itself something existentially disturbing.* One knows that it cannot be done. But the Sisyphean torsions of Bacon's Figures bring home, at once, the hopelessness of the task, and, also, the fact that, *qua* embodied, we will always be thrown back on such a yearning, at times when our body's demands *qua* body disturb us or are sickening. And, of course, this does not have to arise in extreme situations alone. All bodily functions and exertions can feed back a sense of our imprisonment under the *regime* of such things. The normal can seem monstrous in the demands it places on us.

Now, of course, it is one thing to think about or describe what is at issue in the desire to escape the body, but to realize this in paint is to present it in terms that has the possibility of exceeding mere narrative. It is not just a presentation of the relevant idea, but a presentation which is shown to us through the being of another person – the painter. We are involved with the inseparable unity of both.

Some painters may repeat such idea through adopting the style of others, and in these cases, we may well have no more than mere narrative or figuration. But an original presentation engages us with the both painter and what is painted – in a shared aesthetic symbolism that waters and fertilizes the arid formalism of the Deleuzian Figure.

I am arguing, then, that the symbolic–figurative dimension *must* be involved in Bacon's painting as a direct player, otherwise one overlooks a feature that is distinctive to his rendering of Figure. Indeed, Deleuze's claim that the attempt to escape the body and the body without organs are implicit in *all* painting, makes it all the more important to highlight those symbolic features which give Bacon's exemplifications of these, a *special edge*. The existential dimension of painting needs to be given much greater due.

These points are the first marker of what Deleuze's entire approach to painting lacks, namely, an understanding of *individual style* as the central concept in pictorial art. For, in effect, his distinction between Figure and figuration is a distinction between, on the one hand, pictorial art and, on the other hand, pictures that simply represent.

But Deleuze tries to justify this distinction on the basis of painters using the right kind of pictorial devices or strategies – whose use creates Figure, and which are, accordingly, the basis of pictorial art rather than pictorial figuration.

What Deleuze does not think through is how the devices in question apply just as well to pictorial figuration. In this respect, for example, consider the role of Figure and diagram. Insofar as painting is analogical, it creates the means for constructing resemblance from pictorial elements such as marks that do not, in themselves resemble anything other than themselves.

Now there is a sense in which this accurately describes a basic phenomenological structure of painting, as such. Indeed, as we saw earlier, Deleuze himself describes it as 'the act of painting'. Any painter must decide a way of using marks to create an image – a diagram that transforms initial figurative ideas into concrete pictorial actuality.

However, Deleuze's problem is this. He presents Figure in its emergence from ground through the diagram as something basic to painting. But if it is so basic, why do so few paintings actually engage us in such terms? In the majority of cases, we rarely look at paintings except as representations of such and such a kind of thing or state of affairs. They are no more than figurative.

Now, the reason why most paintings do not engage us in terms of Figure and diagram is because they do not create these genuinely, but use, rather, established idioms that have already been established by other painters. If this happens, any paintings so created will not have any interest other than their narrative significance.

In contrast to this, what engages our *aesthetic* attention is when a painter's individual style of treating diagram – of exploring possibility and making discoveries in the potential of marks to make resemblance emerge from them – is one that refines or innovates, and leads to something new or at least unfamiliar.

Deleuze seems to think that diagram must be something overt and discernible in a work. It is constantly 'reinjected' into the whole. This, in itself, tends to privilege modern painting – which lacks 'finish', and where the material structure from which Figure is generated, is more immediately apparent. But one can equally well reverse Deleuze's logic and argue that if an 'organic' painter's work is good, it makes us consider how it was generated – what sort of diagram it emerges from, even if that diagram is concealed by the finish. Indeed, if a work can refer us to diagram that is hidden – which is not constantly 'reinjected' into the whole – perhaps this makes it all the more remarkable as a realization of Figure!

I am arguing again, in other words, that Figure cannot be tied to specific genres of painting. *Individuality of style* is the decisive factor that allows diagrammatic features to be read as Figure, or, (in works which do not have a manifest diagrammatic element) invite us to imagine the invisible ground from which the Figure is generated.

The painter's individuality of vision and expression makes us interested in *how* the figurative elements emerge from the work's ground. And, in attending to such emergence our sense of figuration and symbolic meaning becomes something very different from mere visual recognition of what is presented (a topic that I will return to, in due course). A Deleuzian might object that style is not relevant. What counts is whether the painting has colour modulations that sustain an intense enough range of sensations in our discriminations of them. But immediately, this faces the problem of its immense restrictedness. Many paintings strike us in terms of how they generate figuration from material structure. Figure cannot be tied to the colouristically orientated painters whom Deleuze favours. So, if we are to explain why Figure is able to emerge, we must determine this by reference to distinctive features in the painter's individual style.

And even if we admitted such hierarchical exclusion, and insisted on Figure as emergent from the passage of appropriate colour sensations alone, this would face the problem already encountered. We would have to offer something that Deleuze does not provide, namely an account of why sensations arising from colour modulation in painting should have any significance over those arising from intense perceptions of colour per se. Surely if they do have extra significance, the relevant extra intensity can be explained only because they are recognized as *colour worked by artifice* in a specific way, that is, as colour integrated within an *individual style*.

There is the additional problem of explaining why it is that not every painting with a strong colouristic emphasis is able to engage us in terms of modulations of colour and concomitant sensations. And again, this seems to leave only individual style as the only factor that can explain how we become attentive to these features in the emergence of Figure.

Deleuze's pronouncements on painting's 'task' – namely the rendering of invisible forces through their effect upon visible bodies – also fall victim to these objections. As far as I can see, the substance of this claim is, in itself, *pure stipulation* with no other purpose than to privilege Bacon's painting, and those who Deleuze regards as his forbears. It would only be a task for painting in general, if one persuasively defined its three-dimensional content to consist of the representation of bodies that are subject to force.

However, this is trivially true by virtue of what a body is, and has no explanatory value in relation to the 'task' of painting. And even if it did, we would find the very same problem that we have just encountered. If all painters address this task, why is it that only some of them attract our attention? The answer, of course, leads again to the fact that some painters' individual styles engenders Figure, by virtue of their very individuality.

It might be asked why individuality of style should be a focus of more compelling aesthetic engagement than our sensations of modulated colour. The fact is, that how others see the world is of intrinsic interest to us, because it is only through the understanding and appreciation of this that we become aware of the nature and scope of our own identity. Style as a focus of aesthetic engagement means that that engagement constellates around that which is fundamental to our personal and species identity, and, decisively, *the relation between them.*

Now, as we saw earlier, Deleuze justifies his privileging of Cezanne and Bacon through a broader historical grand narrative. Grand narratives justifying modernist art, are, of course, a major part of the formalist tradition, and can be found in Clive Bell, and Clement Greenberg, among others.

It is interesting that Deleuze derives much of his historical account from the great formalist art historians, Riegl, Worringer, and Wolfflin. These figures have been of renewed scholarly interest of late, insofar as art history as a discipline has been much concerned with reviewing the historical conditions of its own construction. They have also been valued because of their willingness to see differences between fine and applied art and between epochs such as Renaissance and Baroque, *as differences* per se – rather than the basis of a hierarchy.

Deleuze's utilization of these figures, however, inverts these values. He uses them as unquestioned sources of *authority* for his grand narrative of painting, despite the fact that the narratives they provide are teleological and essentialist. On their terms, painting is driven from one way of seeing to another by various conceptions of the 'spirit' of the age or culture.

Now, Deleuze not only uses these accounts for authority, he *reverses* their general tone by using them to justify an essentialist hierarchy. In this respect, we will recall his claims about colourism:

> as an analogical language, painting has three dimensions: the planes, the connection or junction of planes (primarily of the vertical plane, and the horizontal plane), which replaces perspective; color, the modulation of color, which tends to suppress relations of value, chiaroscuro, and the contrast of shadow and light; and the body, the mass and declination of the body which exceeds the organism and destroys the form–background relationship.[62]

However, for Deleuze, the sure and steady historical path to securing this essence is a highly exclusive one. In it, art with a haptic orientation is succeeded by painting that is optically orientated but with a servile (yet necessary) hapticity operating within it. This 'organic' painting is in turn succeeded by a painting determined by haptic sight – emphasizing the features set out in the passage just quoted. It is a kind of *higher* synthesis of the previous tendencies.

Of course, Deleuze does not describe it as 'higher'. However, since he consistently affirms the importance of the Figure over figuration, and consistently assigns 'organic' painting to figuration it is clear that for him, modern colouristic painting is far and away truer to painting's essence than organic idioms.

Through the privileging of haptic-sighted colouristic painting Deleuze is, in effect, relegating 'organic' modes to a lesser, merely figurative status. Such 'organic' art includes all that of the Renaissance, the Baroque, the Romantic era, and academic painting in general, apart from a few select individuals.

Indeed, Deleuze is led to the remarkable conclusion that 'It was with Michelangelo, with mannerism, that the Figure was born in its pure state, and which would no longer need any other justification than "an acrid and strident polychromy, striated with flashes, like a metal plate."'[63]

The quote within the quote here is from Leiris describing Bacon. For Deleuze, it is the trajectory prophesied by Egyptian and Gothic art, and inaugurated by Michelangelo, that issues in painting's congruence with its own colouristic essence in the work of Bacon and other moderns.

Now we have already seen the hierarchical exclusions involved in this. Indeed, they extend further than I have shown hitherto, in that Deleuze presents his general theory of colourism as the analogical language of painting, on the basis of exclusively *western* examples of painting. It may be that some non-western idioms are amenable to such analysis, but, whether they are or not, and can be determined *only* through consideration of the *distinctive style* in which they embody paint marks.

Given these objections, the time has come to follow them through at the very heart of Deleuze's hierarchy, namely the link between colour modulation and sensation itself. What does this relation amount to, in strict phenomenological terms?

The problem here is that with all his talk of colour and sensation it might seem that he is offering a genuine direct description of a key aspect of the experience of painting. He is not. His descriptions are a blend of the phenomenological and the arbitrarily constructed, and the phenomenological emphases he does address are not the ones that are really at issue.

In this respect, let us return to the claim that painting is an analogical language. Earlier, I noted the acuteness of this insight. What is not so acute, is the way in which he develops it on the basis of colour, exclusively. Planes, colour, colour modulation, the mass and 'declination of body' are the constitutive elements here.

Now, if, in ontological terms, painting were no more than the marking of a surface with pigments, then good painting might be based on colour modulations. But, of course, painting in the sense in which Deleuze discusses it, is much more than this. It involves the generation of Figure from diagram – it is pictorial.

Deleuze downplays figuration as no more than a mere means to the generation of Figure, but in even this grudging concession he lays the seeds of his own theory's downfall. The problem is this. If we attend to how colour is laid down on a surface, and the graduations of its distribution, then this might well be described as a passage of sensations.

However, once these colour modulations are tracked not just as real marks on a surface but as realizations of a virtual three-dimensional space, then their significance is changed, *qualitatively*. We are dealing not just with the distributions of colour across a surface, but the way in which this distribution constitutes three-dimensional meaning, that is, opens up and populates a pictorial space.

It might be thought that Deleuze's sustained discussion of the synthetic character of sensation describes this adequately. He claims, we will recall, that,

> It is each painting, each Figure that is itself a shifting sequence or series (and not simply a term in a series); it is each sensation that exists at diverse levels, in different orders, or in different domains. This means that there are not sensations of different orders, but different orders of one and the same sensation. It is the nature of sensation to envelop a constitutive difference of level, a plurality of constituting domains.[64]

This means that in our experience of Figure there is one overall sensation – a direct impact on the nervous system, whose different aspects (or 'order') unfold as one explores passages of colour modulations. However, this is a stipulative redefinition of what is customarily understood by the term 'sensation'.

Sensation is taken, usually, to involve low-level causal impacts wherein stimuli are registered, and (through the mediation of concept awareness) interpreted. Animals may be immersed in sensations as a result of the direct impact of stimuli, but in humans our awareness of colours, tastes, sounds, and the like, is always mediated by awareness of both self and surroundings, and other cognitive factors. Sensation is not separated from perception.

There can be exceptions to this. In the case of extreme and/ or sudden impacts of stimuli, these may overwhelm us with sensations of pain (or whatever) and allow explicit recognitions of what is happening to us, only in the consequent. But even with the most hypersensitive spectator, this surely is not what is involved in experiencing painting.

It follows, accordingly, that the impact of *painted* colour sensations on the human sensorium is never some direct appeal to the nervous system. Such sensations are always mediated by conceptual awareness. They are *perceptions*.

Deleuze is aware of this, but negotiates it in a sly and biased way. To see why, let us recall some other points from him that were noted earlier:

> Sensation has one face turned toward the subject (the nervous system, vital movement, 'instinct', 'temperament', . . . and one face turned toward the object (the 'fact', the place, the event). Or rather it has no face at all, it is both things indissolubly, it is Being-in-the-World, as the phenomenologists say.[65]

In the foregoing quotation, Deleuze is already, in effect, acknowledging that his notion of sensation is a cognitively complex one, rather than the customary sense of the term. However, he then actually misrepresents this cognitive complexity. The human subject's role in it is *reduced* to mere animal features such as the nervous system, and instinct, etc. But it is surely the case that in humans, even bare sensation amounts to much more than this by virtue of our *self-conscious* status, which means that the object also is experienced as more than mere 'place', 'event', or whatever.

Sensation, in other words, is embodied in a complex cognitive *reciprocity* between subject and object, that Deleuze slyly acknowledges, but misunderstands, or deliberately misuses. His account is confused further by his interpretation of Kant's notion of intensive magnitude in sensation. Deleuze uses Kant as an *authority* for the view that magnitude of sensation is registered always through a fall or descent.

However, whatever Kant's position is, or is not on this issue, it should be emphasized that a descent can be logical without also having to be perceptual/psychological. For even if the ascending intensity of a sensation is measured by reference to a base, this need not involve some felt, or perceived, explicit downward 'fall'. Rather we have degree zero as a logical, *tacit* base line against which intensity of magnitude is judged.

Whether a magnitude of sensation is *experienced psychologically or perceptually* as a fall or an ascent – or, better, as an accumulation – is determined by the character of what we are judging in these terms. And in the case of painting this is especially the case.

Now, it might be thought that if we simply allow Deleuze his redefinition of what sensation means, then the theory will work. However, it is more complicated than that. For while he concedes, indirectly, that what he is talking about is a mode of perception rather than sensation, he, at the same time, wants – where convenient to fall back into the customary understanding of the term – to make it seem that painting involves a passage of sensations in direct response to the stimuli of colour modulation.

This is why he emphasizes again and again that Figure impacts directly on the nervous system. Deleuze admits it involves complex cognitive judgement, but then, repeatedly, treats it as though it didn't. Why does he bring these contradictory characterizations together? There are a number of reasons. First, Deleuze is, in effect, redefining our response to painting, in general, on the basis of scattered comments by Cezanne and

Bacon concerning what they took to be at issue in their own painting. He tells us that,

> If the color is perfect, if the relations of color are developed for their own sake, then you have everything: form and ground, light and shadow, bright and dark. Clarity no longer resides in the tangible form or the optical light, but in the incomparable flash produced by complementary colours.[66]

Here Deleuze is freely paraphrasing and elaborating (without acknowledging it) some lines from Gasquet's 'reminiscences' of his conversations with Cezanne.[67] And likewise, in his bizarre claims about the direct impact of colour and Figure on the nervous system, he is drawing on a quotation from Bacon to the effect that 'to know why some paint comes across directly onto the nervous system and other paint tells you the story in a long diatribe through the brain'.[68]

A second reason why Deleuze introduces his whole suspect account of colour and sensation, is to ensure that his systematic treatment of Bacon and modern painting uses familiar Deleuzian notions.

The emphasis on sensation and the body without organs are connected instances of this. They are both major players in his previous philosophy, so obviously, he feels he must give them authoritative status in his discussion of Bacon and modern painting. The fact that Cezanne and Bacon themselves use similar notions, makes this assimilation all the more attractive, whatever distortions might be involved.

For Deleuze, the body without organs is of especial importance. In previous works, he uses it to evoke the fact that the human subject is not just an organism constrained by the limits of its physical, *organic*, capacity. It is, rather, a being that can base its actions on the potential to do this or that – or neither. A human's organic physicality it is tied to the here and now, but in its cognitive being it is always, as it were, alive in different potential scenarios to those of its immediate habitation.

For Deleuze, the body without organs is the signifier of this potential to transcend immediate organic limitations. It is something more than the 'lived-body' of phenomenology. It is the flow (and potential flow) of sensation through different 'orders' – a flow that is recognized through the different levels of intensity that its various shifts and motions occasion, or might occasion.

However, Deleuze's emphasis on different 'orders' to this overall sensation undermines its status as sensation. Whatever we feel – whatever our brute sensation of being alive might be – it is inflected, made meaningful, and given its momentary characterizations (in the passage from one sensation to another) by the cognitive appraisals on which it is founded.

Even if we talk of different orders of the same sensation (a notion difficult in itself), what we are talking about are its different aspects. But to see or feel one aspect rather than another is adopt one cognitive orientation rather than another. It is to perceive. The character of the sensation is dependent on this – unless it is a case of overwhelming brute causal impact alone (which is, of course, as I have claimed already, surely not the case with our experience of painting).

These cognitive orientations are the only possible basis for different 'orders' in the overall unity of our sensation of being alive. However, *they are not quantitative, but qualitative.* They are different *perceptions*, the cognition of different *aspects* to who and what we are.

Now, as indicated in note 1 of this chapter, in *What is Philosophy?* Deleuze and Guattari distinguish percepts and affects from perceptions and affective states. The former are the artist's perceptions and affective states as they are *embodied* in the artwork, and thence made available as sensations for the art audience.

However, it is this very embodiment – or *objective presentation of the artist's style* – that renders the notion of sensation so inappropriate in the art context. To see the works *as* percepts and affects, means to see them *as* complex expressions of high-level aesthetic cognition, rather than as sensations – and this is true even when, as in painting, we are engage with the work's particularity in the most direct sensory terms.

Characteristically, Deleuze distorts what is involved here, even further, through his crudely articulated notion of 'rhythm'. In this respect, we will recall his claims in relation to painting that,

> in the simple sensation, rhythm is still dependent on the Figure; it appears as the vibration that flows through the body without organs, it is the vector of the sensation, it is what makes the sensation pass from one level to another. In the coupling of sensation, rhythm is already liberated, because it confronts and unites the diverse levels of different sensations.[69]

Deleuze's confusions are at their densest here. Having posited a single sensation as the proper response to the Figure, he introduces rhythm as the 'vibration' that leads *from one sensation to another.* 'Vibration' is itself, of course, a quantitative-type notion, whose character, in the context of painting is not explained. It is no more than a 'something, I know not what'.

Conclusion

Given Deleuze's unwarranted hierarchies and conceptual confusions, the question arises as to whether his approach is sustainable in any significant way. The answer is yes.

Whatever its shortcomings, it must be reiterated that his treatment of Bacon and modern art is one that focuses with the most admirable insistency on how these works aesthetically disclose the world. And, in particular, he is especially attentive to the relation that really counts – namely the emergence of Figure from material structure. His analysis of Bacon has a compelling character – as long as we bear in mind the importance of allowing symbolic factors as a valid element of Bacon's style.

As far as I know, Deleuze only talks of Bacon's 'style' once,[70] and even then, makes it appear a suspicious term through putting it in inverted commas. This qualification is ill advised. Hopefully my detailed exposition and discussion of Deleuze's account has shown that everything in it is geared to showing what is at issue aesthetically and ontologically in Bacon's *individual style* and that of modern painting in general. If we eliminate the hierarchical factors, the grand narrative and misguided aspects of his essentialism, he still illuminates, nevertheless, key aspects of modern painting.

And there is one other important way in which Deleuze's theories are of the greatest service. Ironically, these focus on the most confused area of his approach, namely the relation between Figure, orders of sensation, the body without organs, the desire to escape the body, and rhythm.

Interestingly, there are important senses in which Deleuze's emphases of Figure, colour, and rhythm are anticipated in Mikel Dufrenne's *Phenomenology of Aesthetic Experience*. Dufrenne, indeed, uses 'rhythm' as one of his own most important terms.

Deleuze was familiar with Dufrenne's book,[71] and, indeed, his notion of Figure is in large part anticipated in Dufrenne's distinction between the represented object and the 'pictorial object'. The former is that which the picture is of. The latter is our sense of how this is generated from the picture as the product of gesture and coloured marks.

For Dufrenne this involves an originary notion of time. We are told, for example, that,

> pictorial space becomes temporalized when it is given to us as a structured and orientated space in which certain privileged lines constitute trajectories that, instead of appearing to us as the inert residue of some movement, appear as filled with a movement realized in immobility.[72]

Dufrenne uses the Bergsonian term 'duration' to indicate this mode of time which is internal to, and distinctive to, pictorial space. It is time evoked through imagination as a sense of the picture's very emergence into being, that is, the way it is created as the realization of the painter's individual dynamic strategy of gestural and compositional activity.

In practice,

> a painter decides on the relative importance of his colours by choosing his scale and then decides on the manner of treating them, either by modelling them, that is, by multiplying their various hues and tints from warm to cool. Colours are modulated for the purpose either of animating various areas of the canvas and articulating the design by means of colour or of obtaining the greatest intensity of colour.[73]

On these terms, harmonic colour choices and forms, are brought into a rhythmic compositional unity. As Dufrenne continues,

> rhythm belongs to drawing in the same way that harmony belongs to colour. Colour in itself, as harmony strives to grasp its essence and to give it form, cannot constitute a pictorial object. Drawing gives form. Only drawing gives consistency to an object, only drawing establishes discernable and measurable relationships in space where colours can be measured, contrasted, and grounded, and only drawing distributes these relationships and proportions into an order which requires movement. Thus drawing is irreplaceable.[74]

On these terms, then, rhythm is given a more concrete meaning than is found in Deleuze. It centres on the structural formal and compositional organization of the painting. And while Dufrenne, like Deleuze emphasizes the primacy of colour for painting, he sees drawing as the basis of rhythm. He integrates a key notion which is somewhat suppressed by Deleuze.[75]

Given these points, we can say that thinking Deleuze in relation to Dufrenne augments the former so that a more complete sense of what is at issue in Figure and rhythm begins to emerge. However, the augmentation works in the other direction also. Dufrenne's idea of the pictorial object as our perception of emergence through gesture and composition is ill understood through the notion of 'duration'.

The picture, indeed, involves a kind of dynamic emergence that, ironically is perceived through the immobility of the finished work. But this remains a worryingly metaphysical – even mystical – fascination. Can it be made more concrete?

I would say 'yes' – by reference to Deleuze. His notion of different orders of sensation within some overall sensation is a kind of confused characterization of the complex and dynamic unity in diversity of our aesthetic response to painting. But the link to the body without organs, and the desire to escape the body, are more vital clues to some key aspects that are at issue in such responses.

As we have seen, Deleuze gives them a quite distinctive loading in Bacon. But they are key players more generally in the understanding of painting – if we keep the notion of style in mind. In painting, the artist presents his or her sense of what is important in how the visual world is revealed. In ordinary life, we are immersed in things; our style of perceiving them does not exist independently of our body. The painting, however, frees the painter's style from this confine, and makes it exist at a public level – as a possibility of experience for others. It is, literally, an escape from the body for both the artist, *and the spectator*. At the same time, however, while the painting is, in essence, visual, it presents a visual world in a way that – through explorations of depth, and exploitation of the broader associations of colour and shapes, offers a spectacle that is not at all tied to just one organ of sense.

Indeed, the fact that we perceive the emergence of Figure or the pictorial object means that we have an immobile evocation of mobility – something that is at odds with, the horizon of time that the normal unified operation of our senses opens for us.

With the immense stylistic range of modern art, and, in particular, abstract painting, the eye indeed becomes polyvalent. It is not tied to any rigid order of visual perception, but rather takes us to places and aspects that are not normally available for direct visual perception.

What I am suggesting, then, is that Deleuze's notions place the body and its transcendence as central factors in aesthetic responses to style in painting. Instead of us being left with a metaphysical notion of time, we are returned to the ontology of the body – to the possibility of a more searching phenomenological orientation that negotiates both the pictorial object and the spectator's response to it.

And this is only a beginning. By exploding Deleuze's hierarchies, the opportunity for a more pluralistic phenomenological approach is established. The key thing is to follow Deleuze's exemplary attentiveness to pictorial style, and the role of the body, to see how these might be added to by other approaches, and what the results of this fusion might caution us against.

This task will occupy the remainder of this book. Before undertaking it, however, I shall now offer an alternative to Deleuze's explanation of the origins of modern art.

Chapter Two

Origins of Modernism and the Avant-Garde

Introduction

I shall now address the rise of modernism on an alternative basis to that of Deleuze by linking it to the notion of the 'avant-garde'. The terms 'modernism' and avant-garde[1] are often used in a loosely synonymous way to describe that, which, is new, or in some ways at odds with the established order of things. However, there is also a more specific historical usage where the terms are not synonymous, and which involve, indeed, distinctions of some significance. What is at issue in these distinctions is the way in which avant-garde conceptions of art phenomenologically reconceive the relation between art and reality.

Of course, to argue this in conclusive terms would take a book in itself. However, it is possible to outline a speculative, but viable, basis for such an argument. By doing so, it is possible to offer some reasons for the emergence of those general features of modern art that were noted in the Introduction to this book.

I shall, accordingly, in Part One, identify a factor inherent in mathematical perspective namely the *ontological reciprocity* of subject and object of experience. It will further be shown how this issue is implicated in various conflicts within Romantic art practice.

In Part Two attention will be paid to the way in which it then becomes a decisive factor in the rise of that most central of modernist pictorial idioms – impressionism. It will be suggested, also, that the work of Cézanne and Gauguin and his circle mark an important transitional point. For them, the function of art's symbolic means is taken, in effect, to involve a transformation of ontological reciprocity, rather than a mere embodiment of it.

This transformation and also the attempts to create different forms of it will then be explored in Part Three in the context of twentieth-century art.

Part One

First, mathematical perspective is a pictorial device which is not transmitted in a pure state, historically speaking. It is embedded in a whole network of idealizing devices and indeed, theories and institutions, which are known in concert as the 'academic' tradition.

The basis of this tradition is the acknowledged authority of models and theories from classical culture and from the Italian Renaissance. In philosophical terms, the academic view of things is one which demands conformity to 'timeless' canons of excellence and which assigns a primacy to rational constructions – of which mathematical perspective is a paradigm.

The breakdown of authority of the academic tradition is a complex and sustained process, which begins with the Enlightenment, if not earlier. It is also deeply bound up with broader economic and social upheavals. But, interestingly, there are elements within the tradition itself which point in the direction of its eventual disruption.

One such factor pertains to mathematical perspective. Consider the following remarks by Charles Taylor:

> As Panofsky describes it, the new distance (achieved through perspective) 'at one and the same time objectifies the object and personalizes the subject'. Didn't this also in

this way prepare the ground for the more radical break, in which the subject frees himself decisively by objectifying the world? The separation by which I stand over against the world perhaps helps prepare for the deeper rupture where I no longer recognize it as the matrix in which my life's ends are set. The stance of separation helps overcome that profound sense of involvement in the cosmos, that absence of a clear boundary between self and world, which was generated by and contributed to sustaining the premodern notions of cosmic order.[2]

The point is, then, that while in one sense perspective posits a continuity between the observer and a fixed objective order of visual items and relations, it at the same time introduces a sense of distance – a position which invites questioning about the individual's relation to the objective order. Perspective thus loosely anticipates that problematic relation of subject and object of experience, which becomes a key feature of European philosophy from Descartes onward and which is, of course, deeply involved into those more general political and social upheavals of modern society.

There is a sense, indeed, in which nineteenth-century art tendencies associated with the term 'Romanticism' also gravitate around the problematics of the subject–object relation. But there is a more interesting link to be made. To see why this is so, we must note one extremely general but significant line of continuity which runs through otherwise very different philosophies from the Enlightenment onwards.

It holds that the relation of subject and object in experience is not a case of one element being given passively to the other. The relation is, rather one of *reciprocal* interaction and modification. On these terms, the structure of subjectivity and the objective structure of the world are directly correlated. The one cannot be adequately characterized without reference to the other. I shall call this general position 'ontological reciprocity'. This encompasses the traditions of German idealism and Bergsonian vitalism, to the degree that, in those views, the structure of thought and of the objective world is correlated in a mutually defining dynamic.

A reciprocity of loosely the same kind also characterizes key philosophers in the tradition of existential phenomenology (Merleau-Ponty, most notably), insofar as they hold that spatio-temporality is organized on the basis of those practical interests brought to bear on it by the human subject, and that the subject in itself is orientated by its own spatio-temporal finitude.

This leads to a more specific feature in common between all these views. For if the relation between subject and object of experience is seen as an active reciprocity, rather than a static correlation, then such a position assigns a much more radical role to the dimension of *temporality*. Time is not just a necessary condition of experience, but *also* profoundly implicated in relation to questions of its meaning. Notions of change, transience, and historical transformation assume, correspondingly, a *positive* significance.

To understand the significance of this for the visual arts, we must first advert back to that aforementioned ambivalence in mathematical perspective which points towards a problematic relation between subject and object of experience. With the radical challenges to the ideology of academicism in the nineteenth century, this problem begins to surface in art, as it had already surfaced in philosophy.

There are many different manifestations of this. For example, it is customary to draw a distinction between *Poussinisme* and *Rubenisme* as recurrent tendencies in the academic tradition. The rivalry between Ingres and Delacroix is, perhaps, the culmination of this opposition. Ingres is the more officially sanctioned artist, who, in his strong emphasis on precisely defined plastic qualities and finishes, stays closer to classical models, and the notion of art as a fundamentally rational engagement with the visual and moral order. Delacroix, on the other hand takes much greater liberties in terms of composition and colouristic devices, and choices of content.

In naïve dialectical terms, it would be easy to see this well-known conflict in terms of the subject–object problematic, with Ingres epitomizing continuity with the objective order; and Delacroix instantiating the position which questions the subject's relation to the world.

There is *some* truth in this. But the more significant manifestation of the problematic is in the way it is *internalized* by both artists. Ingres (for all his official acceptability) also takes 'risks', especially in the mannered eroticism of his prediliction for the nude and oriental motifs. There is a strong element of subjective fantasy, which – like much academic art of the time – reflects a tension between a public order of morality, and a level of private indulgence which contradicts it.

Again, with Delacroix while the element of fantasy and risk is to the fore throughout his career, it is (in its strongest moments) constrained by traditional compositional devices (such as the structure of diagonals in the *Death of Sardanapalus*, 1827 [Musée du Louvre, Paris]). In this, and in such things as his systematic commitment to historical and literary sources, Delacroix remains (however loosely) within the academic parameters of *history painting*.

Now, the full details and ramifications of the 'positions' represented by Ingres and Delacroix, requires of course much more analysis than I can offer here. But I have said enough to show the signs of a crisis rather than a mere tension. For it is not just that the overt antagonism between Ingres and Delacroix (in both its stylistic and institutional setting) deepens the object–subject problematic; their opposed positions actually internalize aspects of one another's standpoints. The crisis comes about, in other words, through simultaneous sharpening and blurring of positions – a destabilizing of both the content and context of antagonism.

The resolution of this is protracted and intermittent and deeply implicated in the rise of modernism and beyond. It also has important affinities with the phenomenological standpoint, which I earlier characterized as 'ontological reciprocity'.

Part Two

In order to understand these affinities, one might first link lack of 'finish' and the diminution of perspectival accents in early modernist painters such as Manet, Monet, Pissarro, and Sisley, to a striving for spontaneity in terms of both perceptual and emotional responses, and an unwillingness to be bound by the dictates of tradition.

At the heart of all these factors is an insistence on the temporal as exemplified in evanescent atmospheric effects and movement. Just as importantly, however, these effects must also be linked to the rhythm of the urban world itself as exemplified in industry and its artefacts, the dynamic of crowds, the enjoyment of leisure time, and random encounters in public spaces.

In 1876, the critic Edmond Duranty published a brochure on the 'New Painting', which brings out these factors with some force. Consider the following:

> From within, we communicate with the outside through a window, and the window is the frame that ceaselessly accompanies us. . . . The window frame, depending on whether we are near or far, seated or standing, cuts off the external view in the most unexpected, most changeable way, obtaining for us that eternal variety and unexpectedness which is one of the great delights of reality.[3]

In this passage, Duranty exploits both the literal and metaphorical significance of the window to affirm the importance of subjective conditions of perception in connecting individual and world.

Significantly, he then transposes his example into both the hurly-burly of the crowded city street and the motions of nature, and relates it to the strategy of the new (impressionist) painters:

> They have tried to render the walk, the movement, the tremor, the intermingling of passersby, just as they have tired to render the trembling of leaves, the shivering of water, and the vibration of air inundated with light, and just as, in the case of the rainbow coloring of the solar rays, they have been able to capture the soft ambience of a gray day . . .[4]

In these remarks, Duranty sees a continuity between the impressionist treatment of the city, and its treatment of nature. At the heart of both is a relation between transient appearances and a mobile observer. The poetry of the visual work is not realized through contemplative abstraction and withdrawal from it; it involves, rather, a leisurely involvement and successive focusing on its diversity and shifting nuances.

An interesting example to consider here is Manet's *Dejeuner sur l' herbe* of 1863 (see Plate 2, Musee d'Orsay, Paris). The audience of the time was scandalized by the juxtaposition of a naked woman and a semi-dressed one, with two men in dandyish contemporary apparel. In its sexual provocativeness, the painting is a restrained anticipation of later fauve and expressionist 'licence'. Indeed, in even addressing a contemporary scene, it is at odds with academic painting's historical and classical orientations. For present purposes, however, I shall emphasize other factors.

The painting does not conceal the brushstrokes that bring forth its illusionistic content, and, in some areas, indeed, even seems unfinished. In this respect, the work exemplifies that emergence of Figure from material ground or 'diagram' that Deleuze sees as so central to modern painting.

However, the character of this Figure is extremely ambiguous. With a complex group like this, one would expect the painting to strike us as highly composed and thought through. Actually this is not the case. However, contrived the group is, in terms

Plate 2 Edouard Manet, *Dejeuner sur l'Herbe*, 1863, oil on canvas, 208 × 264 cm (81.9 × 103.9 in.), Musee d'Orsay, Paris/Giraudon/The Bridgeman Art Library.

of actual composition, *qua* Figure, it tends to suspend this by making it appear somewhat disorganized. There is, in fact, a strong sense of instability to the work. One aspect of this is spatial inconsistency or oddness – such as the semi-clothed woman appearing much nearer to the viewer than she should, and the curious jumble in the way that the figures in the central group are disposed towards one another – both in terms of gesture and physical juxtaposition.

The visual effect of this instability is to compress pictorial place, and produce a flatter looking painting. But the question is, what is at issue in this emphasis? An answer (in speculative terms, at least) might focus on the dynamic of the group's gazes.

The naked woman appears to be addressing the viewer directly while the frontally presented man is looking at someone a few degrees further over. They are engaged with the viewer, but the man on the viewer's right is addressing his gesture and gaze to his companions – and seems 'out of synch' with the viewer's arrival. Likewise the semi-dressed woman seems to have drifted into a different setting altogether.

I would suggest that what Manet is tending towards through these 'awkward' features is *an evocation of the presence of a participating mobile viewer.* The image is evoking, if not representing overtly, a synthesis of passing or passed moments, wherein the viewer is relating, or has related to the group. Awkward compositional elements, in other words, here suggest the spontaneity and transience of visual perception, and the reciprocal relation between that which is seen and the one who sees it.

Other painters engage with this spontaneity and ephemerality of the visual encounter, on different stylistic terms. Consider, for example, Monet's *Le Pont de l'Europe, Gare Saint-Lazare* of 1877 (Musée Marmottan, Paris). Here, the figures and machines, the daylight and steam, are forms and masses equalized in visual terms. In particular, the drifting clouds of steam serve to both carry the spectator's gaze into the distance, and, yet, at the same time, suggest a gentle counter-motion tending towards envelopment of the viewer. This carries the epistemological implication that the relation between subject and object of experience is not an absolutely fixed division, but rather one which is constantly transformed by new circumstances. The subject and his or her world are, in a constant state of *reciprocal interaction and modification.*

As we shall see in more detail (in Chapter Four) an affirmation of reciprocity is also found – with much more complex emphases – in the work of Cézanne. After the early 1870s he develops a technique, which focuses on the juxtaposition of small planes of colour, rather than tonal modelling. This results in works wherein the plasticity of objects does not disrupt the integrity of the picture plane. Indeed his combination of different perspectival viewpoints in the same plane is one, which emphasizes the plasticity of objects by distending them. Hence, there is an implicit correlation between the character of the objects, the fullness of their presence, and the viewer's capacity to change his or her viewpoint in relation to them.

Some of the further complexities embedded here are well brought out in a brilliant passage by T. J. Clark:

> In Cézanne's art 'seeing' is certain that it takes possession not just of straws of color but of objects made out of them; it believes that it *has* the world, in all its fullness and articulation, and that the world is present *in seeing, strictly and narrowly conceived.* Yet at the same time it seems to grow progressively uncertain as to how its procedures give rise to the separateness and connection of things. Thus the task of representation comes to be twofold: to demonstrate the fixity and substance of the world out there, but also to admit that the seer does not know – most probably cannot know – how his or her won sight makes objects possible.[5]

These remarks indicate just why the work of Cézanne marks a key transition point. The visual world is defined by reciprocity between the viewer and the viewed, but this cannot be adequately expressed within the existing formats of pictorial representation. Indeed, the visual itself is only one aspect of a more total reciprocity involving all the senses and our physical and social setting.

As Clark goes on to observe: 'In Cézanne, . . . painting took the ideology of the visual – the notion of seeing as a separate activity with its own truth, its own peculiar access to the thing-in-itself – to its limits and breaking point.'[6] The breaking point in question here surely centres on the problem of mathematical perspective. The implied continuity between viewer and viewed in such a technique, symbolically ties the observer to an idealized objective order of things. But this static monocular relation is at odds with the visual's complex temporalized relation to both its objects and other pertinent factors.

If art is, therefore, to creatively engage with the visual world in a more searching way, something new, logically speaking, is demanded. The opportunity is created for a radical transformation of pictorial representation's semantic and syntactic code, so as to accommodate a more searching expression of the ontological reciprocity between subject and object of experience.[7]

It is this possibility and the pictorial and broader cultural implications consequent upon it, which make Cezanne's achievement into something much more than 'ideology' in a negative sense. This transformatory approach is also manifest in different and more diffuse ways in some of the artists associated with Gauguin's circle, most notably, of course, Van Gogh and Gauguin himself. In their work, an intensive schematization of form, contour, and colour – subsequently radicalized by the fauves and German expressionists among others – is seen as a kind of mutual liberation of the self, and of the world's expressive possibilities.

As will be shown in Chapter Three, such a Nietzschean liberation – in its very phenomenological intensity – is also taken by some of these artists to have further radical political and social overtones of a utopian kind.[8]

The 'ideology of the visual', then, brings us to the threshold of a qualitative break. It shows that some modernist art involves not only refinements of pictorial strategy so as to address the more temporally insistent aspects of the real, but also posits art itself as *an idiom which comprehends the real in distinctive and unique terms through acting upon it in a direct way.*

Modern art's emphasis on planarity, and new ways of articulating it, might be taken as a tacit recognition of this distinctiveness. The possibility is thus opened up for new semantic and syntactic structures which offer a radical progression beyond the last vestiges of mathematical perspective and its legacy. It should be emphasized that the transition to this point is not one of evolution, but of progressive articulation – bits and pieces accumulating and modifying one another in ways that open up new possibilities.

This involves a complex interaction of new and traditional idioms across a long period of time and which eventually issues in a critical mass of the most radical transformations – exemplified most dramatically in Picasso's *Demoiselles d'Avignon* of 1907 (Museum of Modern Art, New York).

On these terms, then, the term *avant-garde* is warranted, in quite specific and special sense, for the instigators of these transformations. What is at issue in them is not new ways of representing reality, so much *as new possible relations between representation and reality*. Avant-garde art embodies a new relation to experience, phenomenologically speaking. At the heart of this new meaning is the notion of *ontological reciprocity*. This can be exemplified in many different ways. I shall now consider some of these possibilities in relation to the major varieties of avant-garde art.

Part Three

As we have already seen, some of the artists who can be described as avant-garde in the special sense, have a figurative orientation. However, the real energy of the avant-garde finds its main expression in artists of more abstract or conceptual orientation, since it is here that the possibility of new semantic and syntactic structures for art is most open.

But here we have a paradox because the first great example of this tendency – Picasso's and Braque's cubism – comes with no explicit phenomenological programme from the artist themselves. However, it can be argued that there is a genuine phenomenological transformation which occurs in their work so as to bring painting and reality into a closer mode of reciprocal proximity. In this respect, Chapter Five will show, in detail, that cubist works self-consciously and manifestly reorganize visual appearance in such a way as to aesthetically emphasize those characteristics of spatial tangibility and mutability which both demand and inform the organization of such appearance by the human cognitive apparatus.

The reciprocal structural dependence of object and subject of experience is interiorized within the semantic and syntactic structure of Picasso's and Braque's cubism. A rather more overt phenomenological dimension can, of course, be found in the work of the Italian futurists and the de Stijl group. In the former case, we have an extensive use of Bergson's theories as a ratification of metaphysical vitalism, and of the dynamism of all aspects of modern urban culture, and of course machine technology in particular.[9]

Indeed, Italian futurism sees the latter as in profound senses emblematic of metaphysical vitalism itself. For it is through the dynamic rhythms of modern life that modes of personal and collective existence adapt themselves self-consciously to those dynamic forces which ultimately drive and structure the universe's creative evolution. Boccioni, for example, affirms the importance of 'simultaneousness' in art, and defines it as 'an effect of that great cause which is *universal dynamism*. It is the lyrical manifestation of modern ways of looking at life, based on speed and contemporaneity in knowledge and communication'.[10]

Mondrian's de Stijl metaphysic takes us in some very different directions. His writings[11] and artworks embody an often understated neo-Hegelian thrust wherein nature calls art into being but is then spiritually transformed by art into something phenomenologically higher.

By abstracting from natural forms and relations the artist forms a pictorial structure which is more unified than these originals. Through such pictorial reconceptions we can recognize those fundamental dialectical oppositions which organize nature. Our consciousness is thus elevated towards a more universal level of understanding wherein nature and spirit are understood more determinately in their reciprocity.

Another neo-Hegelian explosion of the avant-garde can be linked to those surrealist theories and practices associated with André Breton. It is a commonplace to interpret surrealism as though its primary theoretical ratification is in terms of Freudian notions of the unconscious. This is extremely one-sided. Breton himself said in 1935 that 'even today it is Hegel whom we must question about how well-founded or ill-founded surrealist activity in the arts is.'[12]

Indeed, in the second *Surrealist Manifesto* Breton advocates surrealism as a kind of dialectical expansion of consciousness through complex realms of ontology. Referring to Engel's famous example of dialectical contradiction in the statement 'The rose is a rose', Breton suggests that the surrealist artist should attempt,

> to lure the rose into a movement where it is pregnant with less benign contradictions, where it is successively the rose that comes from the garden, the one that has an unusual place in a dream, the one impossible to move from the 'optical bouquet', the one that can completely change this properties by passing into automatic writing, the one that retains only those qualities that the painter has deigned to keep in surrealist painting and finally the one completely different from itself, which returns to the garden.[13]

This dialectic of artistic intervention upon the object takes some rather more sceptical and hostile forms in other avant-garde artists. In Chapter Six, for example, I will argue (against Thierry de Duve) that Duchamp's unassisted ready-mades, involve a parody which implicitly mocks the pretensions of art to represent reality, and which subverts, accordingly, the elevated cultural status which is traditionally assigned to art.

In the work of the Dadaists, this scepticism becomes a hostile energy that wishes to destroy the role of art and its institutions – implicated as they are, in the maintenance of the repressive social status quo. This being said, there are other aspects of Duchamp, and some Dadaists such as Schwitters which point in a rather different direction, namely the construction of a more complex alternative reality wherein the trivial or discarded objects of everyday life can be aesthetically re-routed into new avenues of signification and art. This does not lead to a completely constituted phenomenological alternative, but rather extends the pleasures of aesthetic form in new directions. (These will be addressed in more detail, in Chapter Six.)

Before considering a decisive transitional case, it is worth thinking about the legacy and fate of the artists and tendencies mentioned, and what this tells us provisionally about the limits of the avant-garde. The key point is that while art's transformative phenomenological significance is at issue within them, it is one whose time has gone. By this, I do not simply mean that these movements have become old fashioned and should be seen as significant only in terms of the art-historical circumstances which gave rise to them.

The problem is rather that they are theoretically overdetermined. If avant-garde art seeks a new route to the absolute, the problem is that once such absolute art is attained, there is no real way for it to continue its own transformation, except through endless variations on the basic absolute format or strategy. The very audaciousness of the avant-garde's transformations condemns them, in most cases to creative paralysis.

The effects of this can even be seen in terms of those artists working in the positive Duchampian tradition where the transformation involved is not stylistic in any straightforward terms. Works by Neo-Dadaists, Beuys, and more recent conceptual artists, operate from the premises that, in principle, anything can be art if it is designated as such by the artist.

The irony of this, is that as a paradigm of creativity this, in effect, empties art of any real avant-garde structure, precisely, because it involves a mere use of objects in the service of vague theoretical or culturally critical ideas. If anything can be art, then art *qua* exploration of significant boundaries has nowhere to go . . . except into further vagueness.

It is important to stress the term 'vagueness' here, for, more often than not, the meaning of such work is determined only by a managerial class of critics, curators, art historians, and gallery owners. The only experimental content or innovation is a sense of the *outré* for its own sake – and even this is negated by insertion into the publicity, media, and managerial structures of the art world, where innovation for the sake of it is a dreary norm. The avant-garde in this context gives way to the demands of fashion and careerism and amounts to no more than that.

Does this mean, then, that the time of the avant-garde has now gone forever? Not necessarily. To see why this is so, we must briefly consider some key points concerning Kasimir Malevich and his intellectual milieu. Like other avant-gardists, Malevich ratifies his work by reference to metaphysics, most notably that of Schopenhauer.[14] However, his visual idioms have a diversity and radical experimental quality, which point beyond any single link between pictorial means and a single absolute conception of phenomenological truth. Indeed, the influence of *Zaum* theory – concerning the possibility of a trans-rational language – gives Malevich's work a special significance.

The reason for this is that, as we have seen, what makes avant-gardism more than the merely new or modern, is its re-thinking of pictorial means so as to codify some central conceptions of phenomenological truth in an aesthetic form. We have also seen that the absoluteness of these conceptions tends to paralyse further substantial creative development in the artists concerned. However, suppose we focus on what is common to all these efforts and ignore the specific answers, which they give.

In these general terms, we might say that to be avant-garde involves the invention of new artistic codes and idioms so as to comprehend the phenomenological *elusiveness* of the real. The scope of Malevich's practice as artist, designer, and theorist is an exemplar of this flexibility. His work is enormously complex and refuses to cash-out in terms of some exact 'absolute' style. This is illustrated marvellously in his *Englishman in Moscow*, of 1914 (see Plate 3, Stedelijk Museum, Amsterdam).

Plate 3 Kazimir Severinovich Malevich, *An Englishman in Moscow*, 1913–14, oil on canvas, 88 × 57 cm (34.6 × 22.4 in.), Stedelijk Museum, Amsterdam/The Bridgeman Art Library.

The foreground, the central figure's form, and the background are fused, using structures that blend a sense of the facet with that of the geometrical solid. These features and their spatial distribution, the overall planar emphasis of presentation, and the use of lettering, all evoke the visual character of cubist space. However, what is more striking is Malevich's stylistic re-appropriation of this. In his work the individual forms are much more distinct than those in Braque's and Picasso's cubist works.

Indeed, in great contrast with their paintings and collages, the pictorial space in this work is *not* created through the distending and merging of the represented object with the surrounding space (or with spatially contiguous objects) or with the picture plane itself. Rather the composition is based on a psychology of visual declaration or association where pictorial elements such as the fish, church, candle, and the ladder, may be reflections in a window or in a mirror that the Englishman is gazing into, or they may be visualizations of things that represent psychological barriers between him and his perception of Russia.

Whatever, the case, this is a kind of playing with space, in every sense. It carries the suggestion that visual reality is not only constantly mobile in terms of the viewer's relation to ever-changing objects, but that this relation is both obscured and clarified, and re-routed through mediation by psychological and cultural *symbols*. And in this case, the symbolism runs to a more metaphysical level. The Russian words in the picture mean 'eclipse' (at the top) which has been divided into two words that suggest 'beyond the dark'. The words towards the bottom mean 'partial' divided so as to suggest the words 'hour' and 'hourly'.

What is evoked by all these terms, is a temporary but partial loss of light that will be overcome in time. It is this which explains the symbolic significance of the represented objects. The church, and the cross formed from the candle and the sword, will, in time, remove the scales (embodied in the fish) from the Englishman's hypnotically fixated eyes, and allow him to see the light. On these terms, then, Malevich's Englishman is himself a symbol of cultural and religious alienation, functioning as both an individual outsider, and as a symbol of a deeper outsiderliness. At the same time, however, Malevich inscribes this pictorially speaking, with the possibility of redemption in both dimensions.

Now an image such as this can be analysed, but in the concrete perception of it, these analytic factors are drawn back, and made strange through the specific manner in which they cohere, inseparably, in the visual unity of the image itself. As a focus of visual and psychological complexity, the picture does not allow our sense of the individual's immersion in visual reality, to settle into some edifying formula.

Given that Malevich's *Zaum* sensibility is centred on the elusiveness of the real rather than some end system that is the recurrent goal of new signifying practices, then this is a clue to what an enduring avant-garde might be. In negative terms such an avant-garde will acknowledge that no world-changing system or utopian ideal will be the result of its activity. It is this ambition, indeed, which contextualizes the avant-garde as part of modernism. In positive terms, the task is to continue exploring possible codes, which articulate elusive key phenomenological structures of the real, but without trying to absolutize the visual idioms in which they are to be expressed.

I have argued, then, that the rise of modernism and the avant-garde centres on a gradual change in how the ontological reciprocity of subject and object of experience is understood in broad cultural, societal, and philosophical terms. The dynamism of the relation finds expression through the rhythms of urban life, and through this, into painting. Eventually, the reciprocity of subject and object of experience is such as to demand new pictorial codes, and a more active involvement of visual art media themselves as elements in this reciprocity. Through all this, the four major stylistic features that I identified in the Introduction to this book, are engaged. As noted earlier, the main argument in this chapter is admittedly speculative. But it offers a viable explanation of why modern art has been so orientated towards stylistic transformations that emphasize process and a re-thinking of the scope and structure of individual media such as painting.

In the remainder of this book, I will consider how these transformations are to be understood in relation to specific artists and tendencies. (Special attention will be devoted to the new avant-garde pictorial codes of abstract art, in the last two chapters of the book.)

Chapter Three

Nietzsche and the Varieties of Expressionism

Introduction

In the Introduction to this book, I identified four general stylistic characteristics of modern art. One of them centres on a handling of paint that is not constrained by academic criteria of 'finish' and compositional norms. In impressionist art it is a feature used, mainly, to evoke the play of light on surfaces. In post-impressionist painters it is often explored for more complex and diverse expressive ends – often bound up with mystical ambitions. Another tendency (often overlapping with the above) is the overcoming of traditional notions of artistic and moral propriety in terms of choice of subject matter.

In the first decade of the twentieth century this overcoming of finish and propriety becomes the insistent basis of a quite aggressive, extreme painterly tendency – notably in the fauves, but markedly and more self-consciously so in the varieties of 'Expressionism'. These artists take the release from 'finish', and from aesthetic and moral constraints, to its most extreme level. Indeed, it becomes a tendency that recurs – in different forms – throughout the twentieth century.

Previously in European art, painters have been described as 'expressionist', on occasion – usually in relation to specific works, or specific periods of their work where there is an emphasis on such things as insistently manifest brushstrokes or brutal or grotesque subject matter, or both. (Late Goya, and even late Titian, are cases in point, here.)

Twentieth-century expressionism exemplifies these stylistic features in a more sustained way – often with a strong polemic social intent. In the broadest terms, the affirmation of such features is taken to be a more direct and authentic idiom of visual communication, that is more primal than the ossified commonplaces of established idioms.

As we have seen, Deleuze does no justice to the more existential dimension of aesthetic meaning – regarding it as a mere aspect of 'figuration'. However, these stylistic features can be probed in searching phenomenological terms if we think them through on the basis of Nietzsche's philosophy of art. Such a thinking through is not concerned, primarily with the direct influence of Nietzsche's ideas on varieties of expressionism, but rather with showing the striking general consistency between Nietzschean aesthetics and the varieties of expressionist art practice. By thinking these two factors through together, the phenomenological meaning of the latter can become manifest.

In recent times, of course, Nietzsche has been culturally stereotyped as an 'anti-metaphysical' philosopher. This is because of his hostility to philosophical *systems*. But a thinker can become *profoundly* metaphysical by virtue of the very intensity of his or her hostility to system. Nietzsche is of this ilk. He offers a distinctive vision of humanity's relation to itself and to the world, by virtue of his radicalization of finitude, and the link between rationality and animality. His philosophy is, in consequence, an aggressively vitalist phenomenology of thought, feeling, and action.

In this chapter, accordingly, I shall, in Part One, outline Nietzsche's philosophy and its understanding of art as outlined (mainly) in *The Will to Power*. In Part Two, I think through some of its ambiguities, and then consider its relevance to German expressionism of the early twentieth century.

Part Three then traces its continuing consistency with other varieties of twentieth-century expressionism. In Part Four, special attention is paid to its relevance for postmodern neo-expressionism, and, in particular, the work of Georg Baselitz.

Part One

The essential context for Nietzsche's claims about art is, of course, his overall philosophical position. This position is encapsulated in the following remarks:

> . . . there is only *one* world, and this is false, cruel, contradictory, seductive, without meaning – a world thus constituted is the real world. We have need of lies in order to live – that lies are necessary in order to live is itself part of the terrifying and questionable character of existence.[1]

By 'lies' Nietzsche means the general production of illusion. Indeed, he goes on to claim that man must be a liar by nature – which amounts, in his terms, to being an artist. In *The Gay Science*, this rhetorical characterization is cashed out in more specific terms, as follows:

> What one should learn from artists. – How can we make things beautiful and attractive when they are not? – Moving away from things until there is a good deal one no longer sees and there is much that our eye has to add if we are to see them at all; or seeing things round a corner and as cut out and framed; or to place them so that they partially conceal each other and grant us only glimpses of architectural perspectives.[2]

Nietzsche is emphasizing here the capacity of artistic style to change the world's appearance. And it is interesting that his characterization of this – with its emphasis on vision exceeding its customary organic confines – is strongly reminiscent of Deleuze's notion of the body without organs.

Indeed, just as Deleuze emphasizes the link between art and sensation, Nietzsche also stresses art's embodiment of it – albeit with a different emphasis. As he puts it,

> Art reminds us of states of animal vigour; it is on the one hand an excess and overflow of blooming physicality, on the other, an excitation of the animal functions through the images and desires of intensified life – an enhancement of the feeling of life, a stimulant to it.[3]

Indeed, 'The demand for art and beauty is an indirect demand for the ecstasies of sexuality communicated to the brain. The world becomes perfect through "love".'[4] The artwork, then is testimony to *an overflow of power* which, in giving rise to rich sensuous configurations and images of how life can be, or might become, serves to enhance the audience's own total feeling of life. It is, as it were, an *embodiment and communicator of sensuous and sensual possibility.*

The overflow of power which gives rise to this is, however, somewhat complex. It is an extreme state akin to certain forms of nervous illness. Nietzsche cites in particular three characteristics:

(1) intoxication: the feeling of enhanced power; the inner need to make of things a reflex of one's own fullness and perfection;

(2) the *extreme sharpness* of certain senses, so that they understand a quite different sign language – and create one . . .

(3) the *compulsion to imitate* . . . a state is divined on the basis of signs and immediately enacted . . .[5]

The art impulse, then, is an overflow of power which becomes both a need for and a heightened sensitivity towards the communicative possibilities of signs and mimesis. The overflow thus demands and finds a structured mode of expression.

This brings us to the most complex aspect of the will to art. It is well known, in his *Birth of Tragedy* (1872), that Nietzsche saw art – especially that of the ancient Greeks – as embodying two distinctive modes of expression, the Apollinian and the Dionysian. In *The Will to Power* he defines these in the following way:

> The word 'Dionysian' means: an urge to unity, a reaching out beyond personality, the everyday, society, across the abyss of transitoriness; . . . an ecstatic affirmation of the total character of life as that which remains the same, just as powerful, just as blissful through all change. The word 'Apollinian' means: the urge to perfect self-sufficiency, to the typical 'individual', to all that simplifies, distinguishes, makes strong, clear, unambiguous . . . freedom under the law.[6]

In terms of its general applications, the Apollinian–Dionysian distinction seems to tie neatly in with other parallel pairs of oppositions, notable between classicism and romanticism, being and becoming, and, in visual art, *Poussinisme* and *Rubenisme*.

By the time of *The Will to Power*, however, Nietzsche is somewhat uneasy about these putative oppositions and parallels. We are told, for example, that,

> The desire for destruction, change, becoming *can* be the expression of an overfull power pregnant with the future . . . (Dionysiac); but it can also be the hatred of the ill-constituted, disinherited, under-privileged, which destroys, *has* to destroy, because what exists, indeed existence itself . . . enrages and provokes it.[7]

On the other hand,

> 'Eternalization' . . . can proceed from gratitude and love – an art of this origin will always be an art of apotheosis . . . but it can also be that of a tyrannic will of a great sufferer . . . taking revenge on all things, as it were, by impressing . . . and forcing them into . . . the image of his torture.[8]

Nietzsche's point in these two quotations is (presumably) to over-come the sharpness of the Apollinian–Dionysian distinction, by highlighting the ambiguous relation which exists between the will to art, and the works which embody it. Characteristically, we will expect dramatic Dionysian-looking works to spring from Dionysian motives: but they can also embody a kind of Apollinian rage for order in the midst of chaos and feebleness. Likewise while we might expect Apollinian-looking idealized art to be a manifestation of plenitude and control, it can also emerge from Dionysian urge to make the world answer to the suffering self.

Given this ambiguity between the art impulse and its embodiments, Nietzsche proposes an alternative distinction which supposedly avoids such difficulties. It is the opposition between, on the one hand, *romantic* art which springs from an extreme dissatisfaction with reality, and is thence an art of 'hunger'; and, on the other hand, *apotheosis* art, which has its origins in the feeling of gratitude for existence, and a sense of 'superabundance'.

Now this pairing has difficulties and ambiguities of its own – notably in the scope of the two terms involved. Indeed, one suspects that it is in part an uneasy attempt to square his own taste (and particularly his dislike of extreme romanticism) with a world view that in his later works is increasingly characterized by him as 'Dionysian'.

However, Nietzsche at the same time achieves something of a more general significance: he in effect overturns the rigid dis-tinction between *all* the parallel paired oppositions noted earlier, namely Apollinian–Dionysian, Being–Becoming, *Poussiniste–Rubeniste*. Under the rubic 'apotheosis art', for example, he groups Homer, Raphael, and Rubens. Clearly, oppositions are coming unstuck here.

I shall now situate this theory in more historically specific terms. In the first decade of the twentieth century, Wilhelmine Germany was an ideologically rigid society, dominated by an imperial ethos of the Fatherland and sustained by a rapidly expanding industrial economy supported in turn by colonial expansion. A rigidly bourgeois society of this sort, of course, sustained fairly predictable canons of taste – classicism and the Ideal in the Academy, late romanticism and impressionism for the more adventurous, and *biedermier* for more popular consumption.

Against this, however, must be measured three disruptive elements. First, industrial expansion brings with it, of course, urban expansion and also the problem of individual identity in the midst of crowds. Second, one of the indirect fruits of colonialism, is a greater availability and awareness of 'primitive' art. Third, there is a relevant specific development in the field of German art history and theory in the early twentieth century – namely a tendency to emphasize that art has its origin not in the perfecting of the mimetic faculty as such, but rather in a more fundamental art impulse which seeks to impose order on the chaos of the sensible world by forming material both abstractly and mimetically. (This view is associated most closely with Wilhelm Wörringer's *Abstraction and Empathy*.)

These disruptive elements connect with the intellectual impetus of Nietzschean philosophy in general, and in particular his doctrine of the will to art. At the general level, his philosophy is a critique of bourgeois rationality, Christianity, and the values of the crowd. His notion of the will to art concentrates this in even more telling ways.

This is because, first, for Nietzsche, art is essential to being human; second, it embodies an impulse which is a sensuous and sensual overflow of the individual's power; third the artist is one apart – not as the lonely genius, but as one hypersensitive to the world of the senses and to the need for and possibilities of, communication; fourth, the art impulse is not simply Apollinian or Dionysian, but rather flows out either to remedy a dissatisfaction with reality, or as a festive superabundance of being.

All in all, Nietzsche propounds a notion of *art as primarily direct communication through sensuous form*. Art seen in these terms is an explosive force. In an ideologically rigid and alienated urban society, it is the possibility of a mode of communication which is fundamental and direct in a way that other stereotyped modes of communication and discourse are not.

Art is not some luxury item – it is a necessity. It is a disalienating factor in urban experience. Indeed Nietzsche's affirmation of art as triumphantly sensuous and sensual, legitimizes a practice which dispenses with, or even attacks alienated canons of bourgeois social and sexual propriety.

At the same time, this theory is one which also differentiates the artist from society. This outsiderliness however, is not elitist in the sense of hinging upon social rank. Neither is it simply a romantic notion of the lonely artistic genius. Rather the artist's alienation is one of the extreme sensitivity akin to that of another group marginalized by capitalism – namely the mentally disturbed.

The artist, indeed, has other allies. For Wörringer's influential notion of the art impulse not only reinforces Nietzsche's account of a will to art, but also, in effect, extends it in the direction of a more sympathetic revaluation of the art of primitive cultures – and this at a time when, as noted earlier, knowledge of such cultures was rapidly expanding.

One might say that, if a will to art is seen as prior, and as determining the mimetic faculties – as is the case with Nietzsche and Wörringer – than the stylized formal reductionism and stark sensuousness of primitive art in general (including here indigenous German 'primitive' art such as the tradition of the *Totentanz* in woodcut, or Bavarian glass painting) might strike the artist as the most primal embodiment of the art impulse.

Nietzsche's philosophy links up with, and illuminates, in other words, various factors that are antagonistic to bourgeois art practice. In the context of such factors, it presents the possibility of art as a means for shattering the alienating distance placed between individuals by urban experience and bourgeois ideology. Indeed, while legitimizing the significance of the individual creator – communicator, it also gives this individual identity a collective dimension – by locating it within a discourse of outsiderliness provided by the mentally ill, by people of primitive cultures, and the indigenous tradition of 'primitive' art.

Part Two

Now, as noted earlier, my main concern is with how Nietzsche's philosophy of art illuminates what is at stake existentially speaking in expressionist styles, rather than questions of his direct influence on them. However, it is worth saying at least something, about the *character* of that influence. It is well known, for example, that Nietzsche's work (especially *Also Sprach Zarathustra*) was well known to Kirchner and other members of the early expressionist groups.[9]

This does not mean that they simply adopted Nietzsche as a kind of manifesto. The relation is much more complex. Indeed, there is much in Nietzsche's thought that pushes in a reactionary direction that would have been wholly unacceptable to *avant-garde* artists. One might cite here the importance he attaches to 'rank' and 'breeding', or (however Dionysian the motives) the importance of restraint and control in the creation of art. Perhaps more important still are his profound reservations about modernity and the worth of modernist culture as such.

However, these reactionary aspects must be measured against another factor. When artists look to philosophy to legitimize their practices or to find ideas for new ways forward, they rarely appropriate a philosophical position in its entirety. Rather they extract insights which square with their own positions or which seem to carve out a space of possibilities in terms of which their position might develop. The rest is ignored.

Interestingly, Nietzsche in many ways invites such a plundering. Consider the following remarks from *The Will to Power*:

Modern art as an art of tyrannising – a coarse and strongly defined logic of delineation; motifs simplified to the point of formulas; the formula tyrannises. Within the delineations and wild multiplicity, an overwhelming mass, before which the senses become confused; brutality in colour, material, desires.[10]

And from *The Gay Science* (1882, revised 1887):

everywhere, . . . , I see the delight in all the *coarser* eruptions and gestures of passion. What is demanded nowadays is a certain convention of passionateness – anything but genuine passion! Nevertheless, passion itself will be reached this way, and our descendents will not only indulge in savage and unruly forms, but will be *really savage.*[11]

Nietzsche is here describing the modern age in ostensibly negative terms. This is his official position. Instinct begins to get the better of will power (in the sense of willing ends and means).

However, there is an unresolved ambiguity in Nietzsche's overall position which also surfaces here, and which might have helped expressionist painters to find a deeper level of compatibility between his thought and their practice. For the will to power in general is a function of the fulfilment both of instinctual drives and existential projects founded on the rational willing of ends and means.

Nietzsche, however, rarely clarifies the relation between the two. Officially he must privilege the rational aspect, but the *instinct* for power must not be lost sight of. Indeed there is a case for saying that given his hostility to rational systems of explaining the world, the will to power as instinct – as a function of sheer physical, sensuous, sensual embodiment, must ultimately be decisive.

At various points in the Nietzschean corpus, explicit emphasis is given to this. However, his main emphasis of it is rather more indirect. It is to be found in the *sensuous thrust of his own intoxicating rhetoric and imagery*. Even as he stresses the need for restraint and rational control in art, the tone of his rhetoric subverts this content. Indeed, while the foregoing quotations from him construe the modern age and its future negatively, they at the same time take a kind of perverse relish in them.

Nietzsche's Dionysian instincts, here, sense that modernity embodies 'will-to-power' in a more primal form, one that is in accord with the overwhelming expressive thrust of his own rhetoric. His doctrine of the will to art, therefore, not only has elements of content – centring on art as a primarily direct and sensuous mode of communication – which would be amenable to plundering by expressionist artists, but is also couched in rhetorical tones which focus this primal aspect. By so doing, the rhetorical dimension serves to cancel out elements in Nietzsche, which would otherwise be hostile to such plundering.

On these terms, the 'feel' of Nietzsche's own rhetorical style – his savouring of *attack* – might encourage a much more sensuously aggressive attitude in painters who were familiar with his writing. This could well point towards those features which characterize German expressionism – namely, a willingness to define forms in emphatically stylized linear or schematic terms and to render both these and broader shapes and masses with unabashed colouristic intensity. The physicality and texture of paint and brushwork is manifest. Elements of tonal modelling and perspectival recession are diminished accordingly.

In terms of content, an art of this sort will be orientated towards subjects that can be sensually provocative – such as the nude – or which have archaic resonances or associations (as in primitive art), or an immediate and direct relation to the artist's own experience of the social and physical environment.

It is worth considering, now, how this will to art might be related to specific expressionist works. In this respect, consider Ernst-Ludwig Kirchner's *Self-Portrait as a Soldier*, 1915 (see Plate 3.1, Allen Memorial Art Museum, Oberlin College, Ohio).

The picture was painted during Kirchner's convalescence during military service. Its colours are vivid and direct but curiously off-key, and sour. They invest the work with a dreamlike intensity, that makes itself *uncanny* by the fact that the basic components of the work – the artist in his studio with a model – are not at all dreamlike in terms of what they are literally.

Kirchner's own features and that of the model in the background, are articulated in the simplified, stylized way

Plate 4 Ernst-Ludwig Kirchner, *Self-Portrait as a Soldier*, 1915, oil on canvas, 27.25 × 24 in. (69.2 × 61 cm), Allen Memorial Art Museum, Oberlin College, Charles F. Olney Fund, 1950, Oberlin, Ohio.
A colour version of this image can be found in the plate section in the centre on this book.

characteristic of the non-western sculptures that were so important for so many *avant-garde* artists at the beginning of the twentieth century. Their angularity invests flesh with a heroism and monumentality – a kind of direct generalization of being human that is in the starkest contrast with the universalizing treatments of the human form in more academic art.

Of especial note is the curious spatial relation between the artist and the model. She is in the background, but with the space between artist and model so compressed that she appears to be almost perched on his shoulder – her gaze addressing both the painting in the background, and Kirchner's military headgear. The perspectival inconsistency on which this conjunction is based, accentuates the psychological loading of the painting. The artist is in the military, but all the things he is as a practicing artist, and as a man with desire for both art and the erotic, crowd in upon his sad present military identity.

Everything in the work converges on the pained relation between the artist's 'hands'. In the painting, the right one is not there (even though Kirchner, himself, had not been so mutilated). All we have is the grotesque symbolic stump. And the left one, while present, is distorted in a dislocated gesture that seems to aspire to hold a paintbrush, but cannot do so.

In this respect, the most personal fear of an artist – to have the means to artistic creation destroyed – are given a direct exemplification, through sensuous means that are themselves brutal.

Now, in addressing works of art, it is always important to avoid reading-in meanings – to interpret in terms of personal associations provoked by the work, but which are not sustained by what is in the picture. In the present case, however, different considerations are at issue. The features that I have identified are inescapable. And this is the point about expressionism. Such works are primally direct in terms of how they evoke the painter's experience. They have the sensual primal *directness* of the Nietzschean will to art, in the most uncompromising terms. The artist is the *greatest* sufferer, and this realm of directness is what art must be about, ultimately.

Consider also, *Woman with a Bag* (Frau mit Tasche) by Karl Schmidt-Rottluff, 1915 (Tate Modern, London). This painting lacks the overt tortured content of Kirchner's picture, but retains its own directness of visual address. There is a sly informality about the way the woman adjusts her hat/hair, and holds her bag – the kind of informality, indeed, that might characterize a photographic snapshot.

However, the woman's facial features are elongated through adaption to the idioms of non-western sculpture. This formal device carries expressive meaning beyond mere stylization. For it makes the woman's gaze enigmatic in the way it returns the gaze of the viewer.

There are many modernist works – such as Manet's treatments of female subjects where the sitter returns the gaze in enigmatic terms (e.g. the celebrated *Bar of the Folies Bergiere*). However, the sitter's context in such works situates the psychological encounter in a kind of matter-of-fact existential environment. This means that her gaze is the kind of enigma we all know and love, and which forms one of the pleasant features of encounters with others.

But in Schmidt-Rottluf's painting, the subdued range of colouring, slight disposition of the head, and melancholic elongation of her facial features, eliminate the matter-of-fact context, and replace it with a space of ambiguity that makes enigma more difficult. Simply, the complexity of encountering the Other, and what the Other is thinking and feeling, are thrust upon the viewer without the mediation of a narrative context. Here, the existential encounter is *all*. It is direct in its presentation of, in effect, the lack of directness in the way the human gaze is returned, sometimes. The space of feeling between people – its uncertainties, and moment-to-moment character, is paramount.

Finally, it is worth addressing Franz Marc's *Animal Fates* 1913 (see Plate 5, Kunstmuseum Basel, Switzerland). The rear of this picture contains the inscription 'And all being is flaming agony'. But even without reference to this iconographic feature, the work conveys such pain directly, within its own internal resources. The work's colouring is intensely vivid, and the environmental forms in the left of the picture are rendered with a lightness and insistent instability. There is at once the

Plate 5 Franz Marc, *Animal Fates (the Trees Showed Their Rings, the Animals Their Arteries)* 1913, oil on canvas, 195 × 263.5 cm, Kunstmuseum Basel. Photograph by Martin P. Buehler.

suggestion of the beauty of a natural habitat, but also its despoiling – especially through the zone of dark forms on the viewer's right, which seem to be *violating* the habitat features on the left, in a destructive struggle. Through this, any spatial distinction between background and foreground is overcome through the tumult of what is being depicted both literally and metaphorically. There is a *panic* of form.

It should be emphasized, also, that these contextual factors at once amplify, and are amplified by, the emphatic death posture of the deer itself. Its thrown-back head exemplifies the actual killing of the creature, and the fact that this death is an effect of a more general anti-life momentum. The work's overall impression, indeed, is of violent destructive frenzy.

In these examples, then, we see exemplifications of an art that aspires to a sensuous and emotional directness which overcomes the customary formal restraints of pictorial representation. There is a kind of intoxication of the psychological – a desire for unmediated primal communication. It is Nietzsche's theory of art that points us, best, to what is at issue in such works – a primacy of sensuous address and focus on existential issues that overwhelms all other considerations in the most aggressive way.

Part Three

It is time, now, to consider the broader art-historical context. The idiom of expressionism has a significance that ranges far beyond German art. As noted earlier, it fits fauvism to some degree, and is relevant also to much American abstract expressionism.

In terms of the latter, this is hardly surprising. Nietzsche was well known in American intellectual and artistic circles by the 1930s. More significantly, these circles were also subject to alienating societal pressures similar to those found in Germany and to an expanded awareness of the possibilities of 'primitive' art. These conditions, indeed, are operative in most twentieth-century capitalist societies. In its primal directness, the expressionist tendency should be seen generally as one particular strategy of resistance to urban alienation and cultural repression – a means of expressing fundamentals of human existence, rather than societal distortions of it.

Again, it is worth considering some specific examples. First, Jackson Pollock's *Number 1A, 1948* (Museum of Modern Art, New York). This work is one of Pollock's so-called 'action paintings' where the painter would pour, drip, and flick paint onto an unstretched canvas placed on the floor. The elimination of studied gesture in the placing of paint, is, in itself, an attempt at some more direct idiom of communication. Indeed, for Pollock himself, this mode of practice seems to have been taken as a means to evoking levels of unconscious symbolism that would be elided by a more conventional easel-painting approach.

And there is more besides. In this respect, it is interesting that Pollock has created the work in very economical planar terms. There is a background plane that supports a shallow central plane packed with writhing forms. This animated effect arises, especially, because the coloured surface that constitutes the background plane shows through – and accentuates the animation of the forms by providing a static context against which they can stand out.

In addressing this work, one should bear in mind, also, that while – as we shall see in Chapter Four – the planar structure of painting involves a virtual immobilization of content – Pollock's abstraction nevertheless evokes a sense of *ceaseless becoming*. And in this he is true to organic process in general. Individual finite things and states of affairs come into being and pass away, but as a general process, this generation and decay does not stop. It has an element of constancy.

Pollock's optical–planar evocation of process means that both the transient individual dimension and the constancy of process, per se, are made complementary, and are, thence, expressed with a directness that eludes more figurative modes of representation.

Another important Nietzschean abstract expressionist is Mark Rothko. He was influenced by Nietzsche's *Birth of Tragedy*, and, in his most sustained piece of writing on art, follows its logic through, quite explicitly, to the conclusion that ' it is through the tragic element that we seem to achieve the generalization of human emotionality.'[12] These remarks were made around 1940–1. In the next seven years or so, he created many rather static and extremely graceful quasi-surrealist works (such as *Slow Swirl at the Edge of the Sea* of 1944 [Museum of Modern Art, New York]) where the dimension of tragedy is not at all explicit.

However, towards the end of the 1940s an important stylistic transformation occurs. The biomorphic elements in his work are gradually eliminated in favour of fragile areas of colours that suggest shape only in the most veiled terms. And, in turn, these are refined further into compositions based on bands of colour – a 'sectional' format that remains with him to the end of his career.

Consider, for example, *No. 14 (Horizontals, White over Darks)* of 1961 (Museum of Modern Art, New York). This work is especially dark in both literal colouristic terms, and metaphorically. Like all Rothko's sectional compositions, the bands of colour are distributed over a relatively uniform background colour plane. In optical terms they appear in front of this plane, or to be bled into it, or, (more rarely) as indented upon it or even behind it.

In the present case, all these relations are present to varying degrees. Of special importance are the boundary areas where the bands relate to the background plane and to one another – the so-called 'areas of violence'. What makes these so important is their recontextualization of the phenomenological significance of the bands. Generally speaking, horizontal bands of uniform colour, are stable – even monumental in terms of their potential visual stability. They echo and reinforce the planarity of painting's basic format.

However, the fineness of their internal differentiation, and their fraying edges in Rothko's work, serve to invert this significance – or, better, *put it in suspense*. There is, indeed, the suggestion of monumentality, but it is achieved through means that evoke its transitoriness in the most direct terms. The reciprocity of Being and Becoming is illuminated through the suggestion of precariousness and dissolution. There is something of this in Pollock's animated forms also, but Rothko takes this to an even more sensuously basic level by evoking it through *colour as form,* per se. Rather than dwelling on the particular details of the transient world, Rothko presents the inseparableness of Being and Becoming (and thence the transience of all things) as *an inescapable absolute* – the universal that determines everything.

It is this which makes Rothko's work an expression of the tragic in the most direct and pervasive sense. And this is true even when his banded compositions employ colours that are brighter and more ecstatic in their connotations. For the ecstatic is bought at the price of knowing that ecstasy – by its very nature – comes, *so as to go.* The fore-knowing of this destiny is implicated in the character of ecstatic experience, itself.

Part Four

Given this analysis, we are now in a position to question the appropriateness of the term 'Neo-Expressionism' in relation to more recent art practice. The term seems to have come into use in the 1970s as a catch-all phrase marking a widespread return to figuration in the visual arts throughout the western world. This return had already been embodied in hard-edged super realist art, where pictorial or sculptural images declare their own origins – as derivations of mechanical techniques of reproduction such as photography or casting.

However, from the early 1970s artist such as Malcolm Morley and Philip Guston began adopting a much freer and painterly mode of figuration. This more painterly impulse caught on in a big way in the latter half of decade, with artists such as

Schnabel, Clemente, Fischl, and Salle coming to the forefront of critical attention.

It also characterized much important work in German art of the 1970s, notably that of Kiefer, Penck, Hödicke, Richter, Fetting, and Baselitz. Interestingly the impulse to extreme painterly figuration in Germany (and, indeed a parallel tendency in British art – represented by the likes of Bacon,[13] Auerbach, and Kossoff) actually pre-dates – at least in some cases – developments in America, but is the American artists who created a market for the tendency, and focused it, as it were, into an international 'style'.

The problem is, however, whether a mere impulse to extreme painterly figuration of itself warrants the term 'Expressionist'. Extreme painterliness may relate to the set of the Nietzschean stylistic traits in terms of which I described the expressionist tendency earlier on, but looseness in the handling of paint also characterizes many other tendencies in art. Indeed to describe painterly figuration as such as 'Neo-Expressionist' is to water down the complex theoretical and practical elements which make expressionism into a quite specific stylistic strategy of resistance to alienation and repression.

However, there is at least one major figure who warrants the term. I refer to Georg Baselitz. Consider, for example, his *B für Larry* of 1967 (see Plate 6, Museum Frieder Burda, Baden-Baden).

This work focuses on a central male figure wearing only a loin garment, with arms splayed in the position of crucifixion. Again, the figure's facial expression is fundamentally passive. What gives the picture its overtly violent dimension are the four savage dogs which surround and hem in the figure. One of these has sunk its teeth into his outstretched arm.

The dimension which energizes a sense of violation, however, is not this literal component. It consists, rather, in an articulation of space which wrenches, dismembers and relocates some of the forms within it. The dogs, for example, are each rendered in terms of a head and half a body, with one exception – which is given in full profile.

Plate 6 Georg Baselitz, *B für Larry*, 1967, oil on canvas, 250 × 200 cm (98.5 × 79 in.), Museum Frieder Burda, Baden-Baden. © Georg Baselitz.

Even so, this dog is itself delineated in a sketchy and incomplete manner, with the two parts of its torso seeming to be torn apart. Baselitz's choice of savage dogs in this and other works is possibly a symbol of male sexuality in its most aggressive mode.

One might even see the overall structure of these works – savage dogs wrenched apart in space – as a kind of sublimation of the violence of the sexual act itself.

Towards the end of the 1970s, the stylizing and schematizing aspects of Baselitz's painterly style come more and more into a dominant position, and define his work of the 1980s. Indeed, they intersect perfectly with another – already established tendency in his work (from the end of the 1960s) namely his painting of images in an *inverted* form.

One of the most impressive instances of this is *Nachtessen in Dresden* of 1983 (see Plate 7, Kunsthaus, Zurich). Here a group of Dresdeners eat their meal at night. Is this the night of the terror bombing and firestorm of April 1945? Even if it is not, the Munch-like sparsity and contortion of the forms and facial expressions connotes the full horrors of this event. And even if one overlooks the name Dresden in the title, the brutality of reductionism *apropos* shape, environment and facial expression, is one that, in its abstractness, connotes primal horror as such.

Plate 7 Georg Baselitz, *Nachtessen in Dresden*, 1983, oil on canvas, 280 × 450 cm, Kunsthaus Zurich. © Georg Baselitz.

The expressionist tendency in art is one which stylizes and schematizes in the manner of primitive art at the expense of tonal particularity; it declares the physicality of paint; it exploits archaic associations, and frequently addresses sensually provocative content. All these elements are manifest characteristics of Baselitz's work. They draw on some sets of societal and artistic conditions similar to those operative in the formation of German expressionism at the beginning of the twentieth century. The consumer society of the post-war Federal Republic has not solved the problem of urban alienation; if anything the problem is more ubiquitous.

In terms of cultural repression – especially in relation to sexual mores – things have changed for the better. The role of art and the artist, however, have not. There is a demand for 'advanced' art, but this is more a reflection of art's function in consumer society – as a bearer of social kudos, than a recognition of art as a necessary part of being human.

Indeed, a great deal of art in the post-war period gives the impression of being mere 'fun', a kind of slightly up-market *biedermier* for the ad-mass sensibility. Viewed in relation to this, primitive art seems all the more potent. Nietzsche's critique of *everything* still seems relevant.

As well as to some degree paralleling the conditions of Wilhelmine Germany, postmodern society has, of course, some aspects relevant to the formation of art practices, which are unique to it. Contemporary society is swamped with visual and written information to an unparalleled degree. The sheer quantity of such information, however, makes it hard to assimilate. We simply snap at the manifold gobbets offered us, rather than chew them over at length, with a fullness of savouring.

Experience accordingly, has, lost its depth. It is disappearing into stereotypes, images, and social role playing which is dispensed to us readymade by the media and advertising industries. We mistake illusion for the real thing. (Indeed, if Baudrillard is to be believed, we regard the illusion as *more* real than the real thing.[14])

In a situation of this sort, certain modes of resistance are possible. The critical deconstructionism of Malcolm Morley and Anselm Kiefer is one such possibility. In their work a diversity of visual information is celebrated.

Another way of reviving experience from its saturated receptive torpor is to create art which communicates with a raw, and even brutal directness. An art which declares its cognateness with the body and the sensuousness of immediate experience and does not disguise its own character, but rather declares it frankly and triumphantly, is the ultimate worth of Baselitz's inversion of the image. It proclaims itself as illusion, as the personal experience of an embodied subject, even as it addresses us publically in the most sensual terms.

This Nietzschean dimension of expressionism, is not simply at odds with tradition and its institutions; it manifests a kind of *rage* of the finite and a yearning for liberation through the transformation of both art and world. It *defines* itself quite explicitly in terms of a sustained antagonistic relation to bourgeois society and traditions. In such terms, it marks a point of intersection between phenomenological significance and broader social factors.

Of course, with the passage of time, and especially in eras such as the present – where all artistic styles are permitted – the antagonistic significance of expressionism will diminish and subside. However, this is not absolute. For it is already clear from expressionism's re-emergence in the postmodern world that changing circumstances can invest it with new meaning. It has a permanent possibility of stylistic and theoretical relevance.

There is, of course, much more to the varieties of expressionism, art historically speaking, than Nietzsche's will to art. In each of its embodiments it is mediated by tensions tied up with the artist's individual relation to his or her particular society.

But at its core, expressionism as a complex stylistic tendency, seeks to overcome alienation and repression by a return to art's primal status – as the impulse to direct sensuous communication. Nietzsche's will to art, in other words, points us towards what is at issue in the phenomenology of modern art vis-à-vis its overcoming of finish and cultural constraints.

I turn, now, to the way in which Merleau-Ponty's phenomenology allows Cezanne's work to be investigated in terms of modern art's other main stylistic features.

Chapter Four

Merleau-Ponty's Cezanne

Introduction

The centrality of Cezanne for modern art has been alluded to already, in the Introduction to this book, and in Chapters One and Two. Given this centrality, it is hardly surprising that Maurice Merleau-Ponty's phenomenology of painting looks constantly to the example of Cezanne for the medium's inspiration and renewal.

As we have seen, already, Deleuze, also, was much devoted to Cezanne. But while Merleau-Ponty focuses on the colour modulation issue, he does so in a way that opens up possibilities beyond Deleuze's restricted notion of 'sensation'. At the same time, however, Merleau-Ponty's philosophical agenda rather overlooks factors bound up with painting's aesthetic status – some of which, again, have been encountered already with Deleuze, and which will crop up again and again in the present work.

In Parts One and Two of this chapter, accordingly, I outline Merleau-Ponty's basic phenomenology at some length, since it both directs his interpretation of Cezanne, and is inspired by the painter's work. (We will have recourse to this phenomenology again, in other chapters – especially the final one.)

Part Two will present, also, the theory of painting that is consequent upon Merleau-Ponty's phenomenology. This rests upon painting's capacity to disclose a 'total visibility' that is the ontological basis of our perceptual relation to the world.

The special significance of Cezanne for Merleau-Ponty's theory is addressed in Part Three. It is shown specifically, that Cezanne is taken to disclose the visible in an 'ecocentric' way, that is, one which integrates the human condition within nature, rather than make it the measure of nature.

In Part Four, Merleau-Ponty's arguments will be assessed.[1] A few potential worries concerning them will be considered and dismissed, but then some severe shortcomings with his general theory of painting will be discussed, also. These centre on the fact that the significance he assigns to painting, and to Cezanne, in particular, are only possible as functions of factors that Merleau-Ponty does not consider.

The factors in question arise from painting's aesthetic status as mode of intervening on, and idealizing our perceptual relation to three-dimensional reality, by adapting it to the planar structure of pictorial media. (As noted earlier, this status will be one of the present work's recurrent topics.)

In the Conclusion, I situate Merleau-Ponty's approach to Cezanne in relation to a broader narrative concerning the emergence of modern art.

Part One

The central tenet of Merleau-Ponty's phenomenology is that our most fundamental perception and knowledge of the world arises *pre-reflectively* through the body's operations as a unified sensori-motor field. In his words,

> My perception is not a sum of visual, tactile and auditory givens: I perceive in a total way with my whole being: I grasp a unique structure of the thing, a unique way of being which speaks to all my senses at once . . .[2]

On these terms, each visible item is characterized within a space of possibility determined by the scope of the perceiving subject's actual and potential bodily capacities and activity, as well by the item's relation to other visual items and levels of light. Recognition of visible things occurs always within this complex relational context. Nothing is simply 'there' as a raw visual datum.

The main impetus of Merleau-Ponty's later philosophy is to find a vocabulary and intellectual strategy that does justice to this reality of perception. Specifically, he develops a dramatic emphasis on the all-pervasive, *reciprocal dependence* of all aspects of the embodied subject and world in the context of perception. The subject can only see because, *qua* embodied, it is itself a visible thing – a thing, indeed, which can see itself in the act of seeing. Cognition's origins lie in this simultaneous immersion in and emergence from, the visible. (Abstract thought is a more generalized competence which is enabled by the body's existence as both seer and seen.)

The affinity between the embodied subject and the world *qua* shared visibility, involves such closeness of ontological bonding that Merleau-Ponty describes it as 'flesh' (which I shall capitalize hereafter). Flesh centres on the 'reversibility' or *total reciprocal dependence* of all perceptual items and capacities at every level of Being. For example, the world would not be visible without beings who could see, but without the possibility of visibility no beings would ever develop the capacity to see.

And again, any individual item is what it is not only on the basis of its immediately present surface aspects and details, but also on the relation between these and a field of general structural *possibilities* which are intrinsic to the thing's nature, and which are realized in contexts whose individual configurations are themselves dependent on the role played by this particular thing.

Reversibility extends also to the relation between individual senses, and even our perception of individual qualities. Each operation with a specific sensory emphasis is informed by all the other senses to varying degrees, it just informs their individual operations; and each perceived quality is inscribed in, and acts upon, adjoining perceptual details, presences, relations, and vectors of possible development and transformation. Even the realm of absence is actively involved, insofar as, for example, things which happen exclude other things from happening, and come about on the basis of things that happened in the past, and in anticipation of future possibilities.

These considerations illuminate exactly why Merleau-Ponty chooses the metaphor of the Flesh. Perceived items are only given partially. The sense of their fullness – their completeness as items – is only emergent through contextualizing their present aspects in relation to previous or possible appearances, and these entail reference to a possible percipient.

Reciprocally, a percipient is only possible insofar as he or she or it is immersed in the realm of the perceptible – the realm of items which are amenable to encounter and re-encounter in a stable and predictable way. There is an ultimate bonding here. The embodied subject and the world are part of each other's full definition.

Part Two

At the heart of the reciprocal bonding just described, is the constellating role of the body. In this context, 'constellating' means the way in which the moment-to-moment orientation of the body both presents items and state of affairs to us under particular aspects, and arranges other items and states of affairs in secondary relation to these.

Of the utmost importance here is the role of depth. For Merleau-Ponty, depth is not, say, the sum of length, breadth, height. It is, rather,

the experience of the reversibility of dimensions, of a global 'locality' in which everything is in the same place at the same time, a locality from which height, width, and depth are abstracted, of a voluminosity we express in a word when we say that a thing is *there*.[3]

As I interpret these remarks, depth is composed of both what is given immediately in perceptual space, and, also, all the avenues of possible positioning, and dimensions of reversibility involved in these, and those which might develop, in correlation with changes of perceptual position.

Depth and its 'voluminosity' is the principle of Flesh in existential practice, and vision provides the most telling cognitive access to it. As Merleau-Ponty observes,

> This voracious vision, reaching beyond the 'visual givens', opens upon a texture of Being of which the discrete sensorial messages are only the punctuations or the caesurae. The eye lives in this texture as a man in his house.[4]

These considerations must be linked, now, to another factor. Merleau-Ponty holds that it is the nature of vision – and, indeed, the senses operating in concert, per se – to characterize the object over and above its basic recognition. In this sense, all perception has an expressive or stylizing aspect wherein subject and object of perception are intimately bonded.[5]

The full significance of this begins to emerge in the following passage:

> Since things and my body are made of the same stuff, vision must somehow come about in them; their manifest visibility must be repeated in the body by a secret visibility. . . .Quality, light, color, depth, which are there before us, are there only because they awaken an echo in our body and because the body welcomes them.
>
> Things have an internal equivalent in me; they arouse in me a carnal formula of their presence.[6]

As we have seen, vision only happens insofar as the one who sees is visible also, and that fact that the full Being of things only emerges through reference to a percipient. This basic affinity is taken to an even higher degree by the fact that, since all visual recognition is stylized on the basis of the individual viewpoint, how things appear is shaped by our own existential orientation and emphases.

It is this which provides the vital clue to the origins of painting. The 'carnal formula' noted above by Merleau-Ponty (and which he also calls 'equivalences') is clearly not a mere after-impression or faded copy of the world, but, rather, a gathering up and concentrating of the visible. It is *the visible stylized from the viewer's particular interpretative standpoint.*

Painting allows this process to be extended into an inter-subjectively accessible domain. The painter, in effect, concentrates the scattered meaning of *ad hoc* perceptions in visual depth, and invests them with a logic of visual unity based on selective exploration through painting.[7] Hence, Merleau-Ponty's further observation that 'it is the expressive operation of the body, begun by the least perception, that develops into painting and art'.[8]

The key task which must be addressed now, is how this stylization process – this concentrating of the visible – is actually made concrete *in* painting. The key concept in this respect is one specific aspect of Flesh – namely what Merleau-Ponty calls the 'invisible'. We are told that,

> Every visual something, as individual as it is, functions also as a dimension, because it is given as the result of a dehiscence of Being. What this ultimately means is that the hallmark of the visible is to have a lining of invisibility in the strict sense, which it makes present as a certain absence.[9]

The notion of a 'dehiscence of Being' here, is one of Merleau-Ponty's most striking metaphors, but one which he never explains in direct terms. His meaning, however, can be explained as follows. Dehiscence is the process of spontaneous opening or bursting that occurs in some kinds of fruit on the attainment of maturity. The analogy with an individual visible thing is based on the thing's dimensional aspect. For

Merleau-Ponty, a dimension is an aspect of Flesh. It presents a general possibility of being that defines a specific range of phenomenal features.

Colour is one such dimension – 'that dimension which creates from itself to itself – identities, differences, a texture, a materiality, a something'.[10] Now an individual visible thing has a determinate range of coloured aspects, and features such as shape, density, volume, and mass. Its specific phenomenal configuration is emergent from these dimensions of Being. But also implicated in its characterization are relations to broader colour contexts and light levels and the way in which all these elements are focussed through configuration's inhabiting of depth, and the viewer's interpretation of the thing in terms of his or her present and past perceptual orientations, and anticipated future ones.

A thing's individuality, therefore, is brought to fruition as an emergence from these factors. It is a gathering up and concentration of the various dimensions of Being into a specific form. The thing 'ripens', as it were, into recognizable individuality, when this depth of dimensional interactions consolidates in a spatio-temporally persistent and determinate configuration.

These dimensional interactions are, in Merleau-Ponty's terms 'invisible'. This means that they are contextual features which enable individuals to be recognized, but are not usually noticed. (One presumes that 'invisibility' in this sense is necessary, insofar as attending to all the details of all the things that we perceive would overwhelm our cognitive capacities.)

Now if individuality brings different dimensions of Being into specific configuration, it also has the capacity to act as a dimension in its own right. This happens when *the character of the individual thing leads us to perceptually explore the details of its appearance*. In this case, the individual acts as a dimension through pointing towards the complex network of immediate properties and relations which it is emergent from, and, at the same time, holds together in a specific kind of unity. Indeed, the individual character of this unity is not imposed on its various parts and aspects as an alien constraint. Each such part will in its own being, disclose something of the individual character of the whole.

It is important to emphasize the scope of this. For the parts of a visible thing as well as the thing as a whole, suggest not only other visible features but also factors bound up with other senses – such as touch – and also movement.

The question arises, then, as to *when* this dimensional aspect of the thing is opened up. In ordinary circumstances this means that we simply put things to use, or do not notice them at all. We do not attend to the *fabric* of its appearance. There are, of course, some important exceptions to this. For example, we may be intrigued by what enables the thing to fulfil its function, and attend to its visual details accordingly. This may amount to little more than idle curiosity. On other occasions, however, our attention to dimensional Being finds an idiom whereby those factors involved in the visual coming-to-fruition of individual states of affairs are preserved and disclosed at the level of visual perception itself. *The idiom in question is painting.* This is an activity whose very essence is to not only ripen into an individual thing, but to do so in a way that discloses the visual 'dimensionality' involved in its emergence to perception.

Merleau-Ponty identifies some of the factors involved here by reference to the shadow cast on the Captain's body in Rembrandt's *Nightwatch* of 1642 (Rijksmuseum, Amsterdam):

Everyone with eyes has at some time witnessed this play of shadows or something like it, and has been made by it to see things and a space. But it worked in them without them; it hid to make the body visible. To see the object, it was necessary *not* to see the play of shadows and lights around it. The visible in the profane sense forgets its premises; it rests upon a total visibility which is to be recreated and which liberates the phantoms captive in it.[11]

In painting, therefore, those normally 'invisible' background features of the visible are made present to perception. The reciprocity of the visible and the invisible is disclosed *manifestly*. Painting is that dimension of Being where a *total visibility* is achieved. It does this 'by breaking the "skin of things" to show how the things become things, how the world becomes world'.[12]

It is this total visibility that gives painting its ontological distinctiveness. Every work – figurative or abstract is 'autofigurative'. It discloses the conditions of its own visibility. With figurative work, of course, this visibility comprehends both the painting itself, and the visible character of that which the painting is 'of'.

But, in such cases, the aesthetic worth of the picture is not determined by comparing the work with its subject. Rather we are concerned with *how* that subject is represented, and, in this, the artist's style of making the subject visible, through the visibility of the work itself, is absolutely paramount. In effect, the total visibility of painting involves a fusion of both the perceptual fabric of the represented object, *and* the painter's *individual style* of rendering it. The two aspects are inseparable.[13]

It is clear that this conception of painting is both a modern and a metaphysical one. As Merleau-Ponty himself observes: 'The entire history of painting in the modern period, with its efforts to detach itself from illusionism and acquire its own dimensions, has a metaphysical significance.'[14]

What is at issue here, is the difference between an art that constantly looks back to pure illusionism – in the form of linear perspective (and its surrounding conventions) and those more complex expressions of visibility bound up with the origins and development of modernism. In terms of the latter, it is Cezanne to whom Merleau-Ponty assigns most importance.

Part Three

For Merleau-Ponty, the significance of Cezanne's painting is not revealed by psychoanalysis, nor is it made clear through looking at the influences on him, or his technique, or even his own pronouncements about painting. Merleau Ponty offers, rather, a phenomenology, that contextualizes all these factors in relation to the question of perception. This approach addresses, in the first instance, the character of Cezanne's immediate artistic precedents, and then, in more sustained terms, his own work.

In this respect, we are told that,

> Impressionism was trying to capture, in the painting the very way in which objects strike our eyes and attack our senses. Objects were depicted as they appear to instantaneous perception, without fixed contours bound together by light and air. . . . The colour of objects could not be represented simply by putting on the canvas their local tone, that is, the colour they take on isolated from their surroundings; one also had to pay attention to the phenomena of contrast which modify local colours in nature.[15]

Such a procedure results in works that do not involve some point-by-point correspondence with nature. They effect rather a generally true impression that arises from the relation between the action of the different parts of the visual manifold upon one another. Such a process, however, in emphasizing 'atmosphere' and breaking up tones, appears to submerge and desubstantialize the object.

The importance of Cezanne is that, in works after 1870 he tries to find the object again *behind* the atmosphere (a point that, as we saw in Chapter One, is raised by Deleuze, also). This involves paintings that do not break up tonal values, but replaces them, rather, with graduated colours, expressed in chromatic nuances distributed progressively across the object.

In this respect, we might consider a major transitional work, namely *The Black Clock* of 1870 (see Plate 8, Private Collection). Here, the drapery is treated in a way that does not obsess over the light effects that play across its surfaces, nor does it delineate

Plate 8 Paul Cezanne (1839–1906), *The Black Marble Clock*, c.1870, oil on canvas, 54 × 73 cm. Private Collection/Giraudon/The Bridgeman Art Library.

the textural richness of the material. Rather, the white colour declares the folds in more insistently plastic terms – emphasizing, indeed, the way in which they are defined by the substantial presence of the table beneath them.

And again, the clock itself, is not presented in terms of reflecting light or of the details of its material, but with a closely modulated, and – one might almost say – *massive* blackness that makes the physicality of the object insistently palpable in direct visual terms. It is because of features such as this that Merleau-Ponty suggests, rightly, that in Cezanne's mature work there is a colour strategy that stays close to the object's form and to the effect of light upon it.

However, it involves, also, considerable licence – in some cases the abandonment of exact contours and the assigning of priority to colour over outline. The effect of all this is very different from impressionism. In Merleau-Ponty's words,

The object is no longer covered by reflections and lost in its relationships to the atmosphere and other objects: it seems subtly illuminated from within, light emanates from it, and the result is an impression of solidity and material substance.[16]

In this way, Cezanne brings about a return to the object, that does not give up the importance of the impressionist aesthetic of nature as model.

The question arises, then, as to the stylistic means whereby Cezanne achieves all this. Interestingly, Merleau-Ponty identifies factors that distinguish Cezanne's work from more geometric, perspectivally orientated ones. He mentions several works in relation to this, including the celebrated *Portrait of Geffroy*. In this work, the table on which the critic is working appears almost up-ended and tilted towards the viewer, and the books placed upon it, seem to be anarchic elements that de-stabilize the unity of the pictorial space which they articulate.

However, this impression only arises if one considers these features individually. But the point is, of course, that this analytic identification of specific pictorial components is secondary to our perception of the work in overall global terms. Then such 'inconsistencies' take on an entirely different significance. As Merleau-Ponty puts it, 'perspectival distortions are no longer visible in their own right but rather contribute, as they do in natural vision, to the impression of an emerging order, an object in the act of appearing, organizing itself before our eyes.'[17]

The radical innovations of Cezanne extend much further than factors bound up with the disposition of items in pictorial space. For, at the very heart of Cezanne's achievement, according to Merleau-Ponty, is a specific relation between brushwork and colour. He describes what is at issue, here, as follows:

If one outlines the shape of an apple with a continuous line, one makes an object of the shape, whereas the contour is rather the ideal limit toward which the sides of the object recede in depth. Not to indicate any shape would be to deprive objects of their identity. To trace just a single outline sacrifices depth – that is, the dimension in which the thing is presented not as spread out before us but as an inexhaustible reality full of reserves.[18]

Cézanne's painting, however, is true to depth. It follows the voluminosity of the object through modulated colours and by indicating several outlines to it. This flexible stylistic means captures the object's shape in the same terms as it emerges in perception itself. Indeed, Merleau-Ponty continues,

> The outline should therefore be a result of the colours if the world is to be given its true density. For the world is a mass without gaps, a system of colours across which the receding perspective, the outlines, angles, and curves are inscribed like lines of force; the spatial structure vibrates as it is formed.[19]

In these remarks, Merleau-Ponty is suggesting that Cezanne presents outline, in effect, as a dehiscence emerging from the inexhaustible pulp of the object's colour and light – just as, in perception itself, the things *qua* discrete entities emerge from Flesh. Cezanne returns us to the primordial conditions of perception.

Given these points, it is clear that already, in 1945, Merleau-Ponty's thinking about Cezanne is pointing to the notion of Flesh which is such a distinctive feature of his later thought. This is one of those rare occurrences when the example of a specific art practice is taken as pointing towards a more general philosophy of perception and Being.

Indeed, there is a further remarkable feature involved. In recent years, it has become fashionable to affirm the importance of Being, and humanity's relation to it, in 'ecocentric' terms, that is, ones which emphasize that the human world is only one aspect of a much broader notion of Being that encompasses the full diversity of organic and environmental factors.

This is precisely the direction in which Merleau-Ponty's interpretation of Cezanne is pointing. Cezanne's work overcomes any dichotomy between nature and art through the specific character of his paintings. In particular, he evokes the reciprocity between the stability of things and the shifting conditions under which they are perceived – the zone where matter takes on form, and where order emerges through spontaneous organization of the perceptual field.

The ecocentric character of this is stated explicitly by Merleau-Ponty, as follows:

> We live in the midst of man-made objects, among tools, in houses, streets, cities, and most of the time we see them only through the human actions which put them to use. We become used to thinking that all this exists necessarily and unshakeably. Cezanne's painting suspends these habits of thought and reveals the base of inhuman nature upon which man has installed himself.[20]

The point is, then, that Cezanne's style discloses Being in a non-anthropocentric way. Conditions of human perception are traced *as emergent* from a more encompassing sense of Being rather than as expressions of a notion of Being that has been appropriated on the basis of instrumental thinking and social attitudes.

Of course, as we saw earlier, for Merleau-Ponty, all painting has ontological significance through its disclosure of 'total visibility', that is, its presentation of a visible item or state of affairs, together with the colour, light, and other relations which are the basis of its presentness to vision.

However, Cezanne's work is more than just this. For, in its specific mode of resistance to a mere illusionism based on 'classical perspective', his painting emphasizes the emergent character of perception itself. Not only is the relation between the visible and invisible disclosed, but is so in terms of that flesh and voluminosity of depth from which the human reality is itself emergent.

One might consider this in relation to a work such as *Gardanne* of 1885–6 (Barnes Foundation, Merion, Pennsylvania). Here, the individual forms and spatial units comprise both natural features and buildings. However, in the way that Cezanne treats these, there is no hierarchy of visual significance. By declaring the more basic geometric features of the building, they are given a kind of matter-of-fact visual substantiality that is true to their character as edifices, but which presents them visually only as palpable articulations of spatiality, rather than as buildings that serve such and such a function. There is an equalization of nature and human artifice that Cezanne achieves through making the contents of pictorial space at once unstable, yet, paradoxically enough, emphatically substantial.

In his later work, Merleau-Ponty extends this interpretation of Cezanne to the painter's final phase – with its relatively free-floating planes of colour, and strategically unfinished white areas of canvas/paper. In 'Eye and Mind' we are told, for example, that,

> there is clearly no one master key of the visible, and color alone is no closer to being such a key than space is. The return to color has the virtue of getting somewhat nearer to the 'heart of things', but this heart is beyond the color envelope just as it is beyond the space envelope. *The Portrait of Vallier* [from Cezanne's last few years of life] sets white spaces between the colours which take on the function of giving shape to and setting off, a being more general than yellow-being, or green-being, or blue-being.[21]

The features described here by Merleau-Ponty as relevant, especially, to the extraordinary series of paintings of *Mont Sainte-Victoire* that Cezanne did between 1900 and 1906. Consider, for example, a treatment of this subject done between 1902 and 1904 (see Plate 9, Philadelphia Museum of Art; Johnson Collection).

Plate 9 Paul Cezanne, *Mont St. Victoire*, 1902–4, oil on canvas, 28.75 × 36 3/16 in. (73 × 91.9 cm), Philadelphia Museum of Art, Johnson Collection.

Cezanne's painting, here transforms the carefully modulated colour passages of his earlier works into broader spatial masses and relations that are expressed through mini planes or facets of colour. These have the effect of further equalizing out the relation of the built landscape and its natural setting.

Indeed, this equalization is so emphatic that it begins to appear that both human *and* natural landscape are modulations of a more fundamental *Being-as-spatializing* – whose generative power is evoked by the brooding agitation in terms of which the coloured planes and flecks of white articulate the painting's surface. In effect, the ontological ecocentrism of Cezanne's first mature period takes on a more metaphysical turn.

We have seen, then, that for Merleau-Ponty, Cezanne's style is of the profoundest philosophical significance. The time has come, therefore, to assess his interpretation.

Part Four

There is an immediate question that must be asked. Merleau-Ponty emphasizes the ontological–metaphysical significance of Cezanne's style, as a distinctive feature. But why should this be regarded as positive? Why should we want painting to provide the kind of insights that are achieved more articulately through philosophical explanation? Indeed, might it not be said, reasonably, that Merleau-Ponty's interpretation, in effect, *reduces* Cezanne's work to a mere bearer of theory?

A related worry arises. The philosophical significance that Merleau-Ponty assigns to Cezanne has not been affirmed by the artist's other major interpreters. *In fact, it is only when viewed in relation to Merleau-Ponty's own work, that Cezanne's work takes on the ontological significance that he assigns to it.* But suppose Merleau-Ponty had never been born, and had, thence, never formulated his philosophy. How would Cezanne's work express this arcane philosophy under those circumstances?

In relation to the first of these problems, it must be emphasized that Merleau-Ponty is emphasizing how reflective thought such as philosophy is secondary – a reflection upon – a more primal level of bonding between the human subject and the world, that he attempts to capture through the notion of 'Flesh'.

Merleau-Ponty, indeed, holds that this ultimate philosophical truth cannot be described adequately in analytic terms. It requires '*hyper-reflection*' – a quasi-poetic mode of discourse that evokes the intimate bonding of subject and Being, through an expressive and unorthodox philosophical terminology.[22]

Interestingly, Cezanne's work has an advantage in this respect. For whereas even hyper-reflective philosophy is still a kind of looking on at the subject–world intimacy from above, painting, *and Cezanne's style especially*, models and discloses the intimacy of that bonding *at the very same ontological level – of visible space occupancy – that the bonding is mainly achieved.*

Before assessing the significance of this, I shall consider the point about how the interpretation of Cezanne would fare if Merleau-Ponty's philosophy was not there to guide us. First, it is important to note a sense in which there is no necessary connection between Merleau-Ponty and the philosophy he articulates. His own idiosyncrasies are involved in the formulation of his philosophical standpoint, but if what was so formulated did not outreach the subjective conditions of its articulation there would be no real grounds for calling it philosophy, at all.

This means that what Merleau-Ponty argues through his philosophy in not dependent on him for its existence. The world is such as to allow the possibility of a Merleau-Ponty-type interpretation of perception, Being, and Cezanne, even if the philosopher himself had never been born.

And in this context, another point is worth noting. Many of our insights about the character of the world have an *intuitive* character. We know something to be the case, or treat it as the case, even though we might not explicitly label it in these terms in the course of most of our dealings with it. There are many things that we negotiate on the basis of extremely complex bodies of knowledge and belief whose relations and individual components, we rarely know explicitly, and perhaps have never articulated at all.

In this respect, consider walking from one's house to a local shop. In order to do this one operates on the basis that this will involve a continuous traversal of the space involved, and that one will not share the same exact spatio-temporal coordinates as another material body as one progresses. One operates also on the expectation that the spatial phenomena one encounters will not suddenly increase or decrease in magnitude, and that neither will the moments of time involved in our journey.

Now this kind of intuitive knowledge is basic to how we negotiate the world, indeed, it is constitutive of our very sense of the physical world. But it is not likely that we ever formulated all the factors I mentioned (and there are many more besides) in explicit terms together. Indeed, many of them will never have been explicitly formulated at all – rather they are negotiated as intuitive expectations based on reality's general consistency.

The kind of interpretation that Merleau-Ponty employs in relation to Cezanne plays off, actively, in the context of such intuitive recognitions. Cezanne's work is a kind of *making strange* that we recognize intuitively as expressing the relation between the subject and the visible world in a new way. And, even without Merleau-Ponty's specific guidance, we would sooner or later look in the same direction, if only by virtue of the way in which Cezanne's painted world actively undermines the stereotyped stability of our familiar visible world. Where we intuitively look for continuity, in Cezanne we find radical discontinuity that is, nevertheless, uncannily familiar.

We can literally describe the paintings, and if our vocabulary is good, we can begin to evoke some of the factors that Merleau-Ponty emphasizes, even if we do not articulate explicitly what they imply in broader philosophical terms.

Now, in the foregoing points, I have emphasized the importance of intuitive recognition. This should be linked to my earlier points concerning the privileged status of Cezanne's work as a disclosure of the bonding of subject and world at the same level at which that bonding is achieved – visible space occupancy.

The upshot is that what Cezanne's style presents is ontological disclosure that is inseparably embodied in the concrete particular. It is a meaning *which is accessible only through direct visual perception*, and whose understanding involves complex intuitive recognitions rather than clear analytical procedures. On these terms, philosophical content is basic to Cezanne's style, *but only insofar as that style is constituted aesthetically.*

Merleau-Ponty himself has very little to say about the aesthetic, except in passing. His discussion of painting and the other arts are always in terms of their status as media of expression, rather than in relation to their aesthetic and artistic features. My point, however, is that this factor has to be foregrounded. It is embedded in Merleau-Ponty's position, and if it is not declared, then his interpretation of Cezanne might appear to be susceptible to the objections that I raised at the beginnings of this section. This being said, while the aesthetic and, indeed, the artistic, are embedded in Merleau-Ponty's position, their full understanding raises further questions concerning his interpretation of Cezanne.

And this leads, in fact, to the fundamental limitation of Merleau-Ponty's entire approach to the arts, and painting in particular. His approach is very much orientated towards how the viewer (be it the artist or audience) perceives the work. *There is little or no sense of how painting transforms its subject matter through the act of representing it in a specific medium.* Merleau-Ponty, in other words, does not offer a phenomenology of artistic creation.

There is a great irony here, for the central factors involved in such creation are especially pronounced in Cezanne. However, before returning to Cezanne, it is important to consider these factors more generally. The nearest Merleau-Ponty gets to them, is in the following observation:

> Pictorial depth (as well as painted height and width) comes 'I know not whence' to alight upon, and take root in the sustaining support. The painter's vision is not a view upon the outside, a merely 'physical-optical' relation with the world. The world no longer stands before him through representation; rather it is the painter to whom the things of the world give birth by a sort of concentration or coming-to-itself of the visible.[23]

Here the relation between pictorial depth and the sustaining support is simply noted as a mystery, and immediately passed over in favour of more metaphysical considerations.

However, there is much more to it than that. The edge of the picture not only marks a physical limit and principle of separateness from its surroundings. It acts also as a principle for organizing how the picture's visible content is made to appear. Indeed, painting can only disclose total visibility through, at the same time, *transforming it according to the demands of the picture's planar structure.*[24]

In real physical terms there are no absolutely two-dimensional entities. Two-dimensionality is an ideal state that some physical configurations approximate or suggest. The picture surface is an example of this. However flat it might look, it is not absolutely so in physical terms. It's flatness is virtual. It forms an ideal planar structure confined within the edges of the picture.

But matters are more complex still. Figurative painting, by definition involves three-dimensional depth, *but so does abstraction* – once a mark or line is placed on a plane surface. Then – depending on its character – the mark appears to be in front of the ground or behind it, as well as occupying a space defined by its own mass. (This is, of course, the famous push–pull effect, described in most detail by Hans Hofmann, and which I shall return to, in great detail, in my final chapter.)[25]

Now, once depth is created through figurative or purely optical illusion, a plane in addition to the surface one is created. Specifically, there is a background plane which the figure/mark is defined against. This plane can be blank; or may deploy secondary figures (aligned so as to accentuate recognition of the main figure). The distance between the surface and background plane defines the overall character of the painting's depth. However, between these boundary structures, any major masses that are created can (through their own character, and/or their relations with other items and masses) suggest secondary planes – in parallel with, or obliquely related, to the frontal plane.

These planar structures cognitively enhance our perception of the painting's content. There are several aspects to this. First, because the pictorial or abstract figure is defined against the background plane the painting, in effect, emphasizes that figure–ground relation which is basic to perception, but whose character is scarcely, if ever, noticed, in day-to-day perception.

Second, in ordinary visual perception, the viewer is mobile. Even in a physically stationary position, the viewer will have slight head and eye movements. Indeed, an entirely stationary viewing position is actually difficult to achieve and maintain over any period of time. Our perceptual attention to figure–ground relationships is *constantly* shifting and directed to new contents through changes of cognitive and/or practical orientation.

In making a picture, in contrast, the artist fixes the figure–ground relation on the basis of the planar structures described above. The viewer and object are related in notionally stationary terms, with the object presented, optimally, through a frontal viewing position that is not too near, and not too far from the perceived object. The subject matter is presented, in other words, from a *virtually stationary frontal viewpoint in relation to a virtually stationary viewer.*

This is so even if the represented subject is represented as in motion (or if an abstract work's optical illusion is suggestive of movement). Presentation in a planar format, in effect, creates *virtual immobility.* The planes *hold* and stabilize pictorial or abstract content and display selected aspects on terms unavailable to normal visual perception. In effect, *the planar basis of pictorial depth is an intervention on, and transformation of, visual perception.* The total visibility that Merleau-Ponty assigns to painting is *consequent upon* those immobile figures realized through the artist's activity.

On these terms, the painting's content and structure is not only bracketed off from the surrounding perceptual context (through its status as an independent material object with defined edges, mass, and volume), *it is also – through the very act of painting in a pictorial format – bracketed off from the phenomenal flow of real time.* It is literally out of the world – a spatial idealization that suspends time.

Photographs also suspend time. But in their case, the suspension does not have the character of an idealization. It is rather, a visual arrest – a literal suspension of time, through a causal extraction of the momentary play of light across surfaces in a limited region of space.

Every photograph, accordingly, presents a scene that had a definite and actual history before the photo was taken, and a definite and actual history after the photo was taken. The captured image is an extract from a history that transpired independently of our, or the photographer's will. We may not know the character of that history, but *that* it actually occurred is a logical consequence of the image being a photograph.

The painting is situated, ontologically, in entirely different terms. We know that the image or configuration that we see, was created through the marking of a plane surface. This means that the state of affairs represented or optical configuration has no previous history, nor subsequent history, except what artist and spectator project for it, in imagination. *It is subject to the will.* It is a scene or configuration with no internal before or after, except what we assign to it.

Merleau-Ponty notes in relation to paintings that depict movement:

> The picture makes movement visible by its internal discordance. Each member's position, precisely because by virtue of its incompatibility with the others (according to the body's logic), is dated differently or is not 'in time' with the others, and since all of them remain visibly within the unity of one body, it is the body which comes to bestride time.[26]

But of course, this suggestion of movement is not just a suggestion of what is *actually* to come, it is a purely imaginary one. And, as Merleau-Ponty admits, the picture works by making the elements in the body's normal motor coordination temporally *discordant* with one another.

Although he clearly does not recognize the fact, this sense of the 'unity of a body' is, *manifestly*, an ideal postulate. Merleau-Ponty is, in other words, conceding (at least indirectly) an *intervention* on how visual reality appears, which, by adapting content to the demands of the planar medium, makes the image ideally rather than actually 'true'.

Merleau-Ponty suggests, himself, that in the representation of movement, the body is 'bestride time'. However, what is actually involved is the painter *releasing* the body from time. We are offered a reality that is manifestly *made*, and, as such is an avenue into an order of imaginary events *different* from those of our actual embodied existence. This is not just escapism of the kind one might get from literature, or the moving image. Those arts exist in time, and have to be read in temporally linear terms in order to be intelligible.

Painting, however, presents itself in a single immediate configuration of planes, whose intelligible order can *qua* spatial item, be perceived without having to explore the parts successively in an exact linear order. It manifestly acts against time in the ways described, yet does so at precisely that level – the visible – which is the major embodiment of space occupancy, and thence real existence. This transport is of decisive ontological significance. Humans are distinctive through their capacity to project themselves to times and places that they do not presently occupy, and to create projections of things, places, and times, that are apart from the actual order of events. This is *our* truth.

Now in literary works and moving images, the same capacity is manifest, but tends, phenomenologically to be submerged in our following of the narrative flow. Painting, however, makes the capacity manifest. For it presents and celebrates itself *immediately* as a virtual alternative to the place and time we presently occupy, and as one that, *qua* virtual, is not subject to the vicissitudes of finitude and mutability. Indeed, the very fact that the painting has edges – often declared by a frame – declares, insistently, that it presents an order of Being separate from that of ordinary reality, even while operating at the same level that mainly defines that reality, namely the visible. What Merleau-Ponty fails to negotiate in other words, is the way in which picturing as an idiom of pictorial representation not only evokes the conditions of visual perception, but intervenes upon them through planar idealization.

Let us now consider this in relation to Cezanne. In this respect, a fine work to look at is the *Bibemus Quarry* of 1898–1900 (see Plate 10, Museum Folkwang, Essen).

What is striking is the way in which Cezanne visually constrains oblique dispositions among the different rock formations, and makes them appear synchronous with the picture plane. At the same time, however, this alignment evokes a visual tension – as though the formations are striving to re-assert their oblique projection. This makes them seem dynamic – as though

Plate 10 Paul Cezanne, *Bibemus Quarry*, c. 1895, oil on canvas, 65.1 × 81 cm (25 5/8 × 31 7/8 in.), Museum Folkwang, Essen.
A colour version of this image can be found in the plate section in the centre on this book.

their form is emergent through correlation with basic bodily movements, rather than with the demands of human instrumental interests in the organization of the landscape (and this, even though the landscape feature in question, a quarry, has been created by human artifice).

Now, of course, this is precisely the kind of feature that Merleau-Ponty takes to be evocative of (what I have called) the *ecocentric* relation of humanity to the world. However, this effect is very much a secondary feature. It is dependent upon precisely the kind of planar idealization that I have described in the foregoing.

The various rock formations are visually discordant with one another. The three-dimensional emphasis of their more oblique projections (which would be dominant in any direct perception of the quarry) have, as it were, been tamed, and redistributed in harmony with the picture plane.

This places the dynamic, emergent character of the painting's content in a very different light from the one emphasized by Merleau-Ponty. There was a Bibemus Quarry, but whereas, as we have seen, a photograph declares its status as a visual extract from the spatio-temporal continuum, in a picture, the before and after of the represented scene is entirely open. In the present case we cannot tell that Cezanne's painting represents an actual physical site purely on the basis of the painting.

Because of this, our perception of the work has an openness in temporal terms. Its emergent appearance does not locate it within some strict linear succession of spatial contents in time, but as an *act of showing*. The only linear temporal succession involved in reading the scene is our sense that it was physically painted by an artist placing marks on a surface, and that when it was complete, the artist became occupied with something else. Temporal linearity, in other words pertains to the act of making rather than being internal to the virtual space represented in the painting.

This suspension of the flow of time vis-à-vis the picture's virtual content presents an interesting challenge to Merleau-Ponty's reading of Cezanne. For while he emphasizes the way in which Cezanne equalizes nature and perception, the paintings themselves, *qua* paintings, prioritize the latter, necessarily. This is because they suspend the natural flow of linear time in an act of pure showing. What is in the picture is so, primarily as *an imaginative presentation by the artist*. We may tend to look at it in terms of what it represents, but if the picture is of the slightest merit, we will be much more attentive to *how* it represents its subject matter.

The 'making strange' that the work effects, arises, only because it is our sense of the artist's personal style that is the destination of our perception, as much as it is the character of *what* is represented. If, in other words, Cezanne's painting evokes the equality of nature and perception, it is only because, in the first place, it arises from the unique individual style of the artist's interpretation of painting. And, as we have seen, this interpretation centres on a distinctive way of emphasizing and idealizing the planar basis of representing three-dimensional virtual content.

I am arguing, then, that Merleau-Ponty's interpretation of Cezanne is a sustainable one. However, we have to recognize that it presupposes that the painter has intervened on visual reality through an idealization that suspends linear time. In making a drawing or painting, the artist performs an aesthetic variety of phenomenological reduction that involves virtual immobilization (even if this also evokes movement in the ways described earlier). Aesthetic intervention through adapting three-dimensional reality to the demands of planar structure is the basis of painting's ontology. Merleau-Ponty's account of painting, and of Cezanne is only complete through reference to it.

Now it is interesting that Deleuze and Guattari, also, offer a criticism of Merleau-Ponty's theory of painting on the grounds that it does not take account of the importance of planar structure. It is suggested that the notion of Flesh, is, at best 'the thermometer of a becoming' that requires a 'second element'. Specifically,

The second element is not so much bone or structure as house or framework. The body blossoms in the house . . . . Now, what defines the house are 'sections', that is to say, the pieces of differently oriented planes that provide flesh with its framework – foreground and background, horizontal and vertical sections, straight and oblique, rectilinear or curved.[27]

All well and good. But Deleuze and Guattari's 'house' metaphor for planarity is here presented in superficial phenomenological terms – as a basic pictorial structure within which Merleau-Ponty's Flesh of painting must be articulated. Indeed, we are told, also, that the planar 'sections' 'are the sides of the bloc of sensation'.[28]

But we must now recall an important point from Chapter One – namely that Deleuze's emphasis on immediate sensation does no justice to the more complex cognitive structures that are at issue in painting. And this is very much the case with the understanding of planarity in the foregoing quotation. Planarity does not just organize what is given in the painting, it is an active intervention upon it, on lines described a little earlier. No doubt Deleuze would regard the idealizing functions that I have clarified in relation to planarity, as no more than aspects of 'figuration'. However, I have shown that such idealization is central to painting's distinctive aesthetic meaning – a factor that neither Deleuze nor Deleuze–Guattari address.

Conclusion

I shall end by relating my account of Merleau-Ponty's theory of painting and interpretation of Cezanne, by relating it to aspects of the historical narrative offered in Chapter Two.

European painting from the Renaissance was dominated both by classical perspective, and a highly 'finished' and idealized representation of form. In artists such as Delacroix and Turner, this begins to be challenged, and with the rise of impression-ism, the challenge is radicalized.

Monet is a significant figure here. Merleau-Ponty rightly emphasizes his spontaneity of handling – with its expression of the transient conditions of visibility. However, there is much more involved. In achieving this spontaneity, Monet and the other impressionists weaken perspectival accents and consist-ency through canvases that lack 'finish' in the academic sense. The upshot of this is that the planar structure is no longer swal-lowed up in the presentation of depth, but presents itself as the bearer – even the creator – of pictorial depth. Paint's intrinsic creative power is affirmed in visually immediate terms.

Cezanne inherits this but also pulls off a remarkable reconfig-uration of the planar emphasis. As we have seen, from the 1870s onwards he develops a brushstroke technique that has the para-doxical ability to both affirm the three-dimensional substance of objects and natural formations while at the same time empha-sizing the virtual two-dimensionality of the picture plane.

This creates the total visibility effects that Merleau-Ponty sees as the basis of Cezanne's importance. I have argued, however, that what is more fundamental is the aesthetic relation between affirming the plane and plastic qualities which give rise to these effects. For it allows the gap between painting's own nature and pictorial formats, and the visible palpability of the subject mat-ter, to be diminished. Indeed (as we shall see in the following chapter), Picasso and Braque's cubism continues this momen-tum to such a degree that the gap is almost entirely collapsed. There is, in effect, a fusion of medium and subject matter. This fusion is basic to the rise of abstract art. Indeed, by the time of Jackson Pollock's action paintings, the relation between subject matter and the act of painting has been totally reconfigured.[29]

Now described in these outline terms, it may seem that what I am talking about is no more than a succession of stylistic inno-vations. But my point is that painting makes things visible in new ways only through innovation and refinement in relation to the planar basis of pictorial formats.[30]

These are far more than questions of technique. They are basic to how painting changes our relation to the visible world, and, in so doing, changes our relation to ourselves and to Being. The idealizations I have described, are responses to the transience and opacity of finite existence. Vision and perception are remade, so that in the midst of their transient motions we find a reflective bearing – a kind of secular redemption.

I shall explore, now, phenomenologically, the key structural expressions of these idealizations in cubism – by way of a critique of its Kantian interpretations.

Chapter Five

Interpreting Cubist Space: From Kant to Phenomenology[1]

Picasso never never spoke of Kant . . .

D.-H. Kahnweiler

Introduction

Of all twentieth-century art movements, cubism is perhaps the most fundamental, yet one of the most difficult to understand. Since its earliest phase, a critical tradition has arisen which holds cubism to be a tendency whose theoretical foundations and physical appearance can be explained best in terms of cognitive and metaphysical factors deriving from Kant's philosophy.

This approach took on a new impetus with the publication of Edward Fry's compendium of early writings on cubism,[2] and Lynn Gamwell's *Cubist Criticism*. Gamwell actually goes so far as to say (of two of cubism's most Kantian commentators) that, 'Raynal and Kahnweiler seem to have given the best overall view of Cubism, as far as understanding the historical roots and the-oretical basis of the style.'[3]

However, in this chapter I will argue that Kant's ideas are not compatible with how Braque and Picasso's cubist works appear. Indeed, we need a more phenomenological approach which emphasizes not just how we perceive cubist works, but also how space is *transformed*, structurally, in terms of the stylistic criteria of modern art that I presented in the Introduction to this book.

In Part One of this chapter, accordingly, I provide an outline of Kant's general epistemology and aesthetic theory (an outline intended, also, to prepare us for issues discussed in Chapters Six and Seven).

Part Two then considers three central interpretative approaches to cubism and argues that their declared links with Kant's philosophy are wholly unviable. More specifically, it is held that the use of the familiar analytic–ynthetic distinction is especially misleading – even if stripped of its overtly Kantian connotations. My arguments here, are sustained by close phenomenological reference to specific cubist works.

The approach is informed generally, and in some specifics, by Deleuze's emphasis on the role of 'diagram' in mediating the relation between Figure and material structure. It is argued that this emphasis – the *fusion phenomenon*, as I call it – is the basis of a highly distinctive new kind of pictorial space.

In Part Three, I argue that the reasons for the continued use of Kantian philosophy in relation to cubism, lie mainly in the ideological self-indulgence of art criticism.

Finally, in Part Four, I consider, at length, a sustained objection by Mark Cheetham to the strategies adopted in the first two parts of this chapter. He is the most recent and insistent proponent of the importance of neo-Kantianism in relation to cubism. His objections have, indeed, the added interest of raising some more general and fundamental issues about the role of artists' statements in the interpretation of their work.

Part One

Kant's basic philosophy is a transcendental idealism. For him, this means that perception and knowledge is not based on simply recognizing the particular items, relations, and states of affairs that are present to perception. Rather empirical recognition of this kind presupposes a more basic, a priori 'synthesis'.

Such a synthesis involves *the material given to perception being connected and ordered in such a way as to enable it to be recognized and classified* through concepts in ordinary acts of judgement. For empirical recognition to occur, our cognitive capacities must have *already structured and given objective form to appearance*. Objectively recognizable phenomena, in other words, are the result of cognition's organizing activity. The stuff which is so organized – the ultimate ground of phenomena – is, in Kant's parlance – a *noumenal* realm of which we can have no knowledge.

In addition to space and time as receptive capacities, objective experience demands the *synthetic* (i.e. connective) activity of the faculty of understanding. This is the capacity to form and apply concepts through judgement, thus providing rules which enable the recognition of what kind of thing, relation, event, state of affairs, or whatever, a particular appearance objectively embodies.

The other major factor in giving objective structure to appearance is the role of productive or transcendental imagination. This is a capacity to generate representations of items or states of affairs that are not immediately present in perception. Through imagination, we can recall the past, and project future possibilities, thus allowing concepts to link and bind phenomena in rule-governed ways that extend our sense of their existence beyond the immediate present. The stream of spatio-temporal appearances are, by means of the productive imagination, assembled in a linear temporal continuity that allows them to be known objectively as structures of one kind or another.

This necessity of the cognitive cooperation of understanding and imagination is also the foundation of Kant's aesthetic theory, as set out in the *Critique of the Power of Judgment* (1790). In concert, the two capacities are the basis of a *sensus communis* which ground the pure aesthetic judgement (or 'judgment of taste' as Kant sometimes calls it). The pure aesthetic judgement has the character of 'subjective finality' or 'purposiveness without purpose'. In this respect, Kant claims that, 'Beauty is the form of the purposiveness of an object, insofar as it is perceived in it without representation of an end.'[4] As an example, we are told, further, that, 'A flower, [. . .], e.g., a tulip, is held to be beautiful because a certain purposiveness is encountered in our perception of it which, as we judge it, is not related to any end at all.'[5]

In terms of natural kind properties relating to 'objective finality', we might simply judge *that* the flower is a tulip. (Most judgements of natural phenomena are of this character.) In a pure aesthetic judgement of the flower, in contrast, attention is concentrated on how it coheres as a phenomenal *particular*. The form of its *individual* appearance, preoccupies us, rather than the form's status as an example of such and such a kind of thing.

This preoccupation is found pleasurable because, by exploring relations of unity and diversity in the form's appearance, our capacities for understanding and imagination are mutually stimulated. Through this, they are 'subjectively final', that is, realize the 'end' or purpose of cognition in general, without involving judgement in terms of some specific concept.

The feeling of pleasure that this occasions, is not just one among others. On the one hand, because of its grounding in the *sensus communis* of understanding and imagination, the feeling of pleasure in beauty is *so* distinctive as to lead Kant to suggest on an occasion, that it is through the pleasure *itself* that we judge the object *as* beautiful. The felt character is decisive, here, because the pure aesthetic judgement is *autonomous*. It is not tied to rigidly recognitional, concept-applying cognitive acts, but, rather, involves a *sui generis* mode of free cognitive interactivity that can only be recognized through the feeling it occasions.

With this account of Kant's basic position in mind, we can address, now, the putative connections between it and the understanding of cubist space.

Part Two

According to John Nash,[6] the critical reception of cubism in France before 1916 was dominated by one interpretation – that the central intention of cubist painting was to render its subject matter in a more 'objective' way than that achieved by conventional representation. This approach is exemplified in Riviere's observation that,

> the true purpose of painting is to represent objects as they really are; that is to say, differently from the way we see them. It tends always to give us their sensible essence, their presence; this is why the image it forms does not resemble their appearance.[7]

On these terms, the cubist painter gives us not simply the appearance of his subject matter but the subject as conceived; that is, its most essential 'objective' formal properties.

Candidates for such formal properties include 'Mass, volume, and weight' (Allard), 'geometric volume' (Riviere), 'precise geometrical bodies' (Puy), and 'the object's form and position in space' (Kahnweiler). Insofar as these writers assert the primacy of thought over sensible appearance, Nash groups them together with Raynal and Olivier-Hourcade under the term 'neo-Kantian Idealism'.

It is worthwhile, however, to pause for a moment, and consider an initial problem raised by this approach. Nash (like most of the critics he is discussing) neglects the fact that while many of the early critics do take cubism to be concerned with the representation of conceived rather than perceived realities (a view hereafter termed the 'conception thesis') two other interpretations are also put forward with almost equal frequency. Indeed, it is only by considering these that we can understand why Kant's philosophy has exerted and continues to exert an influence on the critical response to cubism.

The first of these other significant interpretations is the 'simultaneity thesis', that is, the view that cubist space presents in a single image, the same subject matter but seen from different angles over a period of time. Allard, for example, describes cubism as, 'an art which with little concern for copying some incidental cosmic episode, offers to the viewer's intelligence the elements of a synthesis situated in the passage of time.[8]

In several of the early writers on cubism we find this view, combined with the conception thesis. Werth, for example, notes in relation to the cubist's use of essential geometric forms that, 'these forms alone have the power to transfer on to the plane of the picture the sensation and reflections which we experience with the passage of time.'[9]

The final interpretative approach, and one which is found in virtually all the writers included in Edward Fry's compendium of early writings on cubism, is the 'autonomy thesis' – the view that cubism constitutes a purer or autonomous kind of painting that does not owe its *raison d'etre* to verisimilitudinous correspondence with aspects of the external world. Again, this approach is linked to the 'conception thesis' by critics such as Apollinaire. Hence, 'authentic' cubism is seen as '. . . the art of depicting new wholes with formal elements borrowed not from the reality of vision, but the reality of conception. This tendency leads to a poetic kind of painting which stands outside the world of observation.'[10]

These three theses provide the foundation upon which most subsequent interpretations of cubism have been built. They also have an affinity with three features of Kant's philosophy, although, as I shall now argue, these 'affinities' are of little use in the task of explaining cubism. I shall now consider them.

(1) *Analysis and the Conception Thesis.* As noted earlier, a good many of cubism's interpreters have taken it to be concerned with grasping certain essential features of its subject matter. Now Kant tells us that in an 'analytic judgement', that which is predicated of the subject adds nothing new to it, 'merely breaking it up into these constituent concepts that have all along been thought in it.'[11] It is easy to construe how this might apply by analogy to cubism insofar as the subject matter in cubist works is broken up or analysed into its essential visual features.

Before directly considering the aptness of this analogy, let me
first of all correct a potentially very misleading error found in
an early article by Olivier-Hourcade, and subsequently repeated
by commentators such as Lynn Gamwell and John Nash. Olivier-
Hourcade quotes with approval Schopenhauer's remark that,

> The greatest service Kant ever rendered is the distinction
> between the phenomenon, and the thing in itself, between
> that which appears and that which is; and he has shown that
> between the thing and us there always is the intelligence.[12]

Olivier-Hourcade, Gamwell, and Nash take this remark to mean
that whatever object we perceive is structured by the understanding. This is true of Kant, but hides an ambiguity. The essence of
a perceived object is a function of the understanding's role in
unifying appearances. This 'essence', however, is not in Kant's
terms identical with the 'thing-in-itself' as Olivier-Hourcade,
Nash, and Gamwell imply. The 'thing-in-itself' is the unknown
source of perceived objects, whereas the concept or essence, is a
form imposed by understanding which serves to constitute perceived objects.

This misunderstanding out of the way, I shall now consider the
aptness of Kant's notion of the 'analytic' in relation to cubism. It
is worth pointing out first that Kant holds analytic judgements
to be a function of relationships between concepts. A statement
such as 'all bachelors are men', for example, would involve a
genuine analytic judgement insofar as we would be breaking up
the concept of 'bachelor' and picking out another concept that
is 'thought' in it.

In the case of visual entities such as cubist paintings, however, matters are somewhat different. Here we are dealing not
with concepts, but rather a relationship between what Kant
calls 'empirical intuitions' – in this case, particular subject matters, and particular representations of them. Now although in
a specific case two such 'intuitions' may have numerous visual
aspects in common, it would be entirely misleading to look

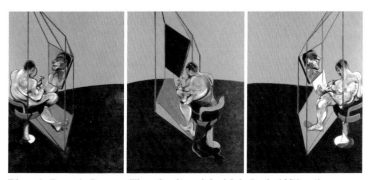

Plate 1 Francis Bacon, *Three Studies of the Male Back*, 1970, oil on canvas, 198 × 147.5 cm (78 × 57.5 in.), Kunsthaus, Zurich. © The estate of Francis Bacon/DACS, London 2011.

Plate 4 Ernst-Ludwig Kirchner, *Self-Portrait as a Soldier*, 1915, oil on canvas, 27.25 × 24 in. (69.2 × 61 cm), Allen Memorial Art Museum, Oberlin College, Charles F. Olney Fund, 1950, Oberlin, Ohio.

Plate 10   Paul Cezanne, *Bibemus Quarry*, c. 1895, oil on canvas, 65.1 × 81 cm (25 5/8 × 31 7/8 in.), Museum Folkwang, Essen.

Plate 17 Wassily Kandinsky, *Cossacks*, 1910–11, oil on canvas, 1118 × 1477 × 74 mm, Tate Modern, London. © ADAGP, Paris/DACS and Tate, London 2011.

Plate 18 Wassily Kandinsky, *Composition No. 6*, 1913, oil on canvas, 195 × 300 cm, Hermitage, St. Petersburg, Russia. © DACS/The Bridgeman Art Library.

upon the paintings as being 'contained' in the subject matter. Indeed, to argue otherwise would be to make a mockery of the artist's whole endeavour.

This is because, ultimately, we expect that an artwork should be distinguishable from its subject matter in a way that enables us to say such things as 'only this artist's style or painting enables us to say this subject-matter in this particular way'. In other words we actually demand that the phenomenal characteristics of the painting should, to a very significant degree, not be contained in the subject matter. This indeed, is the very basis of artistic style.

These points suggest, therefore, that the 'conception thesis' cannot be justified in terms of Kant's notion of the 'analytic', insofar as the fruits of 'analysis' in a cubist painting always take us considerably beyond what was given in the original subject matter. However, what are we to make of the reduction to 'essential' or simplified features of volume, mass, and shape that constitutes the supposed analytic or 'conceptual' character of cubism?

Ironically, it is the two most Kantian of cubism's commentators who provide an interesting alternative approach. Raynal makes telling reference to the cubists' reduction of the subject but it occurs most significantly in Locke's philosophy where it is defined as those qualities,

> such as are utterly inseparable form the body (i.e. material object) in what state so ever it be; such as, in all the alterations and changes it suffers . . . These qualities are 'solidity, extension, figure, motion or rest, and number'.[13]

These are exactly the sort of features which cubism's early, and many subsequent critics take to be the fruits of cubist analysis. Kahnweiler actually makes this explicit. 'In the words of Locke, these painters distinguish between primary and secondary qualities. They endeavour to represent the primary, or most important qualities as exactly as possible: In painting these are: the object's form and position in space.'[14] The link with Locke becomes even more viable when we mention that a substantial minority of cubism's early critics argue that faced with this 'clue' of basic properties, the observer reconstitutes them into an experience of the represented object.

Locke argued a similar thesis in relation to primary qualities (i.e. formal ones) in the object, and the subjective secondary qualities which they cause in the observer. Kahnweiler explicitly parallels this, in his observation that the primary forms found in cubist works, 'suggest the secondary characteristics such as colour and tactile qualities . . . '[15]

Now it is true that cubist works between 1909 and 1912 do tend to emphasize properties of mass, volume, and shape, and make colour values secondary. However, this does not give the grounding of the 'conception thesis' in Lockean 'primary qualities' quite the explanatory value one would hope for. For one thing, while it might be possible through drawing alone to indicate primary qualities without involving secondary colour features, this is surely not the case with painting. Even in so austere a style as cubism, volume, mass, and shape are inescapably and fundamentally a function of tonal values grounded ultimately upon a narrow range of colours. There would, therefore, be something inherently contradictory about articulating primary qualities in terms of a secondary quality orientated medium such as painting, and it seems reasonable in view of this suppose that no competent artist would ever think to undertake such a task.

This leads directly to a second more fundamental problem. To represent primary qualities commits us to an analysis of the subject matter, that seeks to disclose its most objective features. However, as I suggested earlier, it is fundamental to the artistic enterprise that not what is represented but how it is represented, is crucial. One might say that every distinctly artistic representation necessarily carries an implicit proviso to the effect that 'This is how I, the individual artist, interpret this subject-matter'.

Now to link cubism to such a proviso (as indeed we must – if cubism is to be an artistic style and not merely glorified ortho-graphic projection) is to make nonsense of the claim to be rep-resenting the most essential or objective features of the subject matter.

What the artist would in fact be doing, is not so much an 'analysis' in terms of objective primary qualities (with the impersonal methodology that that implies) but rather a highly creative transformation of the subject matter into particular formal and volumetric features, that enables him or her to cre-ate a new entity whose structure is an equal function of both the particular subject matter, and the artist's individual hand-ling of the medium. Of course, all representational painting does this to some degree, but cubism takes the process to such an extreme as to almost collapse the divisions between artist, medium, and subject matter (a point that I will elaborate fur-ther, as we proceed).

This is why it is so misleading to use the term 'analytic' at all in relation to cubism. It fosters the myth that the artist is engaged in impersonal quasi-philosophical investigation rather than a search for authentic artistic expression. Picasso made his opinion on this issue clear:

> The goal I proposed to myself in making Cubism? To paint and nothing more. And to plant seeking a new expression, divested of useless realism, with a method linked only to my thought – without enslaving myself or associating myself with objective reality.[16]

There is an interesting Nietzschean feel to this, and some of Picasso's other remarks about art. Indeed, by focussing obses-sively on the mundane and familiar rather than culturally elevated subject matter, and in taking such extreme stylistic licence with it, both Braque and Picasso, carry out *infringe-ments* with some loose kinship to expressionism – though with-out, of course, being explicitly provocative, in anything other than aesthetic terms. However, even this loosely Nietzschean aspect is enough to bring home the fact that the term 'Analytic' is entirely at odds with the underlying expressive dynamic of cubism.

To underline all this, it is worth looking at a cubist work of 1909 – Picasso's *Bread and Fruit Dish on a Table* (see Plate 11, Kunstmuseum Basel) where a decorative sense of colour still prevails, and where the subject matter is interpreted in terms of geometrical and volumetric properties suggested by its original structure. Here the various objects in the still life are tilted towards the viewer, and tonal values are simplified – especially in the folds of the curtains. However, it would be wholly mislead- ing to describe these stylistic emphases as an 'analysis' of the object. In phenomenological terms, they are better described as visual transformations of it – a strategy that adapts the rep- resented space and objects to the distinctive character of the two-dimensional picture plane.

Deleuze's emphasis on Bacon's treatment of Figure (outlined in Chapter One) provides the basis of a useful contrast here. In Bacon's work, the artist's treatment of the body – is one of deformation. The deformation has its own rhythm wherein the body tries to shake itself free of its organic limitation, by escap- ing into the painting's material structure. In Picasso's *Bread and Fruit Dish on a Table* the central Figure appears to be escaping into the material structure, also, but this time it is through the figure being transformed into geometric and volumetrically emphatic forms.

Even if we consider a work where the subject matter seems to have been broken up completely – such as Picasso's *Seated Nude* of 1909–10 (Tate Modern, London) – the breaking-up has very much the character of a transformation, rather than a deformation. For example, the seated figured is translated into relatively well-defined, and variously sized facets that define the form; but, on the other hand these facets are distributed in such a way as to merge the form with the background environ- ment, and to even create areas of brighter faceting – where the upper torso of the figure, and several parts of the background

Plate 11 Pablo Picasso, *Bread and Fruit Dish on a Table*, 1909, oil on canvas, 164 × 132.5 cm, Kunstmuseum Basel, Photograph by Martin P. Buehler. © Succession Picasso/DACS London 2011.

are pulled forward, as if drawn towards the frontal picture plane.

True, the colour and tonal range in this work is extremely narrow, and has a certain visual austerity, but this does not, of itself, make the term 'analysis' appropriate, and even less so when related to the features just described.

Now, even when cubist space appears most broken-up, as in the 'hermetic' works of 1911, and early 1912, the notion of analysis does not even begin to get a purchase. Braque's *Soda* of spring 1912 (Museum of Modern Art, New York), for example, shows just how opposite of this, cubism's expressive dynamic actually is.

The painting seems to focus on a set of rhapsodic visual variations on the theme of a bottle on a table – elicited by, and made harmonious in relation to, the two-dimensionality of the picture plane. The cheerful tondo format itself accentuates the sense of cubist space as a site of joyous reconfiguration. We are immersed in the broadly concentric visual rhythms, wherein the substance of the represented objects is transformed through its modes of distribution around the picture.

'Analytic', then, (whether derived from Kant or some other source) is a term that is totally at odds with the imaginative pictorial transformation of cubist creativity.

(2) '*Synthesis*' *and the Simultaneity Thesis.* As we saw in Part One, Kant places great emphasis on the understanding's and the imagination's connective syntheses. He tells us that, 'By synthesis in its most general sense, I understand the act of putting different representation together, and of grasping what is manifold in them in one act of knowledge.'[17] Taking this statement literally (as Kahnweiler does, for example) we would seem to have a succinct description of the 'simultaneous' aspects of cubism from around mid-1910 onwards. The cubist work is to be taken as a synthesis of different views of an object, in a single image. It presents thereby, the object as given through time, rather than as perceived from a single viewpoint.

This approach is possibly the most common interpretation of cubist space, of all. However, it faces a radical phenomenological difficulty.

Consider such works as Braque's *Violin and Pitcher* of 1910 (see Plate 12, Kunstmuseum Basel), or Picasso's *Portrait of Daniel-Henry Kahnweiler* also of 1910 (Art Institute of Chicago).

Both these paintings involve subject matter which is transformed into substantial facetted forms that constellate around the basic shape of the dominant forms–seated figure, and the

Plate 12 Georges Braque, *Violin and Pitcher*, 1909–10, oil on canvas, 116.8 × 73.2 cm, Schenkung Dr h.c. Raoul la Roche 1952, Kunstmuseum Basel, Photograph by Martin P. Buehler. © ADAGP, Paris and DACS, London 2011.

salient features of their respective visual appearance. The distribution of facets sits easily *upon* the two-dimensional picture plane, whereas normal forms of picturing would cut more deeply into it, in illusionistic terms.

Now this faceting animates the picture plane with strong visual rhythms. And if there is rhythm, this entails some temporal nuance. But, if we want to describe these formal rhythms as the fusing of different appearances of the object into one simultaneous aspect, we need more than nuance, alone. What is required is a recognizable *visual principle of temporal continuity* – one that allows the simultaneous image to be understood as a gathering up of the object viewed across different moments in time.

In works such as Duchamp's *Nude Descending a Staircase* of 1912 (Philadelphia Museum of Art), or some futurist paintings from 1909 onwards, we find exactly such a principle. There is a visual linkage of forms such that we can recognize the picture as a simultaneous presentation of the object's appearances over different, successive moments in time.

However, there is nothing that even remotely approximates this in the works by Braque and Picasso that I have just described, nor, indeed, can such a principle be recognized in *any* of their works.

There are, however, some remaining ways in which Kant's notion of synthesis might appear to connect with cubist space. One could, for example, follow Raynal[18] in construing the conventional representation as, in effect, a single appearance unstructured by concepts, and the cubist work in contrast as a complex and highly conceptualized synthesis of appearances.

Unfortunately, Kant holds that any intelligible perception which is recognizably 'of' something – be it a bowl, or a picture of a bowl (or whatever) presupposes the application of a concept or concepts in a 'synthesis of representations'. Hence, the conventional picture is also founded upon the unity of concepts, insofar as they provide 'rules' whereby appearances loosely grasped in a so-called 'synthesis of apprehension' are further unified into the perception of some specific object.[4]

It is clear, also, that the 'synthesis' of appearances found in cubist work from mid-1910 onwards inclines towards a less immediately recognizable presentation of its subject matter. It might be argued, therefore, that far from being more conceptual, the cubist 'synthesis' has more in common with the essentially preconceptual 'synthesis of apprehension' noted by Kant.

This means, in effect, that the 'simultaneity thesis' cannot be justified by reference to Kant's notion of synthesis, unless we acknowledge that, in a significant sense, the cubist work is less structured by concepts than conventional representation. It presents, as it were, the shifting succession of appearances which ultimately fuse into distinct objects.

A very contorted version of this view does occur in Kahnweiler, but again there are phenomenological difficulties with such an approach. Painting in general (unless it is wholly abstract) can only take as its starting point objects in the world as they are given under ordinary perceptual conditions. If an artist wished to evoke the pre-conceptual 'synthesis of apprehension', he could only do so by the pictorial transformation of objects as they are customarily perceived. But *qua* transformation, this would count as a development beyond our normal perceptual relation to objects, rather than a return to some more basic perceptual idiom.

In this respect, we might consider Braque's *Still Life with Harp and Violin*, of 1911 (Kunstsammlung Nordrhein-Westfalen, Düsseldorf). Here, it becomes hard to identify what kind of objects are being represented, except on the basis of a few recognizable visual cues provided by details of the musical instruments involved.

Now this work appears to be a transformation of both the substantiality of the represented object, and the intelligibility of three-dimensional space. *This is its pictorial status.* But there is no immediately apparent sense in which this and similar cubist works can be described, phenomenologically, as appearances or aspects of the objects before they are gathered up into recognizable constant shapes. Indeed, the use of vertically heaped broken facets and extensive trellising to link them, suggests, again, an entirely different artistic dynamic.

Far from being a decomposition of the represented objects – one that might be taken as presenting their appearance in some pre-conceptualized form (the Kantian 'synthesis of apprehension') – exactly the opposite dynamic is at work. Braque's and Picasso's works of 1911–12 systematically reconstruct their subject matter by *fusing its plastic mass with the surrounding space and that of the other represented objects.* By these means, the space of the objects represented are brought into a creative harmony with the two-dimensional basis of the picture plane.

What I am describing here – the *fusion phenomenon*, as I shall call it – is a heightened case of the Deleuzian relation between Figure and material structure. We will recall from Chapter One that the emergence of Figure (in modern painting especially) is linked by Deleuze to 'diagram' – those 'nonrepresentative', 'asignifying' trails which form the painting's close-up fabric. Deleuze himself emphasizes Cezanne and Bacon as exemplars of this, but in Picasso and Braque's cubism diagram the nature of diagram is made even more explicit, and may even be regarded as what the entire cubist project converges upon.

In cubism, the accelerating difficulty of separating the central figures from the details of their fusion with the surrounding space and lesser figures, means that the narrative–symbolic significance of the work is suspended. The diagram becomes an aggressive macro-feature in terms of asserting the Figure's reciprocal emergence and return to the material structure.

I shall return to this fusion phenomenon in more detail further on. Before that, it is worth considering one final route whereby Kant's notion of 'synthesis' might appear relevant to cubism. It focuses on his definition of the 'synthetic judgement' (as opposed to 'synthesis in general'). Such judgements '. . . add

to the concept of their subject a predicate which had not in any-
wise been thought in it.'⁵

This has led Christopher Green to say that synthesis in cubism
is pure, and not carried out from the premise of reductive or
de-structuring representation:

> . . . synthesis in Cubism is the process of pictorial conception
> and construction where the component parts used have not
> been derived from the observation and 'analysis' of the paint-
> ing's subject-matter. Seen thus, synthesis and invention have
> become almost synonymous, synthetic cubist images being,
> presented not as reflections of the world we know, but as addi-
> tions to it – new inventions.¹⁹

However, while the synthetic elements in cubism may be
'additions to', rather than 'reflections of' the world, to see
them as 'new inventions' or synthesis is somewhat misleading. For surely it is crucial that the *papier collé* and collage
of 'synthetic' cubism (so called) are introduced precisely at
the point where Picasso and Braque had arrived at canvases
of such extreme inventiveness as to bear almost no relation
to observable reality. While *papier collé* and collage introduce
elements foreign to the painted canvas itself, in other words,
their concrete effect is to restore an intelligible link with the
subject matter.

But what is the nature of this link? Kant's notion of the synthetic judgement provides no real clarification insofar as the
finished painting retains (albeit stylistically transformed) certain specifiable visual aspects of the original subject matter.
Indeed, even the 'foreign' elements are not introduced in an
arbitrary way, but rather serve to draw out aesthetic possibilities
suggested by the original subject.

A work such as Picasso's *Bottle of Vieux Marc, Glass, Guitar and
Newspaper* of 1913 (see Plate 13, Tate Modern, London), for
example, is a complex work.

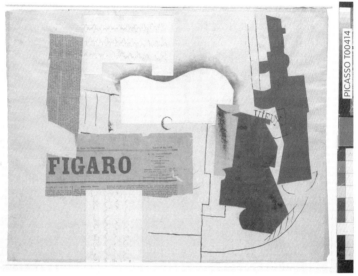

Plate 13 Pablo Picasso, *Bottle of Vieux Marc, Glass, Guitar and Newspaper,* 1913, collage and pen and ink on blue paper support, 467 × 625 mm, Tate Modern, London. © Succession Picasso/DACS, and Tate, London 2011.

The extraneous material that it deploys, has a (usually over-looked) visual interest of its own. By configuring this material to reconstruct the basic shape of the represented subject mat-ter, the artist elaborates that shape, also, and, indeed, energizes the picture plane at two levels of reality – as the virtual support for the drawn elements, and as the real physical support for the collaged elements. (The visual role of the newspaper is espe-cially subtle here, insofar as it both represents itself, and assists in elaborating the other represented shapes.)

Through such compositional strategy, therefore, the 'add-itional' material feeds back on and transforms our experience of both subject matter and medium. The synthetic element is 'contained' in the work. It is fully incorporated.

Interestingly, even if we were to apply the term 'synthetic' to cubism in a wholly non-Kantian way, significant problems would still arise. Apart from its general philosophical associations, the term 'synthetic' has also the inescapable modern connotation of 'substitute reality', that is, a super-imitation which seeks to embody (as complete as possible) the physical properties of some specific natural phenomenon.

Of course, while we might be tempted on these terms to regard certain inanely realist styles as 'synthetic' visual realities we would not be tempted to treat any of the phases of cubism in this way. On the contrary, in cubist works, we find pictorial representation that creatively transforms the subject matter on the basis of some of its fundamental structural features.

Indeed, matters become acutely paradoxical when we recall that a distinctive feature of 'synthetic' cubism, is the introduction of elements such as lettering and scraps of paper, etc. – which are, of course, absolutely real two-dimensional existents and are not 'synthetic' in any sense.

One final approach still remains whereby Kant's philosophy might be linked to the interpretation of cubism. It is to this I now turn.

(3) *Subjective Finality and the Autonomy Thesis.* As we saw in Part One, Kant holds that the pure aesthetic judgement is grounded on the free and disinterested perceptual exploration of the formal aspects of particular appearances in artefacts and nature. It has the character of 'subjective finality'.

Now while Kant is somewhat uneasy about the scope of such appreciation in relation to conventional representational art it is clear how his aesthetic might relate to cubist painting. Whereas, for example, some might claim that in traditional representation the ultimate arbiter of the work's value is its relation to that aspect of the external world which is represented; in cubism we find a configuration of form – a 'subjective finality' which is valued for its own sake, and not for its referential function.

Unfortunately, this autonomy thesis is nearly always found in conjunction with the conception thesis, and the two are inconsistent not just in terms of Kant's philosophy, but also much more generally. Kant, for example, would hold that if cubism is to be interpreted as a revelation of its subject matter's primary qualities, then neither the creation nor appreciation of such works could be counted as the 'disinterested' apprehension of the subjective finality. Cubism would be a mode of conceptual investigation and not a purer, more aesthetic, form of painting. On Kant's terms we must view such pictures as either conceptual investigation or aesthetic object – with no room for any middle ground.

However, even in a non-Kantian context, this conflict of interpretation is still fundamental. Writers such as Raynal and Apollinaire among others suppose that if painting is no longer tied to the direct representation of external reality but rather as conceived, then it must be ipso-facto be purer or more autonomous.

Unfortunately this reasoning in unconvincing, because if cubism is centrally concerned with revealing primary qualities or simultaneous aspects of its subject matter (albeit mediated through 'conception') then it is still and as much logically dependent on some aspect of the world external to the painting itself. In fact, if we push this line of thought, it can be argued that in one sense cubism is even less autonomous than some conventional styles or representation, insofar as it tends emphatically towards a more empirically grounded form of painting. Both classical and Romantic art allow room for the play of imagination and fantasy, albeit in different forms. Cubism, however (at least in the work of Braque and Picasso up to 1914) is tied firmly to variations upon that most empirical of all genres, the still life.

There are two ways of surmounting this conflict of interpretation. Riviere, for example,[20] sees cubism as a 'purer' form of painting not because it is autonomous from external reality, but because it realizes the 'true' purpose of painting – which is to paint objects as they are conceived, that is, in their essential properties.

In other words, the conception thesis is not (as it is with most critics) seen as just one among other possibilities for a painter; it is seen as the true end; and a form of painting which is founded upon it, such as cubism, will be a 'purer' and more authentic form of painting.

Riviere, of course, is supposing that the authentic art form is classical, but offers no justification for this assumption. One can, of course, approach a subject matter and interpret it in terms of its most generalized formal qualities, but equally one can approach it with an eye for the particular qualities which make it just this instance of a subject. To assume that one approach is better than the other, and to posit a hierarchy of styles with classicism at the apex is simple to take an ideological stance – unless (as Hegel does in his *Aesthetics*) we tie it to some well-argued broader conception of the essence of art.

The second way of surmounting the conflict of interpretation noted above, is to argue (in complete independence of the 'conception thesis') that cubist works distort their subject matter to such a degree as to completely negate their referential associations, thus leaving us free to appreciate them on a purely aesthetic level of 'subjective finality'.

This approach has in its favour the fact that between 1910 and early 1912, subject matter in Braque and Picasso's work is so distorted as to be sometimes almost unrecognizable. However, this development has, in fact, an altogether different significance which takes us to the very heart of cubism's importance as the first expression of a radical new mode of pictorial space.

It centres on the fusion phenomenon described a little earlier – when the Deleuzian 'diagram' is related to the Figure in especially emphatic terms. In this respect, it should be emphasized that while the fragmentation of subject matter may inhibit recognition of what kind of objects are being represented, we are still aware of the painting as being 'of' a specific configuration of volume, mass, and shape.

Indeed, such work can make us aware that the tangible, tactile materiality of objects can be encountered and appreciated even (and perhaps especially) within the framework of a two-dimensional medium. As Braque puts it, 'When the fragmentation of objects occurred in my painting around 1910, it was as a means for getting closer to the object, within the limits tolerated by the painting.'[21] In relation to this, it is useful to consider Braque's great work *Le Portugais* of 1911–12 (see Plate 14, Kunstmuseum Basel).

Here, the central human figure is presented allusively through overlapping vertical triangular structures, with facet like brushstrokes emphasizing the stuff and texture of material presence. The distinction between foreground and background, and the foreshortening of the central figure are expressed only ambiguously through small planes and facets. Likewise the individual character of the central figure, which is suggested through scattered details of human physiognomy and apparel. The most clearly recognizable features – namely the sounding box and strings of the guitar – are situated slightly below left-centre, and act as a visual point of gravity for the recognizable smaller details of the picture.

Now in all this, there is not the slightest sense of isolating primary properties or of combining different views of the main figure simultaneously. Rather, three-dimensional reality is here reconstructed in virtual terms, so as to be visually harmonized with the two-dimensionality of the picture plane, and the materiality of painting as a medium. In Deleuzian terms, this is the Figure emerging from/returning to the material structure.

To understand the significance of this one must note that, usually, in looking at a picture, its virtual three-dimensional and two-dimensional aspects are perceptually accessible only in exclusive terms. One cannot *see* the illusionistic content *and* the materiality and two-dimensionality of the picture, at the very same time. This 'twofoldness' (as the late Richard Wollheim used to call it) is fundamental to our perception of conventional

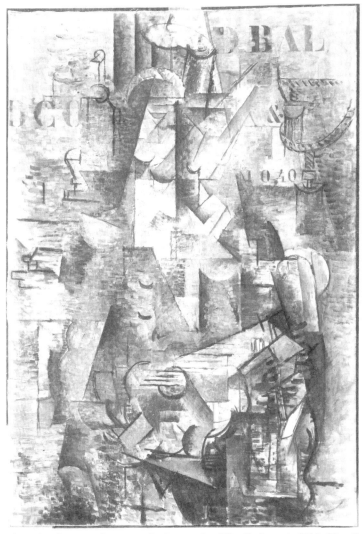

Plate 14 Georges Braque, *Le Portugaise (The Emigrant)*, 1911–12, oil on canvas,117 × 81.5 cm, Kunstmuseum Basel, Photograph by Martin P. Buehler. © ADAGP, Paris and DACS, London 2011.

pictorial structure. However, as we saw in Chapter Two, the emphasis on subjective conditions of perception and the mobility of the subject – from impressionism onwards – begins to subvert this perceptual dichotomy, as does the overcoming of finish and emphasis on manifest brushstrokes that I described in the Introduction to this book.

Now, while these modern factors emphasize the materiality of the painting, impressionism, expressionism, and the other figurative modern tendencies do not inscribe it as an *explicit* factor within the illusionistic space that the painting opens up. The alternating dual-aspect twofoldness of how a picture is seen, remains in place, however it might be challenged.

In Braque and Picasso's cubism, however, this changes, radically. The 'Analytic' phase brings about a distension of the object and – through facet structures – a realignment of it with the two-dimensionality and physicality of the medium. The 'hermetic phase' (from 1911 to early 1912) with its broken facets and trellises, takes this to a new level. We find explicit *reconstruction* rather than realignment. What makes this an entirely new kind of pictorial space is that the virtual third and second dimensions and also the material physicality of the picture are fused into a *continuum* of new visual possibilities. Instead of a twofoldness where material and illusionistic aspects are perceived alternately, we have a distinctive new unity – a pictorial space *sui generis*.

In this respect, *Le Portugais* and the phase of cubism from 1911–12 offer images where three-dimensional content, pictorial space, and the physicality of the medium, form a new – and looser kind of whole – where these individual aspects are presented *as* interpenetrating one another. The painting declares itself, as, *simultaneously*, all these things.

Hardly surprising then, that Braque describes 'fragmentation' as a means for getting closer to objects within the limits tolerated by the painting. If anything, this is understated, for in *Le Portugais* and cognate cubist works the strategy creates the total fusion phenomenon (noted earlier) comprising subject, medium, and artist. *This is as much an existential space as it is a pictorial one.* Within it, artistic interests and the specific nature of the medium are no longer subordinated hierarchically by conventional virtual three-dimensional space and its contents, but rather all these elements modify and change one another in an equalized relation.

In *Le Portugais*, for example, Braque deploys an extremely tightly knit network of small uniform facets, from which the substantiality of the central figure and his guitar, and the background features are generated. However, there is a strong visual sense of the main figures and background being actively *merged* into one another.

I say 'explicitly', here, because of the formal effect of those facets that are grouped together in the appearance of highlights. The remarkable thing is that we have the highlights but without them being assigned to a specific defined body. They float in accents that both express themselves overtly, as painterly devices, and, at the same time, *push and pull* the vectors of pictorial space. By so doing, they generate a sense of the virtual world and its content as *things composed* by, *and emergent from*, the artist's work.

I am arguing, then, that in cubist space, the artist's creative activity in the placing of paint marks and composing of an illusionistic space, is inscribed as a manifest factor within the very realm which it projects. There is a fusion of creator and created – of existence in both the real world of painting and composing, and in the virtual world that the painting and composition opens up. This is a kind of aesthetic idealization. In their finite character, human beings have the escapist yearning to occupy realms of Being other than the one they do, in fact, occupy.

In Deleuzian terms, in cubism the body strives to escape from itself, or to have its eye become polyvalent – wandering beyond the confines of vision, embracing things tactile, and things that can make sound.

At the same time, however (and this is something that Deleuze does not emphasize), the human subject must retain an awareness of the constraints of its organic identity. The retention is needed because the fantasy's whole point is to offer some compensation for a felt lack vis-à-vis the real world. In consequence, the escapist world opened up must be known in relation to the one which is organically real. Cubism idealizes this insofar as it equalizes both the real and represented world. *The imagined scene and the making of it through paint, become pictorially continuous – in a way that is distinctive to cubism.*

Of course, a process like this easily runs the risk of falling into visual unrecognizability. This is probably why the hermetic phase of cubism is accompanied by the introduction of lettering. Letters are two-dimensional entities but which refer to three-dimensional states of affairs. In this way the link between the painting and its subject matter is made somewhat less ambiguous – a factor which is also assisted by the introduction of *papier collé* and collage.

If this reading is correct, then, it is clear that the development of Picasso and Braque's cubism by no means involves the picture being dissolved into a 'subjectively final' configuration of purely formal qualities. The aesthetic dimension, rather, constellates around a new, non-hierarchical way of disclosing the relation of pictorial representation and the world.

In phenomenological terms, the fusion phenomenon that I have been describing is the creation and experience of a new ontology – a state of Being wherein, the visual and material substantiality of the represented subject matter, the two-dimensionality of painting's essential picture plane, and the act of making, are brought into reciprocal harmony, through the artist's creative transformations.[22]

One can describe this philosophically – as I am doing – but the fusion *works* only through what is in the painting, and in the way it transforms our normal sense of visual reality. It is *compelling* in aesthetic terms, primarily. Little wonder, then, that cubist space acts almost as a basic visual grammar for avant-garde artists until the advent of abstract expressionism.

Part Three

I have argued, then, that the link between Kant and cubism is untenable, and that the analytic–synthetic distinction is especially misleading. If anything, such an approach totally distracts us from cubism's real achievement as a new progressive articulation of pictorial space. Given these facts, why is it that art historians and critics have persisted in the use of such an unhelpful interpretative scheme? The answer is to be found in rather broader questions of ideology.

As an especially problematic modernist idiom in interpretative terms, historians and critics need to justify what cubism is doing on the basis of expectations concerning art's high cultural status. Indeed, the use of neo-Kantian also gives cubism a certain technical glamour in keeping with its canonical role in twentieth-century modernist art.

It may even be that the actual awkwardness (in practice) of the Kantian jargon's applicability to cubism, is another reason why it has continued to be used. If the heavy armoury of German idealism cannot make cubism wholly 'transparent' then we must be dealing with works which are very awesome and mysterious indeed!

This means that even if the Kantian jargon cannot actually resolve the mystery, it can still serve as an appropriate external signifier for cubism's internal profundity. It provides, as it were, the appropriate ritual vocabulary whereby the 'meaning' of cubism can be mediated in its mystified form to the congregation of art consumers.

On these terms, in other words, the Kantian jargon has survived in relation to cubism by virtue of its serving the critic's ideological interests. It surrounds such works with an aura of mystery that both justifies the continued existence of the critic, and allows such a person the sophisticated self-image 'guardian of the secret'.

Given this misappropriation by cubism's sympathetic inter-preters, it might be asked why Braque and Picasso did not take issues with it more forcefully. In one sense, the answer is obvious. They were painters rather than critics. But there may also have been an element of practical self-interest involved. A body of critical commentary around an art prac-tice – no matter how far-fetched – can engender interest in that practice as well as ratifying it in relation to a hostile art world.

Neo-Kantian discourse plays just this role. If at the same time the artist should remain aloof from the 'debate' or contribute only apparently oracular utterances, then the underlying mys-tique of his or her work is reinforced and becomes all the more marketable.

Part Four

The kind of arguments broached in this chapter, and a related chapter on cubism in another of my books[23] have been subjected to interesting criticism by Mark Cheetham. He wishes to restore the primacy of the relation to Kant as a means of making sense of cubism.

What makes this criticism especially interesting is the way in which, as well as focusing on cubism, it also opens up vital gen-eral issues about how we should treat artists' statements con-cerning their work in relation to its interpretation. I will now consider this criticism in detail.

First, Cheetham is particularly concerned by the epigram from Kahnweiler (who was Picasso and Braque's dealer) which I placed at the beginning of this chapter. It reads, we will recall, 'Picasso never, never spoke of Kant.' It is claimed, accordingly, that my approach involves an 'unacknowledged and hackneyed hierarchy that apriori, accords artists comments about their work more credence than the commentaries of critics or historians'.[24] Cheetham also claims that I overemphasize the 'phenomenological truth' of the cubist canvas itself – which allegedly, in my analysis, 'appears to exist as raw fact without any interpretation or frame'.[25] I am further criticized for wishing to 'exclude' Kantianism (and, in particular, Kahnweiler's version of it) as a key mode of cubism's historical reception.

My worst sin of all, however, is to be a 'superior' philosopher employing philosophy as a means of disciplining Kant's relation to art. In this respect, Cheetham claims that,

> the very autonomy of philosophy that Crowther invokes in 'disciplining' the separation of Kant and Cubism is one that stems historically from Kant and specifically from his struggles with the juridical proprieties that attend the construction of interactions among art, artists, critics, and philosophers. The vagaries of reception suggest that there can be no purity in history, or philosophy, only the desire for it.[26]

Cheetham suggests, further, that my position perpetuates a very 'unequal relationship' between philosophy and the visual arts. Because for Kant, philosophy pertains to the conditions of thought per se, it is able to test the intelligibility of other areas of experience.

This authority is, according to Cheetham, the reason why Kant has been appealed to again and again in relation to art, and especially in the context of cubism. As he continues,

> Kant established – and then in this and other contexts became exemplary of – philosophy's primacy in the disciplinary hierarchy. To exclude his name from the cubist context is both to override history and to ignore the important sense in which his own strict system of 'conflict' among the faculties

depends on art as a material and empirical other opposed to transcendental philosophy.[27]

I will now review Cheetham's critical points. First, the relation between an artist's intentions and responses to his or her art is of great complexity. And certainly, when it comes to questions of distinctive artistic meaning, the artist's intentions have no necessary logical bearing on our aesthetic judgements (a point I will return to). The relation between Kantianism and cubism, however, is not *just* a question of recognizing distinctively artistic meaning.

There are actually two questions (which Cheetham and most of the early interpreters of cubism conflate). One is whether Kant's *influence* can explain how Picasso and Braque arrived at the particular constructive and compositional strategies embodied in cubism (i.e. did the artists actually read Kant, or summaries of his thought?). The other question is that of whether Kantian ideas per se can help generally explain those constructive and compositional strategies which *enable* cubism's artistic meaning.

Cheetham approaches my arguments as though I am exclusively addressing the latter question. I am, however, addressing the former as well, and insofar as this necessarily involves looking for evidence of familiarity with Kant in Picasso and Braque, then this demands that one attends to what they say, as well as to careful phenomenological analysis of their works.

Even in the case of the second question, it would be very strange not to allow the artists' statements *some* authority in relation to more general interpretations of their work. This authority is by no means absolute, of course; for what an artist says can often be contradicted by what appears in the work itself.[28] But if we can establish basic consistency between the artist's statements and how his or her work *looks*, then this is surely an especially important clue to *how meaning is achieved* in those works (even though, as already noted, one does not have to attend to these statements in order to recognize the meaning as such).

Now, in Chapter One I explored Deleuze's interpretation of Francis Bacon at great length. In the course of this I showed how Deleuze used statements or ideas from Bacon and Cezanne at key points as a basis for his interpretations of both their work and painting in general. Even though Deleuze's use of these ideas from the artists is flawed (for reasons indicated, again, in Chapter One), he at least gets the right sort of inter-pretative balance – placing his emphasis on descriptions of how the works appear, with artists' statements acting in a sup-port role.

This points us towards a useful general interpretative model. Given works by a hypothetical artist *x*, let us suppose that on the basis of an analysis of both how his or her works appear, and his or her statements concerning them, we can come up with a viable *prima-facie* explanation of how the broad artistic meaning of those works is achieved.

Suppose also that another angle of interpretation based on a specific body of theoretical discourse is available, but that the interpretation can be shown to neither understand the body of discourse which it is using, nor or to apply it effectively to the artworks under consideration. In such a case, which alter-native should we choose – the first one that functions economic-ically and has considerable explanatory scope, or the second one which is incoherently articulated and which doesn't fit the works?

Decisions like this face, and are acted upon, by any art his-torian or critic, and to plump for the first alternative doesn't require that one is a Kantian philosopher or, indeed, that one has had any technical philosophical training.

Indeed, what Cheetham stigmatizes as an 'unacknowledged hackneyed hierarchy' which privileges the artist's statements 'apriori' can now be characterized and defended in much clearer methodological terms. *It is the logical starting point for any*

*interpretation which seeks to combine economy and explanatory scope
in accounting for how specific works of visual art come to appear the
way they do.* The principles of economy and explanatory scope
are conceptually basic to effective interpretation per se, and, in
relation to the visual arts, it is the link between the artists' statements and the appearance of the works which combines these
principles most directly.

This link constitutes what I shall henceforth call the *first choice
interpretation.* And, to reiterate, the conceptual grounds which
warrant this title are, of course, basic philosophical criteria, but
of a non-specialist kind. For surely, anyone who wants to explain
anything at all on the basis of the best interpretation will have
recourse to the aforementioned principles in an (at least) intuitive or otherwise informal way.

The first choice interpretation in visual art does not claim to
be definitive – for no interpretation can aspire to that. But until
it is shown that, in a particular application, the artists statements are inconsistent with their works, and/or that a better
interpretation has become available, then it is the *present* justified approach.

It should be emphasized that this justification does not
require that the alternative tradition should then be simply dismissed. It may be that while that tradition is methodologically
unviable, it has, nevertheless been historically important, and
that the explanation of why it has had this importance is a matter of interest in its own right.

Let us now consider this general first choice model in relation to the interpretation of cubism. As well as frequently
affirming the authority of Kahnweiler, Cheetham also declares
that, 'in different ways, Fry, Gamwell, Gray, and Green all
give considerable credence to a pro-Kantian line of interpretation. These contributions allow us to adjudicate between
different understandings of what cubism sought to do and
accomplish'.[29]

*Unfortunately, Cheetham does not offer any explanation whatsoever of
how these 'contributions' are able to 'adjudicate', or why their particular*

use of Kantian ideas should have any interpretative authority in such a context. In particular, he offers no reason why these are to be preferred to the first-choice interpretation noted earlier.

My employment of that interpretation, in contrast, shows the quite specific difficulties which these interpretations face, and it also offers a viable alternative explanation of what cubism 'sought to do and accomplish'. Furthermore – and, despite what Cheetham says – it is not necessarily connected to any formalized philosophical standpoint.

I have, of course been affirming the importance of a phenomenological approach, and have been making use of insights from Deleuze. But it should be emphasized that this has been a relatively informal phenomenology – based on *attending closely to how the works appear* – rather than one based on applying some strict philosophical *system* of analysis. Indeed, my whole point in criticizing the Kantian approach is to show the restrictiveness of its systematic content in relation to the understanding of cubism.

Surprisingly, in relation to my critique of Olivier-Hourcade, Cheetham himself admits that 'I do not doubt that Crowther is correct in this and other precisions he adds throughout his article to critics and historians decidedly undisciplined use of Kant'.[30] Indeed, he claims, also, that 'Crowther's arguments at most allow us to say that Kant and cubism should not be brought together if our goal is to employ Kant's theories carefully or if we hope to describe cubist compositional procedures and chronological developments accurately.'[31] But the 'at most' in this statement is surely what is at issue, most centrally, in the interpretation of cubism. 'Compositional procedures' and their 'chronological development' are not merely formal processes. They involve acting on both medium and world, in a way which realigns the relation between subject and object of experience in complex ways.

It is this *formative* creative artifice which my phenomenological approach gives emphasis to, and the character of which the Kantian interpretative tradition distorts.

A further problem for Cheetham arises from his claim that my approach treats cubist canvases as though they were 'raw fact without any interpretation or frame'. However, not only is my combination of attention to artist's statements and creator-orientated phenomenological analysis, quite manifestly an interpretation in itself, but (as Cheetham also notes in passing, thus contradicting his claim) in my book *The Language of Twentieth-Century Art*, I suggest further that there are actually some interesting broader parallels between Picasso and Braque's cubism and existential phenomenology.

This illuminates, also, a broader contradiction in Cheetham's claims. For while I hold that art and philosophy are distinctive forms of meaning, the basic argument of the aforementioned book by me, is to show in great detail how artists absorb and aesthetically transform philosophical ideas and even rectify some of their shortcomings. Far from placing art in a disadvantaged relation to philosophy, or showing that 'philosophy does not belong in art',[32] I do more or less the opposite, at great length.

Another contradiction arises in Cheetham's approach. I explicitly do *not* exclude the Kantian tradition from the interpretation of cubism, I try, rather, to explain why, in its very inadequacy, the Kantian approach has been historically important – a fact again which Cheetham admits but without considering the ramifications of this admission.

In fact, it is in this context that I apply something like the approach which Cheetham takes to me, in relation to the critical tradition which he favours. He reluctantly accepts this as follows:

> I agree with such explanations for Kant's popularity in this context, but not with their relegation to a secondary status. I would argue that there are only 'ideological', historically inflected and thus 'infected' explanations for Kant's reception as well as for Crowther's rejection of this traditional linkage.[33]

If the second sentence in this quotation is true, one must ask why Cheetham's earlier claim suggesting that the Kantian tradition is able to 'adjudicate' about what cubism 'sought to do and accomplish' should be allowed to have any special interpretative significance. Isn't it just one 'ideological' position among others?

And what about the statement that there are *only* ideological, historically inflected positions concerning the Kantian tradition? Is this assessment mere ideology, or is it a true critical judgement? One assumes that Cheetham intends the latter. In which case he, again, contradicts himself. (I will return to the methodological difficulties involved here a little further on.)

The basic problem which Cheetham faces is that critical judgements concerning the workings and effects – positive or negative – of interpretative traditions involve loosely philosophical criteria of a conceptual kind. We must assess whether the interpretation is coherent and consistent with the object, and how it compares with alternative approaches. Such issues constellate around the striving for economy and explanatory value noted earlier.

It must be reiterated, yet again, that these criteria are *not* the prerogative of a position influenced by Kant, or even by technical philosophy per se. Any critic or historian of the arts – including, of course, Cheetham himself (in an especially emphatic way) – at some point has to make critical assessments. And, if such assessments are made, the underlying assumption is that they are *true*, until something better comes along.

This would argue that first choice strategies in the interpretation of visual art – such as the one which I use in relation to cubism – are not tied to any neo-Kantian 'disciplining' of the relation between art and philosophy. They are simply what, *qua* interpreter, any interpreter, at some point, *actually does*. My interpretation of cubism, therefore, remains justified at all levels.

The question arises, then, as to why an able interpreter of the visual arts such as Cheetham is led into this remarkable morass of difficulties. An immediate answer is that he is trying to make the cubism controversy fit the particular demands of his own broader agenda (in the book where these difficulties arise). These demands centre on the claim (just noted) that Kant's separation of philosophy and other areas of experience allows the former to be used so as to 'discipline' the understanding of visual art.

It goes without saying, of course, that the ramifications of this agenda simply add to Cheetham's problems. His main emphasis is on late works by Kant which are not a part of the major body of that philosopher's *corpus*. Of course, there is nothing wrong with using such works, *unless*, as in Cheetham's approach, the key arguments from Kant's major writings on aesthetics are completely underplayed.

By underplaying them Cheetham faces the following difficulty. While it is a fact that Kant separates philosophy from other modes of understanding it is surely not this separation *as such* which gives Kant's ideas their centrality to art interpretation. The separation is, in fact, only of minor historical interest, unless the basis of the separation involves conceptual material which profoundly illuminates the various factors involved.

If Kant has some 'authority' in the interpretation of art, it is due to the things which he actually says about aesthetics, and the way in which these can explain key features of our dealings with art. Kant's ideas are authoritative, in other words, because of their *explanatory value* in relation to many central problems of aesthetics.

In this respect, it is surprising that while Cheetham entitles his book *Kant, Art, and Art History*, he scarcely mentions – let alone addresses – Kant's theory of fine art. And what makes this omission serious is the fact that the theory in question is one of the few philosophies of art which – despite Cheetham's assertion to the contrary – is artist rather than consumer orientated.

Kant's theory holds that what defines fine art is the originality of the object, and the fact that what is created in it cannot be achieved by merely following rules. This means that such art involves the creating of artefacts which embody both aesthetic ideas and historical difference.

These and the many other complex factors which give intellectual substance to Kant's conceptual distinctions are simply overlooked or, at best, understated by Cheetham. The distinctions are thus made to appear as if their main significance is as expressions of the institutional pressures and academic settings in which Kant operated, late in his career.

This leads us directly to the broad methodological inadequacies which are the major source of Cheetham's problems. He represents (in an extreme form) one aspect of an approach to art history that emphasizes contexts of production and reception. This tends to *reduce* the meaning of the made visual artefact to the social conditions under which it is critically received and transmitted.

In this way, the significance of visual art as a formative activity is distorted in favour of a consumer-based approach. It is telling, here, that while Cheetham's critique of my arguments occurs within a 19-page discussion of cubism, *this discussion does not, at any point, even attempt to describe or analyse any specific cubist work in visual terms.*

Attention focuses exclusively on a particular tradition of interpretation – on discourse *about* cubism. Everything addresses the conditions of cubism's reception and nothing considers the works themselves and what is at issue in them, phenomenologically, looking the way they do. The artwork itself disappears into the conditions of interpretation – reduced to a kind of consumer product adapted to the managerial practices of the world of curators and art historians.

It should be noted, also, that, like many contextualists, Cheetham is somewhat paranoid about philosophy. The fact that philosophical investigation addresses conceptual distinctions and factors rather than historical ones is taken as some kind of 'ahistorical' authoritarian threat. It is not. Neither is it necessarily connected to Kant.

Kant is the first to establish a clear conceptual separation between philosophical and other forms of analytic procedure and experience, but many philosophers outside the Kantian tradition also make similar distinctions, and develop them much further.

It should be strongly emphasized that distinctions of this kind do not mean that what is thus analytically separated is taken, thereby to exist in some absolutely purified autonomous form. Philosophy and art, for example, have their own logically distinctive meanings, but in many existential contexts they infuse one another (in ways shown throughout this book). The analysis of any phenomenal object or activity *in concreto* requires that a conjunction of conceptual *and* other perspectives – such as historical ones – should be brought to bear.

This being said, it should not be thought that such perspectives can 'overcome' or eliminate the philosophical dimension in genealogical terms. Indeed, as my first choice interpretation shows, critical practice in art history and criticism *itself* makes use of conceptual distinctions in an informal way.

We are led, thus, to a final (somewhat ironic) contradiction within Cheetham's specific strategy. He takes himself to be criticizing philosophy's 'disciplinary' role, but does this only by instituting a different, and, if anything, much more prescriptive disciplinary narrative. His position is that of the superior contextualist historian legislating the conditions whereby visual art should be understood as a discursive practice.

Cheetham's strategy, in effect, privileges, a priori, the commentaries of critics and historians over the objects of their analysis. Contextualist history of this imperialist kind *disciplines* art, philosophy, and *everything*. The phenomenological depth and distinctiveness of cubist space *qua* visual, is reduced to a dummy giving voice to contextualist ventriloquism.

Now in the final part of this chapter, I have been defending Kant's importance in relation to the understanding of *general* problems in aesthetics. However, just as his philosophy is of no significant value in understanding cubism as a specific tendency, neither is it viable for the understanding of other key factors in modern art *qua* modern. In the following two chapters, I shall take this claim further.

Chapter Six

Duchamp, Kant, and Conceptual Phenomena

Introduction

Braque's and Picasso's papier colle and collages have one extraordinary and (most likely) wholly unintended by-product. For their use of material (such as newspaper, rope, and lino- leum) not made by the artist personally, invites the question of how far such material can be incorporated into the artwork and still remain the work of that artist, or, indeed, remain a work of art at all?

Through asking such questions, the tantalizing possibility emerges, also, of an art removed from conventional notions of skill. Marcel Duchamp engaged with all these issues through his invention of the 'ready-made' – a step that changes the course of modern art.

The ready-made is a commercially manufactured item that the artist designates as art. *The Bottle Rack* of 1914, for example, is a mass-produced multi-pronged metal device on which bot- tles can be dried. In buying it, Duchamp took himself to be buying a work of 'sculpture', ready-made. Another famous example – *Fountain*, is a ceramic urinal, that Duchamp signed 'R. Mutt 1917', and presented as 'art' at a show organized by the Society of Independent Artists. Some other ('assisted') ready- mades involve physical modifications effected by Duchamp. An example of this kind is *Bicycle Wheel* of 1913 – consisting of a bicycle wheel mounted on a stool, and capable of being spun.

Now the decisive point is that by using ready-made material as the basis of the artwork, Duchamp is eliminating the need for the artwork to have been physically made by the artist. He or she can simply designate existing objects or states of affairs as art, or modify them, or assemble them in configurations that invite them to be regarded as art. Indeed, it becomes possible for such works to be created by other people following the artist's instructions concerning how the materials should be organized and assembled.

In Chapter One, we encountered Deleuze's distinction between digital and analogue representation. It illuminates an important theoretical question here. Digital representation involves signifying elements whose meaning is established by convention – a code which stipulates that 'this' is to be taken as standing for 'that'. Analogue representation, in contrast, involves a sensuous created isomorphism. Painting, for example, *makes* resemblance out of paint marks, that do not, in themselves, resemble that which the picture represents.

Coded reference is of special relevance to the Duchampian context. In an interesting comparison, Deleuze and Guattari link abstract art to the creation of 'sensation' and contrast this with a key example of conceptualism. It is a work that involves,

> a thing, its photograph in the same place and on the same scale, its dictionary definition. However, . . . it is not at all clear that this . . . leads either to the sensation or the concept, because the plan of composition tends to become 'informative', and the sensation depends upon the simple 'opinion' of a spectator who determines whether or not to 'materialize' the sensation, that is to say, decides whether or not it is art.[1]

The work which Deleuze and Guattari are alluding to here is (quite obviously) Joseph Kosuth's *One and Three Chairs* of 1965 (Museum of Modern Art, New York). Kosuth's work is exactly as they describe it – namely an informational configuration whose aesthetic meaningfulness (if any) is decided by the spectator's decision whether or not to regard it in such a way. Whereas, in analogical art, the generation of Figure is something that is the very basis of how the work appears – and thence is a necessary feature of its meaning and identity, *in codified works this is not the case.*

In them, the relation between the object and artistic meaning is a contingent one. The aforementioned work by Kosuth is a good example of this. In terms of its basic identity, the work *just is* the conjunction of a chair, a photograph of a chair, and a label with the dictionary definition of a chair. For this conjunction to signify artistic or aesthetic meaning, it has to be designated as significant on such terms through some convention that the spectator can choose to follow or not. Meaning is here digitally encoded into recognizable pre-existing things, rather than created analogically.

And, if this is the case, then, surely it is even more so with Duchamp's ready-mades, and other conceptual 'art' that does no more than present 'found' material without making any significant modifications to it. Here, there appears to be no room for style in a distinctively aesthetic sense. All we have is encoding.

However, Thierry de Duve[2] has offered a very different interpretation. He posits, in effect, some overlap between conceptual issues and the phenomenon of style. These are based on an ingenious and extremely sophisticated interpretation of Duchamp which assigns a kind of style-in-the-negative to him – based on the character of what he *refrained* from doing.

For de Duve, the understanding of this, requires a sustained thinking through of Duchamp's practice in the context of both artistic modernism and Kant's aesthetic and moral theory. The upshot of this, is that de Duve takes modernism to have aesthetic depth of a deep and unexpected kind based upon an artistic freedom of decision and primacy of feeling that is exemplified in the work of Duchamp. In effect, de Duve displaces the real meaning of style into the realm of what sorts of decision the artist makes.

In Part One of this chapter, therefore, I will offer an analysis and critique of de Duve's Kantian approach to Duchamp. I will argue (using Deleuzian criteria), that the ready-mades cannot sustain, phenomenologically, the decisive significance that de Duve assigns to them. They have been empirically important in the development of modern art, but on theoretically flawed grounds.

Part Two, however, will go on to argue that found material can still be used to construct analogical *conceptual phenomena* of genuine aesthetic worth. By way of conclusion, I will consider this further in relation to more recent art practice.

Part One[3]

For present purposes, the most important of de Duve's arguments are those concerning the significance of the tube of paint in relation to both the literal and the intellectual technology of modern art. In this respect, de Duve builds upon Duchamp's point that in using tubes of paint, the artist is mixing elements which he or she acquires *ready-made.*

In de Duve's own words, 'for Duchamp as for Kandinsky, the tube of paint is the locale of an initial choice in which the making of a painting is grounded. But where for Kandinsky it is an origin, for Duchamp it is a given.'[4] Indeed, 'not only does Duchamp's tube remain sealed, it also remains concealed in every readymade, as a secret example of choices that of course the artist never acted out, and of which snow shovels and bottle racks are the *allegorical appearance.*'[5]

For de Duve, then, the ready-mades signify the fact that Duchamp has refrained from painting. The grounds for this withdrawal consists in a sense of the artist's uselessness in an industrial society dominated by mechanically produced artistic media and images. As the importance of academic tradition and its concomitant values of skill and 'finish' decline, the distinction between artist and audience is erased.

Hence, as de Duve puts it *apropos* Duchamp, 'when he equated art with making and making with choosing, he gave this redistribution ethical value, conferring on the viewer a share in the responsibilities of aesthetic choice.'[6] And this is the point; Duchamp's ready-mades are both made possible by, and signify, the changed status of painting, artist, and audience. They negotiate the advent of a more generic and flexible notion of art, rather than one which is closely tied to specific art genres and media such as painting.

However, there is an important ambiguity here. For while, in psychological terms, painting may seem impossible for those of *avant-garde* disposition, it is, of course, not so objectively speaking. Artists can continue to paint if they choose to do so. The rationale for this activity is then sought in utopian theories about art's emancipatory function, or in formalist approaches.

In relation to this de Duve explores the latter possibilities at some length, giving special emphasis to the relationship between Greenberg's formalism and Joseph Kosuth's seemingly antithetical relation to it. What de Duve seeks to show is that both these writers fail to interpret Duchamp in the right terms.

For de Duve, a proper emphasis on Duchamp enables the construction of a new narrative of modernism in the visual arts:

> this narrative is institutional but it is also aesthetic throughout. If worked out in detail it would show itself not just as artworld politics, although it is that too, but also as the history of institutionalised aesthetic judgements. Such a narrative presumes that "conventions" in art – and there are no conventions without a certain degree of institutionalisation – do not mean properties of the medium (as if the medium could, of itself, stake such ontological claims) but rather a given momentary state of the social consensus . . .[7]

The point is, then that de Duve wishes to understand modernism not as a succession of styles bound up with the properties of painting as a medium (*à la* Greenberg) nor as the artist's mere idea of what counts as art (*à la* Kosuth). Rather, he switches the emphasis to the artist's choice construed as a set of institutional-ized *aesthetic decisions*.

In this respect Duchamp is decisive. For in his ready-mades, the allegorical link to painting ensures that there is a connec-tion to painting's past and continuing existence. But at the same time, the ready-mades also exemplify the fact that art's institutional conventions are not tied to specialized media and their properties.

Given these points, therefore, Duchamp appears as the key figure in defining artistic modernity and linking its many strands. His ready-mades declare the institutionalized aesthetic judgement which is at the base of all artistic activity.

For this theory to be vindicated, however, what de Duve has to do is to explain *how* the ready-mades relate to the notion of aesthetic judgement, and to consider some of the broader ramifications which follow on from this. His key strategy here is to reinterpret Kant's approach to the aesthetic judgement in the light of Duchamp. Specifically, he suggests that we should substitute the judgement 'this is art' for Kant's preferred notion of 'this is beautiful'.

Such an aesthetic judgement is not, of course, compelling – if someone says 'x is art' we do not *have* to agree. However, the judgement at least has the form of universality. This is because in making such a judgement, we draw on a *sensus communis* which is shared by all human beings.

On the basis of his reinterpretation of Kant, de Duve claims that the presumed *sensus communis* then becomes a *faculty of judging art on the basis of feeling* common to all men or women. As he puts it,

> The readymade . . . also erases every difference between mak-ing art and judging it, so that we must suppose that, by the same token, this faculty also becomes a *faculty of making art by dint of feeling*. The artist chooses an object and calls it art, or, what amounts to the same, places it in such a context that the object itself demands to be called art . . .[8]

On these terms, then, the significance of the ready-made is not only that it is an object of aesthetic judgement, but also, more fundamentally, that it is the *vehicle* of such a judgement.

If de Duve's approach were valid, a number of important points would follow. First, it would justify the institutional definition. For what has been lacking in this definition is a viable reason why merely designating something as art should be of any interest to anyone whatsoever.

To see such designation – as de Duve does – as the embodiment of an aesthetic judgement is to offer such a reason. It also offers a means for comprehending the ongoing emancipatory significance of artistic choice as simultaneously aesthetic and ethical. On these terms, whatever the failed utopian aspirations of the various modern movements, there is an emancipatory element – of judgement rather than project – which remains.

The problem is, however, that much of de Duve's analysis is incomplete or mistaken. The incomplete dimension pertains primarily to Duchamp. For if de Duve is correct, much of Duchamp's importance consists in what he refrained from doing, rather than in what he did do. But whether the ready-mades can carry the burden of signifying this restraint is an enormously difficult question. Certainly de Duve makes a case, but it is one without decisive criteria and which substantially underestimates the significance of the ready-mades as ironic and critical gestures. If anti-art is to have meaning, it really must be '*anti*' and not art.

The fact that de Duve can assimilate the ready-made *as* art is, of course, due to him regarding it as an embodiment of aesthetic judgement. However, his deployment of Kant in relation to this is mistaken all along the track.

The key transition – from judgements about beauty to judgements about art – is, in particular, hugely problematic. For Kant's treatment of beauty is fundamentally orientated towards nature. Art is given an entirely different approach which is actually provided in sections of the *Critique of Judgement* which de Duve dips into in only the scantiest way.

This, it must be emphasized, is more than just an academic point about de Duve not getting Kant right. Aesthetic judgement is the key element in *Kant after Duchamp*, but de Duve simply shifts its significance without considering *why* 'this is art' should be regarded as an aesthetic judgement.

Certainly judgements about art can have an aesthetic character, but they do not have to. And in judging a work in relation to its historical position or theoretical significance, the aesthetic aspects seems especially elusive.

Indeed, *contra* de Duve, one cannot judge by virtue of feeling alone, because feelings over and above instinctive gratifications arise *as a consequence of judgement*, or appraisal. Asking whether something is art or not, does not have to involve feeling. It only does so when we are engaged through this particular case mattering to us. Feeling, in other words, can emerge from aesthetic judgement but is not a mode of judgement in itself.

It should be emphasized, also, that even if there was an idiom of judging through feeling, this would not elevate the ready-mades into art. For even if we get hot under the collar about something's claim to artistic status, the feeling that is involved here is a personal state. It does not mean that the object of our judgement is rendered aesthetic by virtue of us having feelings about it.

What de Duve fails to engage with in all this, is the fact that if the aesthetic is a logically distinctive mode of human experience in Kantian terms, it is so through being grounded in direct cognitive exploration of sensible or imaginatively intended particulars. It is logically and phenomenologically distinctive, a distinctiveness – which, as we have seen – is powerfully asserted in Deleuze, Nietzsche, and Merleau-Ponty.

Hence, while de Duve's emphasis on aesthetic judgement seems to give Duchamp and, indeed, the institutional definition of art a new content and vitality, under analysis this content and vitality are revealed as standing on a merely phantom notion of aesthetic judgement.

If this criticism is correct, the significance of Duchamp's ready-mades is nothing like as decisive as de Duve holds. They are

objects used *as if* they were artworks, but whether they are entitled to that status or not, depends on phenomenological criteria.
Is, for example, the object so designated visually interesting in
a way that engages aesthetic attention? If the 'idea' component
exceeds the work's visual vitality, then we would have no reason
for regarding it as any more than an illustration of theory.

De Duve's phenomenology of aesthetic judgement, then, is
at the heart of his various problems. Ultimately, things come
down to this. All the choices and decisions Duchamp might or
might not make are theoretical, but they do not issue in analogically meaningful *conceptual phenomena.*

By this I mean *works involving ready-made material whose appearance gives them an additional, and artistic layer of meaning, over and
above what they are recognized to be in other terms.* Many of Duchamp's
ready-mades are not of this character. They are merely things
that have been re-encoded, by convention, so as to have supposed artistic meaning. But this meaning is only contingently
related to the object. Whether we recognize it in these coded
terms or not, is a matter of choice.

If, in contrast, a thing is visually interesting in its own right,
then no matter what kind of practical artefact it might be,
aesthetic meaning is inseparable from its particular identity.
This is a first step towards the conceptual phenomenon. The
phenomenon is realized when the artist actually produces the
visually interesting dimension through modifying or conjoin-
ing found material. The fact that the found material is still
manifestly an aspect of what is thus made, means that the artefact is different from art as traditionally conceived – it has an
'idea' aspect. But, at the same time, it is configured in such a
way that its visual distinctiveness as a particular, or token of a
type, is essential to understanding its 'idea' in the fullest terms.
Duchamp's unassisted ready-mades fall short of this. He could
have 'created' his ready-mades by using a different bottlerack,
snow shovel, or urinal, and yet made exactly the same conceptual point through them.

Now it might be objected, that irrespective of my objections,
the art world has wholeheartedly embraced the ready-made,

and that any questions about its artistic status have been rendered irrelevant by this acceptance. However, *de facto* criteria are not compelling without the support of *de jure* ones. The acceptance of the ready-mades has more to do with art business and markets (a fact cynically exploited by Duchamp himself – in his later multiple 'editions' of the early ready-mades) than it does with truth.

The Deleuzian distinction between analogue and digital representation is the more truthful insight. There is something primal and originary about the analogical emergence of Figure from ground – something that links human beings across space and time in the endeavour that is painting and image-making.

Digital encoding is entirely secondary to this. To interpret the ready-mades as artistically fundamental, is, in effect, to remake the essence of art on the basis of western consumer society's snide sense of self-irony. However, the principle of creativity involved in ready-mades is, as I have shown, *qualitatively* different from that involved in art.

All this being said, there are, nevertheless, some works (by Duchamp, and others) that are genuine conceptual phenomena, in the sense described earlier. It is to these I now turn.

Part Two

A useful starting point is Duchamp's more complex art practice. As we have seen, some of the ready-mades are 'assisted', that is, involve modifications being made to the found object. Duchamp actually took this a long way – by making (much more visually interesting) works *constructed from* ready-made items and materials.

Notable in this respect, is *The Bride Stripped Bare by Her Bachelors' Even* (*The Large Glass*) completed in 1923 (Philadelphia Museum of Art, Philadelphia), and *Etant Donnes* (Philadelphia Museum of Art, Philadelphia) on which Duchamp worked from 1946 to 1966. In these, and other constructed works, Duchamp offers an imaginative investigation of the analogical basis of sensuous resemblance. In *Etant Donnes*, the main image (of a naked woman lying on her back holding a gas lamp, in an urban parkland) can be seen only through a peep hole in a wooden door. Overall, the work is constructed from a diversity of found materials, some of which (e.g. undergrowth) are real specimens of what they represent, but the overall tableau is more than just found material – it is created resemblance in the Deleuzian sense.

Other artists have developed this strategy with very interesting results. Kurt Schwitters's *Merzbau* is a case in point. It involved a gradual transformation of a number of rooms in his family home in Hanover, between about 1923 and 1937.

In this work there is a genuine dissolution of the boundaries between art and life, insofar as the living space is overlain with aesthetic construction based on found material, and dedicated constructed elements. Schwitters's choice of specific materials may have an arbitrary element (dependent on what material was physically available to him) but once constructed, the artistic space becomes a unique configuration – wherein all the parts are necessary to the appearance of the whole. The work becomes, thereby a genuine conceptual phenomenon rather than just a vehicle for ideas.

Another telling (and related) example, is, again, furnished by Duchamp himself. It is the *Mile of String* from 1942. The work was created for Andre Breton's retrospective exhibition of surrealist art – *First Papers of Surrealism* staged in New York. Marcel Duchamp used string to thread a giant web through the entire exhibition space.

By means of this strategy both the exhibited works, and Duchamp's intervention on their display space created a remarkable and genuine – if temporary – conceptual phenomenon. Indeed, the filamentary structure evokes (through its very fragility) the aesthetic experience of its own transience, and perhaps even the transience of all sites and places, in general. Again, Duchamp might have chosen to disport the string in different ways to the one that he actually did adopt. The result might have been the same in broad aesthetic terms, but equally, it might have negotiated the space in a very different way. As it is, he did it just *this* way. We do not need, in other words, to *infer* Duchamp's decisions and ideas from the work. They are made concrete in the exact character of what was done. *The 'idea' is made present through the uniqueness of the made configuration.*

It is interesting to consider both the *Merzbau* and *Mile of String* in terms of Deleuze's notion of analogical art. In one sense neither of them resemble anything – or, at least, not in the same sense that *Etant Donnes* resembles the disturbing scene which it represents. However, the point is that found material is here put to use – to create something that is a visual whole that exceeds the individual items of material used for constructing the respective spaces. The artist's creative operations suspend the material's immediate ready-made meaning – treating it as 'asignifiying' – and then make it resemble something else, namely an idea whose ramifications cannot be summarized in neat terms.

As embodied in the conceptual phenomena, the idea evokes many associations – but not in an arbitrary manner. A viewer of such works may be led to associations that are based exclusively on his or her own personal experience. But there is a more compelling factor involved.

Schwitters's *Merzbau* and Duchamp's *Mile of String* have a literal character that is inescapable. They are 'about' respectively, the ability of art to colonize unexpected environments, and to open a continuity (in Schwitters's case) or a disruptive interaction (with Duchamp) between practical and artistic space. The works resemble these relations through *exemplifying* them in strikingly inventive ways. The inventiveness of the exemplification here means that the relations just described go far beyond the mere idea of them. They are bases for imaginative experiences that are guided by, rather than reduced to, conceptual content (in the manner of the ready-mades, per se).

On these terms, therefore, we have conceptual phenomena that are analogical, even though the materials used for composition are not 'made' by the artists in any traditional sense. What is decisive is *what they are made into.*

Conclusion

I shall end this chapter with some more general reflections on the scope of conceptual phenomena. The works I have discussed anticipate, and, indeed, create the conditions for, much subsequent conceptual, installation, and assemblage art. And the criteria I have considered in relation to Duchamp and Schwitters apply just as much in these subsequent contexts.

There are many 'works' (such as almost everything done by Martin Creed) that are little more than extensions of the ready-made's stunted scope. Other conceptual and minimal work – such as Robert Morris's *Slab* of 1966, or Don Judd's, work (both involving metal cast to the artist's specifications) can be as simple as ready-mades in bare literal terms, but go much further. This is because the actual perception of them centres on their exemplifications of presence and absence – factors whose character is tied exactly to that of the object in all its particularity. Mere descriptions of these works cannot be a substitute for the direct visual experience of them. They are conceptual phenomena.

It is possible to introduce some further critical gradations to the criteria I have explored. An artist such as David Mach, for example, has used ready-made material to, literally create representations that are, in effect, three-dimensional pictures. A case in point is his *Polaris* of 1983, using around 6,000 car tyres to construct a life-sized simulacrum of a nuclear submarine. This, and many other of Mach's works have a strong visual interest, and can sometimes be imaginatively funny. However, it might be argued, also, that they constitute a kind of wacky 'figuration' rather than 'Figure' in the Deleuzian senses.

In contrast, some other artists use found material in more enigmatic ways. Indeed, an interesting dynamic of later modern art is to explore the very scope of what found material might amount to.

An interesting example, here, is Peter Suchin's online work of 2007, entitled *Thirty Picture Postcards Posed and Composed for Poe* (see Plate 15).[9] Here we are dealing with, in effect, *found visuals*, composed of snapshots – probably taken in the artist's flat, or of odd corners of places visited, or details of images seen by him. Some of these shots involve (as it were) found compositions, while others appear as unexpected or curious *encounters*.

All the images can be looked at individually, but the enigmatic quality comes as much from taking them as a sequence, as from consideration of the subjects selected, individually, and, where appropriate, the particular way in which they are rendered.

One has a sense of fragments from a life composed as an allusive narrative that shows something of the artist's world – but

Plate 15 Peter Suchin, *Thirty Picture- Postcards Posed and Composed for Poe*, no. 27, 2007. Online at http://www.slashseconds.org/issues/002/002/articles/pesuchin/index.php

without impressing itself upon the viewer as merely a record of some of his experiences. Through this allusiveness, the viewer too can occupy the sequence on his or her own terms. It is a sequence from *a possible life*.

The title of the work itself works an interesting switch. The decay of experience into ephemera and loss is dramatically vivified in Romantic terms by Poe. But in Suchin's sequence the dynamic of presentation is posed rather than theatrical. By 'posed' here, I mean that the shots are taken and/or composed and linked for deliberate effect – one that directs us towards the *aesthetics of finitude*.

This aesthetic takes the form of redemptive bits of the mundane and transient, *mementi mori*, and the momentarily special, that are, sadly, all that is available to us in a rigidly consumerized and administered society. Suchin's 'postcards' carry a message – of interwoven loss, preservation, and transience that coheres, analogically, as an affecting conceptual phenomenon.

In this chapter, then, I have argued on Deleuzian lines that Duchamp's ready-mades should not be assigned a privileged theoretical role in modern art, and that de Duve's Kantian criteria, especially, cannot sustain such privileging.

However, found material can be used to create conceptual phenomena, whose visual interest gives them a phenomenological distinctiveness with its own special aesthetic worth. The decisive question is whether the individual character of the work *qua* visual, illuminates its meaning analogically, or whether it simply indicates it, digitally.

I turn now to another Kantian 'explanation' of developments in modern art, namely that of Clement Greenberg.

Chapter Seven

Greenberg's Kant and Modernist Painting

Introduction

In the previous chapters, I have emphasized the key significance of planarity in relation to all aspects of the phenomenology of modern art. I am not, of course, the only one to have emphasized this. The most familiar proponent of the significance of planarity is Clement Greenberg. He sees the flatness of the support, indeed, as the definitive feature of 'Modernist' painting.

Greenberg's theory of this is highly economical, but, in theoretical terms, also extremely sophisticated. It utilizes both a Kantian conception of aesthetics, and a more general Kantian 'infra logic' to account for the emergence and justification of modernist painting.

I will argue, however, that Greenberg's reading of this striving for autonomy is deeply flawed. To show this, I shall, in Part One, highlight the difficulties inherent in Greenberg's understanding of both Kant's aesthetics and his general 'critical' philosophy. In Part Two, I will trace the way in which these problems continue into, and are added to, in Greenberg's analysis of the relation between modernist painting and its planar emphasis.

Part One

In a well-known remark, Greenberg once observed that Kant's aesthetic theory is '. . . the most satisfactory basis for aesthetics we yet have . . .'[1] This remark, together with his frequent references to the primacy of 'aesthetic value' and 'formalism' have led many commentators to suppose that the real basis of his position is therefore a Kantian-style aesthetic formalism.

David Carrier, for example, suggests that Greenberg adheres to (among others) the following points: '(1) the aesthetic is a distinct source of experience based upon feeling, not taste as intellectual comprehension; (2) the aesthetic is an experience of formal values of the artwork . . .'[2] Now if either of these two points could be established unequivocally in relation to Greenberg, he would indeed be an aesthetic formalist in the tradition to Kant.

Unfortunately, he vacillates. For example, in a paper of 1967 he describes the aesthetic judgement as '. . .immediate, intuitive, undeliberative, and involuntary . . .'[3] – a description very much in keeping with Kant's own characterization[4] of the aesthetic judgement's apprehension of formal qualities.

However, it is when we come to Greenberg's more recent (1972) and most emphatic account of aesthetic value that problems really begin. We are told that,

> Quality, esthetic value originates in inspiration, vision, 'content', not in 'form' . . . 'form' not only opens the way to inspiration; it can also act as a means to it; and technical preoccupations, when searching enough and compelled enough, can generate or discover 'content'.[5]

Elsewhere,[6] indeed, we are told that 'inspiration' and even 'intuition' are synonymous with 'conception'. On these terms, then, a judgement which discriminates aesthetic value is very much a case of intellectually comprehending conceptual 'content' in a work, rather than the enjoyment of formal qualities through feeling.

This intellectualist grounding of aesthetic formalism is contradictory, since the formalist would hold that (to put it in Kantian terms) a concern for some conception or inspiration exemplified in the painting imports an 'interest' to our appreciation whereas the aesthetic apprehension of its formal qualities is a wholly 'disinterested'[7] pleasure, indifferent to questions of conception or technique.

It must not be thought, however, that this vacillation between the Kantian formalist and non-Kantian intellectualist account of aesthetic value is simply a case of Greenberg moving from an early formalist to a more mature intellectualist position. Evidence of the intellectualist standpoint can even be found in his claim from the late 1930s that, '. . . the ultimate values which the cultivated spectator derives from Picasso are derived at a second remove, as the result of reflection upon the immediate impression left by the plastic values'.[8]

Greenberg's vacillation is, therefore, symptomatic of a tension in his very notion of aesthetic value rather than a modification which occurs in the course of his theoretical development. This tension arises from the fact that Greenberg vacillates between construing aesthetic judgement *psychologically*, and construing it in its logical sense.

To illustrate this let us first consider the notion of a judgement being 'immediate and intuitive'. As it happens, almost all of our cognitive acts are like this. To recognize a friend on the street (indeed even to be able to walk down a street), involves cognitive activity which is, psychologically speaking, immediate and intuitive. We engage in such activity without being *explicitly* aware that we are making cognitive judgements. However, despite this psychological immediacy, such cognitive acts would not be possible without a complex network of background knowledge. We could not recognize our friend unless the judgement of recognition was informed by our previous experiences of him.

We know it is he, *because* he has that familiar gaunt face and reddish beard and is carrying the knapsack which always accompanies him on his travels. Despite its psychologically immediate and intuitive character, in other words, our judgement *logically* presupposes a specific kind of background knowledge which gives it a rational justification.

This, I would suggest, is also the case with aesthetic judgements. Psychologically speaking, we may know immediately that an artwork is of value – it simple 'looks' right. Of course, we may not at first be able to explain why it strikes us as being so good, but the very fact that we can even recognize it *as* an artwork – let alone evaluate it as good – logically presupposes that we are bringing complex networks of experience and ideas about art (i.e. an intellectual dimension) to bear on our judgement.

Given these consideration, I would suggest that when Greenberg describes the aesthetic judgement as 'immediate and intuitive' he is veering towards its psychological aspect, and when he stresses its intellectualist conceptual dimension he is veering towards its logical aspects.

The question which now arises is which of these aspects *ought* he to be emphasizing? In this respect it must be noted that my example of recognizing the friend shows that forms of judgement other than the aesthetic can be characterized as immediate and intuitive. This means that if we wish to define what is unique to aesthetic judgement – and this is what Greenberg *does* want to do – we must concentrate on its logical aspects, that is, on the specific kinds of quality which it is directed towards and the specific intellectual competences which the discrimination of such qualities presupposes. We must, in other words, concentrate on Greenberg's intellectualist notion of aesthetic value, rather than on his psychological interpretation of it.

A key point to note here is that it is in relation to the definition of what is intellectually unique to aesthetic value, that Greenberg introduces a rather more significant thread of

Kantianism into his theory. The crucial linking concept here is that of 'modernism'. Greenberg informs us that,

> The essence of Modernism lies, as I see it, in the use of the characteristic methods of a discipline to criticise the discipline itself – not in order to subvert it, but to entrench it more firmly in its area of competence. Kant [deemed by Greenberg 'the first Modernist'] used logic to establish the limits of logic, and while he withdrew much from its old jurisdiction, logic was left in all the more secure possession and what was left to it.[9]

These points are then applied analogically to the historical development of modern art:

> What had to be exhibited and made specific was that which was unique and irreducible not only in art in general but also in each particular art. Each art had to determine through the operations peculiar to itself, the effects peculiar and exclusive to itself.[10]

Greenberg's major point, then, is that to avoid being assimilated by other forms of human activity, painting (among the other art forms) has had, since the late nineteenth century, to adopt its own version of Kant's critical method in order to secure and display the unique effects of painting as a medium.

Now for Greenberg, when this (as he puts it) Kantian 'infra-logic'[11] is worked out successfully, what emerges is the declaration of painting's essential 'flatness'. However, it is important to note here that while Greenberg indeed construes flatness as the central feature of modernist works, he is not thereby saying (as Deane Curtin, for example, claims) that the flatness of the picture plane is 'a characteristic absolutely unique'[12] to modernist painting.

Rather, the successful realization of modernism's Kantian 'infra-logic' shows that the exemplification of flatness is the one effect peculiar and exclusive to all good painting. It is the distinctive source of value for painting as a medium.

Interestingly, Greenberg also suggests that, 'Modernism defines itself in the long run not as "movement" much less a programme, but rather as a kind of bias or tropism; towards esthetic value, esthetic value as much, and as an ultimate.'[13] Now if we take this claim that modernism is defined by its ultimate goal of aesthetic value (in the intellectualist sense of the artist's 'conception' or 'inspiration'), and link it with the other claim that modernism is defined by an 'infra-logic' whose ultimate goal is exemplification of the medium's essence, then it is clear that, for Greenberg, aesthetic value must consist in the way a particular work exemplifies the art-ist's conception of, or attitude towards, his medium's essential and unique features.

In the case of painting, as we have seen, this means specifically his conception of, or attitude towards, flatness. It is of course precisely this very narrow grounding of aesthetic value in a defi-nite sort of conception about art, which gives Greenberg's posi-tion its distinctive and controversial character.

We must, however, be very careful to note the exact scope of Greenberg's claims. He is not, for example, saying that only modernist painting has aesthetic value but rather that it is more 'intense, explicit, and self-conscious'[14] in its pursuit of aesthetic value than is traditional painting. On these terms, it would be quite conceivable, say, for a poor modernist work to actu-ally fail to affirm the flatness of painting and hence possess no aesthetic value but for a good traditional work to transcend its representational content, exemplify the artist's conception of, or attitude towards painting's essence, and become thereby a source of aesthetic value.

We find, then, that Greenberg uses primarily an intellectual notion of aesthetic value that owes nothing to Kant's aesthetic formalism. The link with Kant does become more meaningful, however, when Greenberg gives aesthetic value a distinctive con-tent by defining it (in effect) as that successful exemplification of flatness whose character is made most explicit by the realization of modernist painting's Kantian 'infra-logic'.

As I shall now show, it is through this use of the analogy with Kant's Critical method that Greenberg is led into his most serious problems.

Part Two

The most general direction from which Greenberg can be criticized is in his unargued reduction of aesthetic value to artistic quality. For him, we will remember, aesthetic value is grounded in a certain class of artefacts (namely art works) successfully and uniquely exemplifying the essential condition(s) of their own kind of artefactuality.

Now this definition seems immediately implausible insofar as it forecloses on nature as a source of aesthetic value. One way around this would be to argue that aesthetic value arises whenever any object (by whatever means) successfully exemplifies the defining properties of its class or essence. However, this would not only take us beyond the scope of Greenberg's theory, but would also make problematic those formal properties which are customarily understood as aesthetic (e.g. organic unity) but which do not overtly exemplify the definitive properties of the class of relations of which they are particular instances.

It might be thought further that if we simply modify Greenberg's terminology here, and for 'aesthetic value' read 'artistic quality', then his theory will become correspondingly more viable. Unfortunately, the specific way he understands (in our modified terminology) 'artistic quality' in relation to painting raises serious difficulties of its own.

The basic problem is that, as we have already seen, for Greenberg it is in its exemplification of virtual flatness that painting's unique essence and, thereby, its ultimate source of artistic quality resides. As he puts it, 'Because flatness was the only condition painting shared with no other art, Modernist painting oriented itself to flatness as it did to nothing else.'[15] Unfortunately, the two clauses in this statement are simply false.

To see why this is so, we must clarify what Greenberg actually means by 'flatness'. First, I would emphasize that he does not mean *physical* flatness, but rather the flatness of the *picture plane*. If we look very closely at the surface of a painting we see that it is not physically two-dimensional because the brushstrokes and application of the pigment render the surface uneven. However, under normal observational conditions, we do not notice this unevenness; the painting *appears*, rather, as a purely two-dimensional plane which gives – either through optical or representational means – the illusion of three dimensions.

If Greenberg's idea of flatness thus refers to that of the notional picture plane it is easy to see why he takes this to be unique to the medium of painting. It contrasts with, say, the printed page of poetry or the photographic image, insofar as these media are fundamentally flat in physical and real rather than planar and notional terms. It is painting alone which is flat *only* in the planar sense.

Or is it? The problem here is that Greenberg does not seem to consider the most obvious counter-example to his theory, namely that of *drawing*. If we look at a drawing closely enough we see that the lines of graphite, chalk, charcoal, or whatever, are physically on top of the surface, and this means that (however minutely) the surface is rendered uneven. It has notional planar flatness rather than the physical variety.

Hence one might say that the contrast between the flatness of painting and that of drawing, is one of mere physical degree; but it is not in any sense a difference of kind. Now it may be, of course, that Greenberg does not consider drawing to be an authentic art medium, but he provides no justification for such a view, and, indeed, it seems wildly implausible to even imagine that such a view could, in fact, be justified.

I am arguing, then, that Greenberg is wrong to regard planar flatness as a feature unique to the medium of painting. He is also wrong to suppose that modernist painting orientates itself fundamentally towards such flatness more than it does towards anything else.

In this respect, for example, it is theoretically more economical and historically more plausible to argue that the basic impulse of painting after Manet is to assert its distinctiveness from photography. While, relatively speaking, such paintings are flatter looking than the products of earlier epochs, there is no reason why we *must* see this feature as anything other than an *epiphenomenon* arising from broader interests – such as the artist's desire to affirm the centrality of human perception in the creation of painting (as I argued in Chapter Two), or painting's capacity to symbolize spiritual values. Indeed, if one were pushed to define the essence of painting at all it would surely consist in something like 'an arrangement of paint marks upon a plane-surface'.

Now this definition would have at least one interesting consequence, in that it would follow from our definition that the 'painterly' work with its emphasis on handling and brushstrokes would exemplify more securely the real essence of painting (a position which, as we saw in Chapter One, Deleuze is committed to). Greenberg, however, would almost certainly reply to this in terms of the following argument (used in his paper 'After Abstract Expressionism').[16]

The fused and blotted masses of the painterly work have their original *raison d'être* in the heightening of illusionism; and even in a work where painterly effects are not employed to this exact end, there is still a tendency for their use to set up 'descriptive [i.e. naturalistic] connotations', or suggestions of illusionistic depth. The non-painterly modernist work in contrast, if it deceives the eye at all, '. . . it is by optical rather than pictorial means; by relations of colour and shape largely divorced from descriptive connotations'.[17] This line of reply is the only one really open to Greenberg, yet it basically serves to illustrate the unjustified partiality of his critical judgement.

On the one hand, it is a very contentious historical point as to whether, indeed, it even tends to set up such connotations. There is, for example, a good case to be made for linking painterliness with the realization of expressionist rather than illusionistic ends, and this is especially true of such post-war moderns as Jackson Pollock (as we have seen in Chapter Three). On the other hand, one also suspects that there is rather more optical illusionism inherent in non-painterly modernism that Greenberg is prepared to admit; and that such illusionism will tend to make us read such works in terms other than the affirmation of two-dimensionality.

Indeed the ostensibly optical effects of such Greenberg-favoured artists as Mark Rothko and Barnett Newman have a veritable fecundity of descriptive connotations some of which have been well brought out by Rosenblum, in his paper 'The Abstract Sublime'.[18] This is a point I shall return to a little further on.

Even more serious problems pertain if we allow Greenberg his claims about flatness, and see where the argument leads. For example, we are told of Newman, Rothko, and Clyfford Still, that,

> The question now asked through their art is no longer what constitutes art, or the art of painting as such, but what irreducibly constitutes good art as such. Or rather what is the ultimate source of value or quality in art. And the worked-out answer appears to be: not skill, training, or anything else to do with execution or performance, but conception alone.[19]

This is where Greenberg's theory of modernism is given its most extreme exposition. The modernist work in its purest state is one where artistic quality is grounded in conception alone, and where the painter is put into something of an external relation to his work, insofar as (in principle) it could be physically made by someone else simply following his instructions.

That is why the occasionally made objection[20] that Greenberg's emphasis on 'quality' overlooks the fact that a number of hugely

important post-war modernists (such as de Kooning) were trying to avoid the creation of physically 'well-made' painting,
turns out, in fact, to be completely unfounded. For Greenberg,
it is not the 'made' aspect in which quality resides, but the artist's conception of his medium's flatness.

However, while Greenberg is not open to this particular
empirical objection, his theory does lead to several other insur-
mountable problems at a more conceptual level. In the first
instance, there is good reason for saying that the primacy which
Greenberg affords to conception would entail a move into the
realm of something different from art.

Even if one does not want to go this far, it is at least clear
that the emphasis on conception rather than securing what is
unique to painting would serve very much to reduce its creativity to the order of that of craft or technology – where the end
product is fully planned out before execution, and where the
designer does not have to physically make the work himself.

Indeed, something like this outcome to Greenberg's theory
was promised as soon as he introduced the analogy with Kant's
critical method. An art which makes the essentially conceptual
task of self-criticism or definition paramount takes on thereby
the characteristics of theoretical discourse, with the distinctive
sensuous physicality of its medium gradually reduced to the status of a mere bearer for some intellectual idea.

Now there is one line of response open to Greenberg in
respect of this accusation. He insists for example, that, '. . . self-
criticism in Modernist art has never been carried on in any but
a spontaneous and largely subliminal way. [. . .] it has been altogether a topic of practice . . . and never a topic of theory.'[21] In
addition, we are told that, 'No artist was, or yet is, aware of it,
nor could any artist work freely in awareness of it.'[22] This would,
of course, mean that artistic (or 'esthetic' as Greenberg terms
it) quality resides in the successful exemplification of the artist's
unconscious or unreflective attitude towards his medium.

However, this not only conflicts with the spirit of Greenberg's
emphasis on 'conception' and 'inspiration' but also flatly

contradicts his claim that what is distinctive about modernism is its 'intense, explicit, and self-conscious' bias towards 'esthetic value, esthetic value as such, and as an ultimate'.

Indeed, artists such as Morris Louis and Kenneth Noland were so strongly influenced by Greenberg (Greenberg even provided Louis with titles for his works) that they could hardly fail to relate self-consciously to the modernist tendency. Yet, far from judging them necessarily unsuccessful (as his claim above requires) Greenberg actually saw them as exemplifying all that was best about 'quality' painting in the early 1960s.[23]

Even more fundamental, perhaps, is the fact that if modernist art's securing of aesthetic value really was unknown to the artists themselves, then, far from being secured by practice alone, it would be logically dependent upon critical discourse for its emergence and full display. The actual work would, in a sense, be a mere dummy awaiting the critic ventriloquist.

The full implication of this dependence upon critical conception and theory is strikingly illustrated by the strong continuity that exist between Greenberg-favoured-and-influenced Post-Painterly Abstractionism, and Minimal Art and Conceptual Art in the 1960s and beyond.

Greenberg's claim, for example, that 'conception is alone decisive'[24] seems to embody the basic attitude which runs through all three styles noted above. It results, of course, in art gradually diminishing, and then shedding its sensuous particularity, to end up as quasi-philosophical statement of a dubious kind. Taken to its logical extreme, in other words, the modernist tendency results in the death of the visual arts' distinctive media and, thereby, their claim to uniqueness.

On these terms, we find that if Greenberg's theory is followed through, modernist painting not only fails to secure its 'area of competence' but fails to do so in direct proportion to the purity of its modernism. This is the fundamental contradiction which vitiates Greenberg's theory.

Even at the less general level there is absolutely no support for his line of interpretation in the cases of many of the specific artists he considers, such as Newman, Rothko, and Still. The most striking aspect of their work is the deployment of colour-fields which overwhelm by sheer emotional impact and intimations of mortality rather than intimations of flatness.

This is no chance effect, but is, rather, utterly integral to Newman's, Rothko's, and Still's own personal conceptions of what art is ultimately about. Rothko probably spoke for them all in his assertion that, 'I am not interested in relationships of colour or form or anything else . . . I am interested only in expressing the basic human emotions – tragedy, ecstasy, doom, and so on . . .'[25] Even in those artists who were actually influenced by Greenberg (such as Morris Louis) one feels there are more central issues than the questions of conception or flatness. It is telling in this respect that Greenberg himself said of Louis' work, that 'if these painting fail as vehicles and expressions of feelings, they fail entirely . . .'[26]

It is a shame that Greenberg did not explore the notion of 'feelings' in much greater detail. For what his approach lacks, ultimately, is any real sense of what is distinctive to the *individual styles and tendencies* of modern painting – and the complex and contrasting effects that these bring about at the visual level.

Given the internal weakness of Greenberg's theory, why has it failed to attract more searching criticism in relation to these specific philosophical problems? One reason is, I think, that the real terms of the debate with Greenberg have been largely misunderstood through his finding an unwarranted shelter beneath the theoretical umbrella of Kantian-style aesthetic formalism and the metaphysic of 'Kantian infra-logic'.

A second reason is that at a time when abstract expressionism was threatening to shatter conventional critical canon and idioms, Greenberg came up with an urbane and unextravagant style of analysis (in keeping with the tenor of Eisenhower–Kennedy polite society) that related the new works to a culturally respectable Great Tradition of modernist painting. Given this 'achievement', questions of actual interpretative

validity assumed a secondary importance. Abstract expressionism had been made safe for good taste.

This leads us, then, to a final moral. If we choose (*à la*
Greenberg) to give modernism a quasi-Kantian phenomenological depth or 'infra-logic', then what is gained in terms of
a satisfying unity of critical comprehension is utterly lost in
terms of the conceptual or art-historical distortion that ensue.
There are some dominant trajectories and shared beliefs, but
these are mediated by different historical circumstances and
personalities.

It will have been noted that, while Greenberg's theory of modernist painting is not specifically addressed to the understanding of abstract art, its basic momentum, nevertheless is one
which fully integrates, and attempts to explain salient aspects
of such art.

However, as well as being problematic on lines considered
already, it does little to explain what is distinctive about the
ontology and meaning of abstract art, per se. Given that this
tendency is so uniquely modern, any adequate phenomenology of modern art must, however, negotiate the grounds of this
uniqueness.

As a first step towards this, I return, now, to the starting point
of this study – Deleuze's theory of painting.

Chapter Eight

Deleuze and the Interpretation of Abstract Art

Introduction

The detailed study of Deleuze's theory of painting offered in Chapter One, did not address his interesting account of abstract tendencies. This account is fully integrated in that theory, which, as we have seen, is very much geared towards the ratification of Cezanne and Bacon's 'haptic' pictorial space.

Given this, the task arises, again, of expounding Deleuze's hierarchical and essentialist account and then criticizing it, to see what valid insights will emerge.

In Part One of this chapter, accordingly, I set out the basics of Deleuze's approach to abstract art, and then, in Part Two, subject it to critical evaluation. Finally in Conclusion, I identify the worthwhile features and an important clue for a comprehensive theory of abstract art (that will be followed up in the extended final chapter to this book).

Part One

Deleuze's approach to abstract art is an unorthodox one, insofar as he identifies two qualitatively different modes of it, reserving the term 'abstraction' for only one of them. However, his starting point for both is the same – namely, that notion of 'diagram' which I discussed at length in Chapter One. We will recall that it consists of asignifying marks from which the painter creates resemblance, and thus allows Figure to emerge. According to Deleuze, 'Where painters differ is in their manner of embracing this nonfigurative chaos, and in their evaluation of the pictorial order to come, and the relation of this order with this chaos.'[1]

For Deleuze, there are 'three great paths'[2] which modern idioms of painting follow in relation to the diagram – abstraction, *art informel,* and the kind of style which he most favours, namely that of the Figure (exemplified by Cezanne and Bacon). He characterizes abstraction through a contrast:

> Figure is the sensible form related to a sensation; it acts immediately upon the nervous system, which is of the flesh, whereas abstract form is addressed to the head, and acts through the intermediary of the brain, which is closer to the bone.[3]

Deleuze emphasizes the 'cerebal' orientation of abstraction, again and again.[4] He sees it as something ascetic and involving a deep effort to attain a kind of spiritual salvation, by raising itself above the figurative givens, and turning the chaos of the diagram into a stream that must be crossed so as to attain abstract form.

An art of this kind operates with a process of homogenization and binarization. Such a process is, according to Deleuze, constitutive of digital coding and is based on binary as opposed to random choice.[5] Such coding involves the 'maximum subordination of the hand to the eye'.[6] Indeed, the hand is 'reduced' to the finger, insofar as it is involved only in choosing units that correspond to pure visual forms.

Now, as I argued in Chapter Six, Deleuze's notion of digital coding seems especially suited to Duchamp's ready-mades, and simple idioms of conceptual art that repeat the ready-made's basic strategy. However, in his book on Bacon, he links digital coding to some rather surprising artists.

Kandinsky, for example, is considered in such terms. We are told that,

> 'Digits' are the units that group together visually the terms in opposition. Thus, according to Kandinsky, vertical-white-activity, horizontal-black-inertia, and so on. From this is derived a conception of binary choice that is opposed to random choice. Abstract painting took the elaboration of such a code very far . . . . It is the code that is responsible for answering the question of painting today. What can save man from 'the abyss', from external tumult and manual chaos? Open up a spiritual state for the man of the future, a man without hands.[7]

The key point here, is that abstraction's ascetic orientation is based on its affirmation of optical space that is no longer subordinate to manual or tactile elements. Deleuze suggests, indeed, that such painting will amount to an almost exclusive emphasis on horizontal and vertical relations in its attainment of spiritual purification.

But, given these considerations, what is it that separates such painting from the mere presentation of geometrical form? Deleuze suggests that such painting retains a 'tension' which internalizes both the manual movement whereby the form is created, and the invisible forces that determine this movement.[8]

This is made possible because,

> the abstractionists often happen to be great painters, which means that they do not simply oppose to painting a code that is external to it; on the contrary, they elaborate an intrinsically pictorial code. It is thus a paradoxical code since instead of being opposed to analogy, it takes analogy as its object; it is the digital expression of the analogical as such.[9]

These remarks are difficult, and are not given much elaboration by Deleuze. One might, however, try to explain them as follows. Abstraction uses a digital code in that the painting does not generate Figure, as it were, experimentally, through developing the diagram. Rather, Figure is composed in advance as a basic design – a design meant to resemble spiritual realities and relations.[10] It is this design factor, rather than the act of painting itself, which attempts to realize Figure. The analogical function of painting is, thereby, displaced into coded presentation – and is thence a 'cerebal' experience, rather than one of 'sensation'.

Now, it might be asked why such works are experienced as anything other than mere geometric configurations per se. Deleuze's answer is based on the 'tension' mentioned earlier. Mondrian, Kandinsky, and Malevich are good painters. So, despite their digital orientation, we are aware of the effort of painting that has brought these forms forth. There is a kind of positive feedback that amounts to (though Deleuze himself does not put it like this) to a kind of redemptive ghostly analogicality that haunts the presentation of the code.

Of course, this means, in effect, that the quality achieved by great abstractionism is, in a sense, *in spite of itself.* Again, Deleuze is employing a quite explicit hierarchy here. As he says,

> The code is inevitably cerebral and lacks sensation, the essential reality of the fall, that is, is the direct action on the nervous system. Kandinsky defined abstract painting by 'tension', but according to Bacon, tension is what abstract painting lacks the most. By internalizing tension in the optical form, abstract painting neutralized it.[11]

On these terms, having given abstraction a certain dignity by virtue of a creative tension between the code and our sense of it's being something painted, Deleuze is at pains to show that there are, nevertheless, more authentic idioms of painting.

And it is this light that he considers the second major path of modern painting, namely *art informel* – a term which Deleuze takes to include the great American abstract expressionists

(notably Pollock) as well as the post-World War II French painters to whom the term is applied, customarily.

Deleuze regards this as the opposite extreme to abstraction.
We are told that,

> This time the abyss or chaos is deployed to the maximum.
> Somewhat like a map that is as large as the country, the dia-
> gram merges with the totality of the painting: the entire paint-
> ing is diagrammatic. Optical geometry disappears in favour
> of a manual line, exclusively manual.[12]

According to Deleuze, the eye has difficulty in following such a
line, because it does not form a contour that delimits anything
or creates a sense of inside and outside, or of concave and con-
vex.[13] In this regard he mentions Pollock's all-over paintings,
and Morris Louis's stained canvases. They and similar painters
exemplify a line that does not pass from one point to another,
bur rather, passes *through* points, and constantly changes directions in a way that exceeds any digital organization.

Deleuze suggests, also, that other abstract idioms remain figurative – but does not consider how this claim might be justified
through reference to specific examples. He is content, rather, to
observe that the manual line of *art informel* is anticipated by those
great figurative painters – such as Turner – who, in effect, *paint
between things*, and achieve a kind of decomposition of matter.[14]

This is pushed to its extreme by Pollock. In his all-over works,
painting becomes a catastrophe – being both painting, and
painting diagram simultaneously. Here, there is not an inner
vision of the infinite, but a manual power that occupies the
painting in its entirety.[15]

The upshot of this, is that,

> In the unity of the catastrophe and the diagram, man dis-
> covers rhythm as matter and material. The painter's instru-
> ments are no longer the paintbrush and the easel, which still

conveyed the subordination of the hand to the requirements of an optical organization . . . The diagram expresses the entire painting at once; that is, the optical catastrophe and the manual rhythm.[16]

Interestingly, Deleuze suggests that this momentum is continued to a higher stage in artists after Pollock. Specifically,

The current evolution of abstract expressionism is completing this process by realizing what was still little more than a metaphor in Pollock: (1) the extension of the diagram to the spatial and temporal whole of the painting (displacement of the 'beforehand' and 'afterward'); (2) the abandonment of any visual sovereignty, and even any visual control, over the painting in the process of being executed (the blindness of the painter); (3) the elaboration of lines that are 'more' than lines, surfaces that are 'more' than surfaces, or, conversely, volumes that are 'less' than volumes (Carl Andre's planar sculptures, Robert Ryman's fibers, Barre's laminated works, Christian Bonnefoi's strata).[17]

I will return to the curiosity of Deleuze's extension of 'abstract expressionism' to these artists, further on. Before that, it is worth considering Deleuze's response to an alternative interpretative position, namely that of Clement Greenberg and Michael Fried.

These critics emphasize the exclusively optical character of the space which Deleuze has described in relation Pollock and *art informel*. He suggests that there is just an ambiguity of interpretation at issue here.[18] What Greenberg and Fried are emphasizing, in effect, is that the aforementioned pictorial space is one which has lost those tactile referents (depth, contour, relief, etc.) used by classical painting to define and emphasize the relation of figure to background.

However, Deleuze cites the points which we encountered in Chapter One. The tactile referents of classical representation involve a relative subordination of the manual to the visual. In this context, what the abstract expressionists do is not to affirm the purely optical, but, rather, to make manual space visible.

This is done by emphasizing the planarity of the canvas as a vehicle for expressing the impenetrability of the painting, and the gestural character of colour – features that impose themselves on the eye as expressions of a foreign power that allows the eye *to find no rest*. In this way, such 'optical' painting actually reverses the classical hierarchy, by subordinating the eye to the hand.

Deleuze goes on to suggest that Bacon was not drawn to abstract expressionism because it leaves 'sensation' in an irrevocably confused state. Even a line that delineates nothing still has something of the contour about it. Indeed, it is important that 'The diagram must not eat away at the entire painting, it must remain operative and controlled. The violent methods must not be given free reign, and the necessary catastrophe must not submerge the whole.'[19]

Figuration, in other words, should not be dispensed with. Rather, 'a new figuration, that of the Figure, should emerge from the diagram and make the sensation clear and precise.'[20] According to Deleuze, this is exactly what is achieved in Bacon's 'malerisch' period, where,

> the precision of the sensation, the clarity of the Figure, and the rigor of the contour continued to act beneath the color patch or the traits – which did not efface the former, but instead gave them a power vibration and nonlocalization of random traits and scrubbed zones. Bacon thus follows a third path, which is neither optical like abstract painting, nor manual like action painting.[21]

On these terms, Bacon again sets painting to rights – by affirming the figure's analogical emergence from the diagram, and thus avoiding the error of taking the diagram to be the analogical flux, itself. This means, of course, that Deleuze's hierarchical predilection for Bacon and a haptic 'third path' – based on making the tactile and optical complementary – asserts itself, once more.

Part Two

I will now offer a critical review of Deleuze's position. First, his approach is built on a quite definite hierarchy. 'Digital' abstraction issues in some worthwhile works but is always constrained by striving to articulate analogical meaning. Art informel, in contrast is analogical, but remains arrested at the level of the diagram – absolutizing it, instead of putting it to work. It is only with the 'haptic' third way of Cezanne and Bacon, that modern painting is true to what he takes painting to be about – namely the emergence of Figure. But, put this way, however, it is quite clear that, in general terms, Deleuze's approach compels us to regard abstract art in all its forms as something which, by virtue of its specific ontologies, falls short of painting's highest possibilities. Let us, therefore, put this hierarchy to the test by considering his conception of abstraction, and *art informel*, in turn.

Abstraction – in Deleuze's sense of the terms – accrues to those artists whose work is composed primarily through a process of planning or design, in terms of compositional structures and colour. An artist such as Mondrian, for example, presents (in his De Stijl works, at least) geometrical forms based on perpendiculars, horizontal lines and bands of determinate thickness, and areas of pure colour. The work's final state declares only these, and gives us no sense of the work as something created *through* the artist's gestures in handling paint.

The effect of such a creative strategy is to make the act of painting itself, into something *contingent* (though Deleuze himself does not put it in such express terms). In principle, someone else could simply do the painting by following instructions as the size of the individual compositional forms and the colours they are to adopt.

Now, much abstraction of the geometric, post-painterly, and 'Op Art' varieties is indeed like this. And in some cases, indeed, the painting is actually done by the artist's assistants – such as Bridget Riley's *Arcadia 1* of 2007 (National Gallery, London) which was painted by them directly on to the gallery wall on the basis of Riley's instructions.

However, one must question what hangs on this contingency of the act of painting. Admittedly, this way of creating a painting is different from that of *art informel* or the emergence of Figure in 'haptic' painting, *but there is no intrinsic reason why we should regard this as anything other than difference, as such.*

If a work is compositionally interesting, it will invite us to consider how the final form emerged – it will refer us to that realm of 'invisible' factors (bound up with the work's planning and execution, and relation to other works) which enabled this highly distinctive painterly outcome. Indeed, as we will recall from Chapter One, Deleuze himself, in one of his various characterizations of the 'task' of painting, makes 'invisible' factors central to what it presents.

Now, it is true that Deleuze suggests also that good abstraction will embody a 'tension' that refers us to how the painting was made. It will evoke the analogical aspect of painting indirectly. But if this is so, then it rules out any hierarchical distinction between abstraction and other idioms of painting. For we could argue that in such work, the sense of painting's analogical dimension is exemplified with a particular kind of enigmatic – even *apparitional* – character that is not available to *art informel* or figurative work.

It is important to emphasize that the enigmatic quality in question here, is ontological, rather than normative. Such a feature makes abstraction different from other idioms; it does not make it superior to them. For just as the emergence of Figure (in other forms of painting) depends on the quality of the work, so too, the emergence of abstraction's enigmatic or apparitional character is dependent on the inventiveness of the individual work's style.

No doubt Deleuze would object to this equalization on the grounds that – as we saw earlier – for him, abstraction, by its nature is only a 'cerebal' address to the brain. It is unable to impact directly on the nervous system and generate that all-important 'sensation' which, for Deleuze, is the central effect of painting

However, in this respect, let us consider another work by Bridget Riley – namely *Fall* of 1963 (see Plate 16, Tate Modern, London).

Plate 16 Bridget Riley, *Fall*, 1963, emulsion on hardboard support, 1410 × 1403 mm, Tate Modern, London. © Bridget Riley 2011. All rights reserved, courtesy Karsten Schubert, London.

We will recall how much Deleuze emphasizes the idea of fall as a basis of our experience of sensation in painting. Riley's painting addresses this phenomenon quite explicitly. Deleuze would probably claim that such a work merely 'represents' Fall rather than makes it a factor in how Figure is perceived to emerge from material ground.

This would be a mistaken response, however. What is striking about the painting is the way it immerses and overwhelms – descending from immediate optical impact into an evocation of flow and counter flow that appears impressed into the surface of the work. There is an evocation of tactile referents, no matter how shallow the illusionistic involved in these. *Vision as sensation* rather than 'cerebal' recognition is paramount.

The point is, therefore, that while *some* works of 'abstraction' in the Deleuzian sense may strike us cerebally, others will involve much more of a direct address to the 'nervous system'.[22] Which of these (if either) is involved, is entirely down to *the individual style of the work*. We cannot simply assign patterns of response *a priori* on the basis of the ontology of such works.

I turn now to the case of *art informel*. It must be noted at the outset that while Deleuze emphasizes the manual emphasis in such works, he does not attend to the complexities of this.

For example, while Pollock's works may trace a manual line in the terms described by Deleuze, we must recall also, that they were often created using dripped, flicked, or splashed paint. The effect of this is, in fact, one which tends to *suspend* any sense of the manual as a form-creating factor.

In this respect, one might consider Pollock's *No. 14: Gray* of 1948 (Guggenheim Museum, New York). Here the artist has poured paint on to a gesso soaked paper, thus ensuring that the continuous black lines have a feature that could not have been added through direct manual handling – namely, a continuous silver halo, where the black soaks into the wet gesso background. The suspension of manual factors is emphasized, also, by the way in which the poured lines culminate (as in most of Pollock's action painting) in a blob or head.

This invests them with strong organic overtones, suggestive of the appearance of simple life forms, and processes of generation.

These culminating forms, indeed, mean that the spectator's attention is not driven constantly towards the edge of the painting, but is looped back, and redistributed. This creates a strong *sensation* of visual energy *in momentum* – a feature that is accentuated further by Pollock's frequently used device of ending the distribution of forms before they reach the edge of the picture. The effect of this is to make the forms appear as though they are *in front* of a ground.

The upshot is that, in Pollock's work, there is a major dimension of *allusive Figure* that is made emergent from the diagrammatic elements. This is not the manual space that Deleuze describes, but, rather, one that has affinity to his favoured notion of haptic space – wherein the optical and the manual are integrated.

Now the Pollock work I have just discussed is the one which, as far as I can tell, is closest to the manual line emphasized by Deleuze. However, as we have seen, it quite clearly exceeds the reductive Deleuzian interpretative framework. And all Pollock's other works, and that of other *art informel* practitioners bring this home even more. In their painting there is the emergence of allusive Figure. As we have seen, Deleuze himself suggests that much abstract art is 'figurative' but does not offer any more detailed discussion of this slightly pejorative characterization.

This is extremely unfortunate. For the pervasive weakness of Deleuze's approach to abstract art is its unwarranted essentializing. He presents abstraction and *art informel* as opposite extremes, with 'figurative' abstraction covering the rest, as a kind of poor outsider.

However, this does absolutely no justice to any of the painters individually considered. Deleuze, for example, quotes from Kandinsky's theoretical texts, so as to make him appear as a digital abstractionist. But Kandinsky's paintings themselves

– even the later ones, are immensely complex in specifically painterly terms. *How* they are painted is paramount – even if the resemblance to spiritual reality is determined in more general terms, through theory and compositional design.

Deleuze's analytic violence against the concrete individual painter's style is exemplified also in the way he applies his terms. In this respect, we will recall his strange description of Carl Andre's planar sculptures, Robert Ryman's fibres, Barre's laminated works, and Christian Bonnefoi's strata, as developments of 'abstract expressionism'.

Figures such as Andre and Ryman are customarily associated with minimal and conceptual art, and – in the case of Andre, at least, have much more affinity with Deleuze's notion of digital abstraction. This is because many of Andre's sculptures are not made by him physically. They involve, rather, assembling or bonding ready-made material. In his work, the act of making by the artist, personally, is contingent. Someone else could just as easily make the work by following the artist's instructions.

Ryman is more complex, since he steadfastly affirms that he is in the business of making physical configurations that are not meant to signify anything other than themselves (hence his description of his own work as 'realism'). Now, if one stretched the notion of diagram enough, it might be argued that Ryman's configurations of material are, *in effect*, asignifying factors that are, as it were arrested before they can be invested with figurative meaning. But the problem with this, is that they were created to be, and exist *as*, interesting material configurations, per se. There are no grounds for relating them to diagram at all. And with an artist such as Bonnefoi, while many of his works involve a distribution of forms all over the canvas, they mainly involve definition through manifest contours – with nothing like the 'manual line' that Deleuze takes to be at issue in abstract expressionism.

The point is, that Deleuze's approach does not pay due attention to the use of 'found' material in abstract art, nor to the many different *individual styles* of abstraction. He tries to fit artists into his categories of abstract art, without considering the way in which their individual styles *reconfigure* the significance of the ontological structures involved in these categories.

On these terms, therefore, Deleuze's approach to abstract art lacks compelling *comprehensive* explanatory value.

Conclusion

To end, it is important to stress what is of worth in Deleuze's theory. His ontological distinction between abstraction and *art informel* is viable in the sense that it maps out the two opposite limits of creativity in abstract art.

On the one hand, some idioms (notably of a geometric or minimal kind) are based on creative design with the actual act of painting by the artist subordinate to this, and, in principle, rendered contingent. On the other hand, *art informel* privileges exploration through the act of painting as a basis for generating composition.

Despite Deleuze's treatment of it, there are no valid hierarchical implications to this distinction, and it is a useful analytic tool – as long as it is not used bluntly as a means of dividing all abstract art into two great opposing camps, where membership of one or the other is obligatory.

As we have seen, there are some works that do not fit in with this pairing, and in the cases of artists whose work does seem to, the vital point is to test the distinction in terms of exactly *how* it applies in their individual case, and, in particular, to note ways in which some artists modify it.

Of the utmost importance here is – once more – the primacy of individual style. However, this primacy does not simply entail that Deleuze's criteria should be modified in the light of its demands; rather it should be acknowledged, also, that the criteria can help understand what is distinctive about such individual achievement.

Now while Deleuze's theory of abstract art does not have comprehensive significance, there are aspects of his general theory of painting which can still point us in the direction of a more comprehensive theory.

We have seen how, already, in my analyses of the Bridget Riley and Pollock paintings, that there is, in effect, and emergence of Figure – albeit Figure of an allusive kind. The question is, what is the basis of this – what sort of resemblance is created through allusion?

A first step towards the understanding of this is provided by one of the most important concepts discussed in Chapter One – Deleuze's notion of the body without organs. It will be recalled from there, that the effect of Figure is to bring about a diversification of our perceptual relation to painting. We can enjoy explorations of depth, and the broader associations of colour and shapes in a spectacle that ranges far beyond the purely visual organs of sense.

The emergence of Figure involves an immobile evocation of mobility – something that is at odds with the horizon of time is customary in the unified operation of our senses. Modern art, and, in particular, abstract painting, enhances this 'polyvalence' of the eye. It is no longer tied to any rigid order of visual perception, but can comprehend places and aspects that are not normally available for direct visual perception.

Some remarks from Deleuze are useful here:

Painting gives us eyes all over: in the ear, in the stomach, in the lungs (the painting breathes . . .). This is the double definition of painting: subjectively, it invests the eye, which ceases to be organic in order to become a polyvalent and transitory organ; objectively, it brings before us the reality of a body, of lines and colours freed from organic representation. And each is produced by the other: the pure presence of the body becomes visible at the same time that the eye becomes the destined organs of this presence.[23]

One can develop these insights in more specific terms. A mode of painting freed from 'organic representation' is not only one that emphasizes the emergence of Figure from material ground, it is one that can explore aspects of the visible that are not available to us under the normal conditions of perception. Quite literally, it can present configurations and relations that are normally invisible because of the organically constrained sense of sight.

This is a most vital clue to the meaning of abstract art. However, Deleuze himself does not provide material for taking it further. To do this requires an approach which can both think through the character of pictorial media in a more compelling way than Deleuze's, and then link it to a more specific criterion of the invisible – one that can account for the emergence of allusive Figure.

In order to do this, I shall address now the theoretical work of the great abstract expressionist Hans Hofmann, in relation to more ideas from Merleau-Ponty.

Chapter Nine

Plane Truths: Hans Hofmann, Modern Art and the Meaning of Abstraction

Introduction

The time has come, finally, to bring modern art's most unique creation – abstraction – into a more comprehensive phenomenological perspective. As we have just seen, Deleuze points us in a certain direction, but does not offer more.

Interestingly, there is another thinker – an artist – whose ideas on this topic have been much neglected, namely Hans Hofmann.[1] His importance as a teacher is often remarked upon, but what he taught has received comparatively little attention from contemporary art theorists and aestheticians.[2]

Like Merleau-Ponty he offers a theory of painting that is unified. By this, I mean that it can encompass both figurative *and* abstract modern art. Of course, given the diversity of abstract tendencies and their historical contexts, it might seem that no overarching account of their general meaning will be possible.

However, while all visual artworks embody their creator's specific intentions and broader societal attitudes, they presuppose, also, engagement with those features that are distinctive to the relevant medium. And through this, a more universal level of meaning (bound up with the specifically *visual* character of pictorial art) is built into the work as a precondition of its broader narrative and stylistic significance.[3]

Hofmann's linkage of planarity and optical illusion provides the basis for understanding this. But it needs to be developed so as to encompass not only figuration, but also the universal basis of meaning in specifically abstract art.

Such a development offers a more comprehensive theory than is available from Deleuze or Merleau-Ponty. This being said, however, Merleau-Ponty still has an important role to play by virtue of his notion of the 'invisible'. We will recall from Chapter Four that, for him, the invisible is disclosed by painting per se. And, while Merleau-Ponty describes some abstract or semi-abstract works in this context, he does not address abstraction in terms of its more specific character.

However, by thinking Merleau-Ponty's approach through, it becomes possible to identify more specific aspects of the invisible that can be taken as the basis of abstraction's distinctive meaning, and the styles in which it issues. This strategy offers, also, a means for completing Hofmann's theory of art. Its completion means, as noted above, that abstract as well as modern figurative art is done full justice to in phenomenological terms. In this way, my study can end in a satisfyingly comprehensive theoretical overview of modern art.

The completion is effected as follows: Part One presents Hofmann's account of the relation between visual metaphysics and pictorial creativity. Part Two, then investigates his notion of 'plastic' art in more detail – emphasizing the primacy he assigns to planarity, 'triplexity', and optical illusion.

In Part Three, the strength and comprehensive scope of this approach is identified. Part Four extends it beyond Hofmann's own account so as to explain the specific basis of meaning in abstract art, *as such*. This involves the notion of *transperceptual space* (introduced as a modification and extension of Merleau-Ponty's notion of the 'invisible').

Part Five argues that the link between abstract art and transperceptual space is a compelling one – rather then a mere interpretative 'choice'; and, in Conclusion, I offer further defence of the idea of a general theory of abstract art per se, and offer some summarizing remarks concerning the scope of this book as a whole.

Part One

Hofmann's sense of abstraction is informed by a metaphysic that assigns a key role to the human spirit. We are told that 'Metaphysically, a thing in itself never expresses anything. It is the relation between things that gives meaning to them . . .'[4]

In terms of visual perception, the well-known duality of two-dimensional *appearance* and three-dimensional *reality*, is the most decisive relation. The retinal image is two-dimensional, but the reality which is the emergent 'effect' of our engaging with this, is perceived, visually, as three-dimensional, and emerges through the connective activity of human cognition or (as Hofmann prefers to put it) 'spirit'.

Experience in its most fundamental sense, is, for Hoffmann, an effect of the complex, spiritual mediation of retinal appearance. It is important to emphasize that experience in this sense is not some bare recognition of the mere fact of three-dimensional relations. Rather it involves an 'inner-perception'. Hofmann elucidates this by way of a contrast:

> The physical eye sees only the shell and the semblance – the inner eye, however, sees to the core and grasps the coherence of things. The thing, in its relations and connections, presents us effects that are not real but rather supersensory and thereby transcend nature. Therein lies . . . the essence of the thing. By means of our inner perception, however, we grasp the opposing forces and the coherence of things, and primarily in that manner, the essence of things becomes comprehensible to us.[5]

On these terms, while there is a realm of Being that exists independently, it can only be experienced as a three-dimensional *world* insofar as the relations and properties of space-occupying masses are centred – that is, comprehended *as* wholes – through spirit's connective activity. It is spirit that allows *appearances* to be understood as enduring three-dimensional *realities*.

At the heart of this comprehension, is the awareness of movement. Space is imbued with movement and rhythm (in ways that will be described further on), and life itself cannot exist without spatial movement, just as movement cannot exist without life.

The three-dimensional world emerges through our perceptual immersion in static and dynamic spatial relations, and swings between these *mutually dependent* modes of relation. Nature's unity is comprehended as a function of opposites and relationships. Again, in Hofmann's words,

> We recognize that form only exists as light, and light only by means of form, and we further recognize that colour is only an effect of light in relation to the form and its inherent texture. In us everything is bound up in the acknowledgement and the presentation of the whole as a unity. Where man is[,] there is the centre of the universe.[6]

The 'metaphysic' that Hofmann is presented has very strong affinities with the phenomenology of Merleau-Ponty. In this respect, for example, the latter asserts that,

> each thing can offer itself in its full determinacy only if other things recede into the vagueness of the remote distance, and each present can only take on its reality only by excluding the simultaneous presence of earlier and later presents. . . . Things and instants can link up with each other to form a world only through the medium of that ambiguous being known as subjectivity, and can become present to each other only from a certain point of view and intention . . .[7]

I will note a further strong affinity between Hofmann and Merleau-Ponty in my notes, *en passim*. However, the key point

of substance is not only that Hofmann has an unusually sophisticated ontology with distinguished affinities, but, rather, that
he is able to explain visual art's definitive structures on the
basis of it.

This involves showing that *the fundamental duality of two-dimensional retinal appearance and spiritually mediated three-dimensional
reality, is repeated in* the *relation between the picture plane, and its
capacity to open up pictorial space.* Through mastering the laws of
the medium, the artist integrates two-dimensionality and the
virtual third one in a developing 'spiritual effect'. This does
not simply reproduce existing spatial relationships. The effects
qua spiritual, influence one another, and this is continued, the
more the creative process proceeds.

Each stage advances through our spiritual action upon what
has been done so far, and the new and different outcomes
that this issues in. They are stages of appearance driven by a
conception of the real which will be realized when the work is
completed. The 'experience' of the finished work is then the
springboard to new creative endeavours.

Given this general outline, we can now consider how Hofmann
understands it in relation to the phenomenology of painting in
more specific terms.

Part Two

Hofmann offers a theory of what he calls 'plastic art'. He uses
this term because 'plasticity' is an ontological feature that is
basic to working on a two-dimensional surface. If the surface is
marked, the mark will appear to push towards or pull away from
the viewer, and, in achieving such an effect, it will automatically
generate the other effect, as its corollary.

A form that appears to push into the surface, for example,
will make the surrounding area appear to pull away, towards
the viewer and reciprocally, a form that appears to pull away
from the surface, will achieve this effect only insofar as the

surrounding areas seem to stay behind – pushing towards the surface.

In this respect, we are told that, '*A plastic animation "into the depth" is answered with a radar like "echo" out of the depth, and vice versa.* Impulse and echo establish two-dimensionality with an added dynamic enlivenment of creating of creating breathing depth'.[8]

The push–pull effect, in other words, is an optical illusion of depth that is intrinsic to working with a two-dimensional surface. Artistic creativity consists in thinking in terms of this intrinsic plastic animation, rather than in terms of visual narratives or decoration, or the like.

Plasticity as a practical issue for the artist centres on that which is, for Hofmann, most basic to painting as an expressive medium – namely the picture plane. On his terms, indeed, the plane is the basis of *all* the plastic arts including sculpture and architecture. Hofmann's claim here is based on taking the line to be a further development of the plane. In his words,

> The line originates in the meeting place of two planes. The course of a space line always touches a number of space-planes. Only in science is the line, in itself, mobile. The line divides, combines, flows. The line and the plane are the vehicles of free, searching effects. The plane and the painted portion are always confined by a number of lines.[9]

But *why* should we regard the line in these terms? Hofmann's answer – as I understand him – is that once a line is located in a three-dimensional space, it becomes an active space – defining form. However, to be located thus, is not a matter of simply placing a line *in* space; rather, space itself emerges as lines are linked with one another to form planes (a point that will be illustrated in more detail, a little further on).

Space and form, indeed, are mutually dependent insofar as, through planarity, we are able to distinguish between, and negotiate, space *in front* of the object, the space *in* the object, and space *behind* the object. It is this planar 'triplexity' which invests our perception of space with the 'push and pull' effect of expanding and contracting forces. Through it, a sense of active volumetric structure – involving a dynamic reciprocity of presence and absence – can be experienced.

Hofmann holds that space discloses itself to us through volumes, objects are positive volumes, and vacancies between them are negative ones. But even negative volumes are concrete, and force themselves upon us when objects expand their limits and move into new space.

The negative volume is a potential site of positive volume, and thence functions, in effect, as an object in its own right. Hofmann concludes, accordingly, that 'The unfulfilled space and the objectively fulfilled space together resolve into the unity of space.'[10] In this conception of volume, Hofmann could be thinking – with equal felicity – of our perceptual immersion in the experienced three-dimensional world, or of the painter's creation of representational space. What links the two senses of volume is the all-important role of movement.

Without movement, form is the mere 'shell of life'.[11] Form only discloses itself as something living through the relation between its 'super surface tension' and the negative tensions of empty, unfulfilled space that contextualize its appearance.

Indeed, for Hofmann, the triplexity of space – with its planar dynamics – is the basis of both our emotional immersion in the world (insofar as it involves a spiritual conception of the unity of things and the natural rhythm of life and creation) and of the expressive significance of pictorial art.

However, there is a crucial difference between our experience of the real and pictorial creation. The picture plane cannot produce real physical depth, only the illusion of it. Likewise, one cannot create real motion in the picture plane, only a virtual expression of it. But this leads us to the very essence of the pictorial medium.

Hofmann illuminates it through a brilliant phenomenological analysis. He considers the example of putting a line on a sheet of paper. The character of the line – in terms of its length and direction – can only be determined when another (shorter) line is added. Then a network of meanings is established through the mutual configuration of the lines. Putting it in broader terms than Hofmann himself does, one might say that the linear whole just described is emergent from its parts, and in its emergence, invests them with characteristics that they do not have as individuals considered in isolation.

This can be taken further. For by adding another line, a tension between the two lines, and also a tension between their unity and the outline of the paper, is created. Through this relation, the lines and the paper now constitute a unified entity of an ideal kind. It is ideal because it is something emergent from two features – the lines and the paper – that are physically different from one another.

With the addition of more lines, the configuration becomes more defined and qualified. It takes on a definite pictorial character. The paper is transformed into a pictorial space, through the movement and countermovement – the plane-creating activity – of the lines in relation to one another, *and in relation to the edge of the paper.* These movements express force and tension and may suggest more specific representational content. Hofmann himself, for example, suggests that 'the lines may now give the idea of being two shooting stars which move with speed through the universe.'[12]

I turn now to the other major factor in pictorial creation – colour. As one might expect, while Hofmann nominally assigns equal importance to planarity and colour, his conception of the latter is closely guided by the mediation of the former.

Colour is a pictorial means of creating intervals, that is, colour harmonies that emerge from special relationships and tensions, and the reciprocal relation of colour to colour produces. The 'mysterious order' involved in this stimulates certain 'moods' in us.

The mediation of all this by planar relations becomes apparent in the following remarks:

> The psychological expression of colour lies, . . . , in the relationship of the colours themselves and their contrast circumstances; the expression of colour is in addition influenced by the texture contrast of the colour planes, since the texture is also light-forming. The spatial and plastic unity as well as the light and colour unity is of equal importance with the two-dimensional character of the picture plane.[13]

There is one factor – immanent to the foregoing points – that is the underlying and distinctive feature of Hofmann's phenomenology of pictorial creation. It is this. Since pictorial space exists two-dimensionally, creation that is orientated exclusively towards the presentation of a 'naturalistic space' of three dimensions, is incomplete. For two-dimensionality – the significance of planar structures – is absolutely basic to, and thence an inescapable feature of painting.

Works that function only as sources of visual information or persuasion on the basis of three-dimensional narratives are, in a sense, in denial about the nature of the pictorial medium. However, with pictorial art (and modernist and abstract works, in particular) a different possibility emerges. Here depth can be created without destroying the two-dimensional essence of the picture plane. This amounts to a 'conceptual completeness'[14] of plastic experience.

At the heart of this is that push–pull structure basic to plastic art which we noted earlier. As Hofmann observes:

> The forces of *push* and *pull* function three-dimensionally without destroying other forces moving two dimensionally. . . . To create the phenomenon of *push* and *pull* on a flat surface, one has to understand that by nature the picture plane reacts automatically in the opposite direction to the stimulus

received; thus action continues as long as it receives stimulus in the creative process.[15]

For Hofmann, Cezanne's understanding of colour– especially in his watercolours – involves a sustained expression of the dynamics of planes and volumes and their interrelations, achieved through *push* and *pull.*

A delicate pencil and watercolour study of *Mont Sainte-Victoire* from 1902–6 (Museum of Modern Art, New York) can be used to illuminate Hofmann's position. The brushstrokes are mainly in the form of relatively uniform-sized dabs – each one functioning as a small plane. The contrasting colours embodied in these, and the wispier forms that swirl across them or stand upright, have a striking twofold effect.

On the one hand, the dynamics of push and pull between them, creates a sense of recessional depth. But on the other, they also create rhythms that strike up, and play across the picture plane. Indeed, the delicate transparencies of these mini planes overlap and merge with one another, in surprisingly vigorous terms. In this way, pictorial depth and planar insistence are mediated in a free unity.

Now, of course, the planar insistency of Cezanne's later work is very familiar from earlier chapters, but Hofmann regards it, also, as a major factor in pre-modern art. We are told, for example, that 'push and pull' is the secret of Michelangelo's 'monumentality' and Rembrandt's 'universality'.

To see what is at issue, here, it is useful to consider these two artists in rather more detail than Hofmann does himself. Michelangelo's early *Doni Madonna* of around 1503, for example, represents the Holy Family in a tondo format where the foreground area presents extremely emphatic three-dimensional effects that almost appear to spring towards the viewer. At the same time, however, the main body of the group and a background band of nudes, provide strong horizontal emphases that constrain the visually explosive plastic effect in a firm but – as it were, friendly, planar ground. I say 'friendly' here, because the factors involved in this constraint – notably the shallow ledge that traverses the entire lower horizontal centre behind the main group – are ones which achieve it through reinforcements of the plane that actively counterpoint the energy of the main group.

The strategy of creative planar constraint characterizes all Michelangelo's painting – even down to his late group scenes *The Last Judgment* (1534–41), and *The Martyrdom of St. Peter* (1546–50). In the latter work, what should be a profoundly recessed area of space comprising the main action and background crowds and landscape, is compressed into a much shallower area, with rectangular edges that almost become square.

This makes the three-dimensional space evoked into a claustrophobic one that underlines the darkness of the event represented, and ensures that the crufixion group itself is the visual force around which the surrounding figure groups and their episodic interchanges constellate, manifestly.

Rembrandt relates to the planar emphasis in a more complex way. For example, in *The Anatomy Lesson of Dr Nicolaes Tulp* (1632), the cadaver is cut-off by the picture's edge and is disposed obliquely in relation to the main picture plane. The direction of the gazes of a couple of the figures in the painting follow this oblique angle, however, others address the viewer, and Tulp's own gaze goes in the opposite direction. The result is not a mere scattering of gazes but rather a rhythm of pulling the viewer into the picture while, at the same time, pushing it across the picture's internal pictorial space.

This pull and push effect serves to both involve us in the scene depicted and to respect the fact that our presence is as a pictorial viewer rather than one who is actually present at the events represented. This is universality that is distinctively pictorial rather than one based on human insight in a purely narrative sense.

On these terms, then, Hoffman is quite right to link the pictorial distinctiveness of Michelangelo and Rembrandt to their overt treatment of planar factors. (Indeed, it would be possible to illustrate this in much greater detail than I am able to offer here.)

Now, over and above the decisive role of planarity, Hofmann sees only two other considerations at issue in painting. One of them is 'taste' – in the sense of pleasing arrangements of the 'external' physical elements of pictorial composition. But this is mere decoration unless it involves the second factor.

This consists in the artist's power of *empathy* for the intrinsic expressive qualities of the medium. Through these qualities the medium comes to life. To think in terms of, and to master the push–pull logic of pictorial space, is to be in harmony with both the nature of the medium and the broader natural duality of appearance and reality which the medium internalizes. It is this harmony which allows the creation of pictorial art to be experienced *as* a reality that has been constructed from appearances.

Having expounded the general substance of Hofmann's theory, the time has come to focus on its strengths and limitations.

Part Three

As we have seen, for Hofmann, the picture plane is the appearance which supports the further appearance of three-dimensional content, and it is the artist's articulation of these which creates the work as a *real* expression of spiritual activity.

Now what is decisive about this is not only its affinity with the relation between the two-dimensional retinal appearance and our perception of three-dimensional objects and relations, but also the fact that the planar structure of pictorial art is based on the triplexity described earlier. On these terms, any volume occupies its own physical space, and has, in addition, space in front of it and behind it. These latter negative volumes are the spaces of possible movement. They are, in perceptual terms, pregnant with movement. It is relation between them – the tri-plexity – which is the pictorial key to expressing the ontological truth of perception as emergent and dynamic.

It is interesting that many other theorists of pictorial representation seem to regard planarity as a feature that is decisive only for linear perspective.[16] Hofmann, in contrast, realizes its broader significance as the basis of any pictorial meaning. Once a mark or line is put on a plane surface, it appears to be in front of, or cut into the planar support, or to be behind it. The more pictorial elements are added the more complex the relation becomes; more complex planar relations are set up.

Of course, the planar structure that we find in pictorial art may seem extremely stiff or even artificial in comparison with the constant mobility of our ordinary perceptual 'takes' on objects. Surely, we scarcely ever perceive real space in terms of planarity. But one can reverse this logic. Planarity – in the sense of in fronts, behinds, and the spatial extension of objects (both as perceived, and in terms of the disposition of their dominant 'constant aspects') is embedded in perception as a largely unre-flected upon principle of perceptual organization.

Pictorial art, in contrast, thematizes this as the basic structure of its relevant media. This means more than being 'obvious'. The fact that it is rendered as a suggestion of movement or tran-sition in static terms, means that it presents an idealization of its three-dimensional content. In effect, we see it as virtually immo-bile – but with possible vectors of movement suggested through the artist's stylistic and compositional means. Spatial reality is made to stand still through pictorial intervention. This is not the physical arrest of time involved in photography; rather it is one that enables spatial relations to present temporal possibility (in the form of suggested movement).

Indeed, such intervention presents its content under aspects that – in their motionlessness – are amenable to visual inspection and appreciation by the spectator, in a way that they are not during the flux of ordinary perception. Planar structure clarifies what it presents visually, through releasing it from temporal transitoriness.

The unique effects of pictorial art come down to mediation through planarity. Deleuze, as we saw in Chapter One, is aware of planarity as a key factor in painting, but Hofmann has a much more developed sense of its importance.[17] Indeed, he has one further – and even deeper – insight, whose significance must be developed, now. It concerns his belief that pictorial art can attain 'conceptual completeness'. The means of this (we will recall) are pictorial art's capacity to represent three-dimensional content, in a way that does not, nevertheless conceal its planar basis.

This needs to be explored further. For the planar emphasis is not just an extra ingredient that makes pictorial works different from other artistic idioms. It is *the* decisive formative power, insofar as it depends on an organization of push and pull effects which are the basis of creating any pictorial space *whatsoever*. The 'triplexity' noted earlier is what enables shapes inscribed or placed upon a plane surface to resemble some three-dimensional item or state of affairs.

Having the right sort of shape is not enough. There has to be a space of planar layers that allows this shape to be placed in optical depth. It is the emergence of this through the disposition of lines and masses in relation to one another that makes them appear three-dimensional (or as active in a three-dimensional context). On these terms, the picture plane is not just the 'support', it is the principle of layering that created any possible pictorial depth. And the phrase 'any possible pictorial depth' here is of decisive significance. For it means that *a planar orientation is one which discloses the pictorial phenomenon at its point of origin. It is ur-pictoriality.*

It is quite clear that, for Hofmann, while all figurative art has a planar orientation, it is modern art that brings it to the fore, and allows its distinctive expressive potential to emerge in the most manifest terms. However, this raises the more specific question of how abstract art relates to this.

To understand what is involved, it is worth making, first, some rather general observations. Figurative art occupies pictorial space through optical illusion based on resemblance between the specific forms in the space, and those shapes and visual textures that individuate specific kinds of three-dimensional items or states of affairs. The role of resemblance here is not a direct causal one, that is, we do not recognize the picture as 'of' a such and such because we judge, each time, that it resembles a such and such. Rather we have learned resemblance as a convention of reference. Having learned that plane surfaces can resemble three-dimensional items and states of affairs this disposes us to *perceive* such forms 'in' the work. Resemblance is, as it were, naturalized as a basis for pictorial perception.

However, it is not at all apparent how the optical illusion set up by abstract works has representational significance. Some element of resemblance may be involved, but it is much less clear than that involved in figuration, and other factors besides may be involved.

Ironically, Hofmann's own position on this is somewhat ambiguous. I say 'ironically' because while his theory is presented in terms applicable to figuration and abstraction, it is clear that his theory has arisen more in response to questions raised by the latter, rather than the former.

It is a matter of urgency, therefore, that Hofmann's position be interrogated in relation to the specific demands of explaining abstract art. He appears to hold that the plastic artwork is an autonomous visual whole, whose artistic construction involves focussing on, and operating with, push–pull planarity and integrated colour intervals.

We are told, for example, that,

Relations operate on levelled differentiations – experienced as tensions, or contracts [sic] and opposites – within the inherent laws of any given medium of expression. Thereby, a new reality is produced in the aesthetic form of intervals on which plasticity and any other form of creation is based.[18]

Hofmann's idea is that the 'new reality' of the plastic artwork, is a kind of heightened configuration of emotionally significant forms. In this, he is close to formalism. But this raises the problem that bedevils all such approaches (and, indeed, Deleuze's). Why is form significant; what is it about some colour 'intervals' that makes them expressive in a way that other ones are not?

Emotional responses to people and states of affairs are not irrational and inexplicable. They are based on cognitive appraisal of the relevance of those factors to the individual's existence. In the case of art, we must be able to offer some explanation of why forms are found expressive in specific ways.

Now it is a great pity that Hofmann does not answer this question. For his theory has great promise, insofar as it is based on both an interesting general ontology, and one specific to plastic art itself. Indeed, he sees these two as linked. As he puts it, 'Had our mode of seeing not been two-dimensionally oriented [i.e. the retinal appearance] we could never conceive the illusion that a picture, that is a painted surface, is three-dimensional.'[19] This offers a clue as to how Hofmann's theory could be extended. The plastic work may be a new reality, but perhaps the means of creating and responding to that reality may return us to the ontology of visual perception per se.

Now, one might say that figuration involves presenting an aspect of a three-dimensional something where the constancy of form that defines the something in question – and enables its recognition – is the basis of representation. However, this recognitional dimension is not sufficient to characterize visual perception. For, as we saw earlier, Hofmann emphasizes that the recognition of three-dimensional things involves connective spiritual activity. We do not just recognize a specific kind of visual form. Rather our recognition of it is based on an awareness of its more specific details, and broader relations.

The possibility arises, then, that abstraction has a connection with this deeper relational nexus – the fabric of appearance – that our recognition of the three-dimensional visual world is built on. By showing this connection, Hofmann's theory can be extended into a comprehensive phenomenology of abstract art. It is to this I now turn.

Part Four

It should be emphasized that, in what follows, I am going far beyond what Hoffmann says himself explicitly. However, the points I will make are perfectly congruent with his position.

First, whatever the differences between figurative and abstract art, our patterns of interchange and expectation (based on the former's display formats and contexts of presentation) determine how we are orientated towards the latter. Specifically, a cultural convention is established, which I shall call the *presumption of virtuality*.[20]

This presumption takes abstract works to be about something over and above what they are in strictly physical terms. Of course, many minimal works are created with the intention of not being about anything over their bare physical presence, but of course, this affirmation of bare physical presence can be of virtual significance in itself.

We see the work as being about physicality. It is *autofigurative*. (There are other, related possibilities of virtual content here, that I shall come to in due course.) Indeed, *once an abstract work is presented as art in the relevant kind of context, none of its immediately visible properties are virtually inert or neutral.*

Now, the presumption of virtuality gets a purchase over and above mere presentational contexts because figurative art and abstract works both share a common ground, namely optical illusion. As we saw through Hofmann's account, the placing of a line or other mark on a plane surface serves to set up relations whereby the marks appear to emerge from or be situated behind the surface (depending on the character of the particular mark and that of the surface). This creates a pictorial space which constellates around the way in which a mark's own extension is situated in relation to a space in front of it, and one behind it. Pictorial space comes into being, in other words, as a function of the push–pull effects involved in such triplexity.

There is also a further, ontological basis for the presumption of virtuality. In this respect, we will recall Hofmann's point that the relation between the plane and pictorial space is analogous to the relation between the two-dimensional retinal image, and the three-dimensional world which the embodied subject negotiates through its connective cognitive activity.

Given a plane surface, therefore, it is only natural for us to repeat the basic impetus of perception itself, by looking for three-dimensional forms suggested by this particular configuration. This means that the presumption of virtuality is more than just a convention, it has an ontological foundation – it repeats, in virtual terms the basic trajectory of the origins of visual perception, from the two-dimensional to the three-dimensional. True, pictorial space is not real in literal terms, but it is so, in virtual terms – as something that emerges through the embodied subject's cognitive development of a two-dimensional surface.

Before considering all this as the basis for a general theory of abstract art, it is worth getting a sense of how optical illusion can be read in terms of virtuality by reference to important historical examples – where the pictorial space characteristic of abstraction first emerges.

In a work such as Wassily Kandinsky's *Cossacks* of 1910–11 (see Plate 17, Tate Gallery, London), for example, the headgear and suggestion of lances provide visual cues that – in conjunction with the work's title – allow the viewer to develop the title's thematic as an imaginative visual fantasy.

Plate 17 Wassily Kandinsky, *Cossacks*, 1910–11, oil on canvas, 1118 × 1477 × 74 mm, Tate Modern, London. © ADAGP, Paris/DACS and Tate, London 2011.
A colour version of this image can be found in the plate section in the centre on this book.

In the same artist's *Composition VI* of 1913 (see Plate 18, Hermitage Museum, St Petersburg) the familiar three-dimensional visual forms have been loosened more radically. Forms and colours balloon in a tumultuous sense of generation that is at once atmospheric, technomorphic, and biomorphic in terms of what its optical illusion suggests. There is a sense of bursting out of the background plane that state of hyper-activity that precedes a crystallization into more stable planar structures.

The work presents push–pull relations as the dynamics of a process of visual emergence. And in this, it is suggestive of the visual aspects of natural micro and macrocosmic processes wherein matter takes on form.

Mondrian's work from around the same time takes us in very different directions. Here the pictorial momentum involves a gradual crystallization of the tumult of the three-dimensional world of nature, into a purified network of relations based on

Plate 18 Wassily Kandinsky, *Composition No. 6*, 1913, oil on canvas, 195 × 300 cm, Hermitage, St. Petersburg, Russia. © DACS/The Bridgeman Art Library. A colour version of this image can be found in the plate section in the centre on this book.

planar relations embodied in pure colours and insistent perpendiculars. The sense is very much one of *abstracting from* nature.

In *Composition 8* of 1914 (Guggenheim Museum, New York), for example, what started out as a tree is abstracted into a structure of platelets and planes within a restricted colour range of greys, pinks, and light browns. The only concession to natural organic appearance is the curvilinear corners of the individual platelets and planes.

By the time of *Composition with Grid VII* of 1919 (Kröller Muller Museum, Otterlo), this concession has been removed. Planes in the form of absolutely regular squares and rectangles (with the same subdued colour range as in the earlier work) preponderate. If this work started out as a creative abstracting from some familiar three-dimensional natural or artefactual form, then the identity of that form has been lost in the transformation.

We are left with a self-contained whole whose optical illusion might be taken as alluding to micro-cellular or crystalline structures, windows, or the tiles of a mosaic, or to some imaginatively rendered urban configuration seen from above in a schematic plan.

The allusive possibilities here are very open, but they are not so in an 'anything goes' sense. If someone insists that the work evokes lions attacking a herd of zebra, we can point out that the push and pull effects of the planar structures in this work do not allow the individuation of those specific three-dimensional entities that the viewer claims to see there, nor the specific kind of recognizable action that he or she takes to be represented.

One can then point out that allusions to micro-cellular or crystalline forms, windows, tiles, or urban landscapes can be cashed out on the basis of similarities of form whose recognition draws on common cultural stock.

And a similar range of associations with broader human artifice can be invoked, even, in relation to Mondrian's sustained mature style – with its more economic visual structures. In this respect, consider the *Composition with Yellow, Red, and Blue*, of 1921 (Tate Modern, London). This work presents a kind of geometrical trellising that is evocative of the *internal* structural filamentary features of many natural and artificial visual phenomena – that is, it is suggestive of how they might appear, if they were made visible. In another respect, Mondrian's picture isolates certain micro features that might characterize the surfaces of many varieties of organic and inorganic material – if we could see them magnified enough.

Now, in selecting these examples, I have not only been addressing two of the artists who are most fundamental to the emergence of abstraction, but also the two most basic stylistic roots of that tendency. They exemplify the distinction (discussed in the previous chapter) which Deleuze makes between digital abstraction and *art informel*. Mondrian exemplifies the former, and (though Deleuze himself would no doubt dispute this) Kandinsky is a case of the latter.

In this respect, Mondrian creates a static idiom of optical illusion that involves purification of both shape and colour into very basic forms. Kandinsky, in contrast, represents a very pain-terly idiom of optical illusion comprising activity developed through differentiated, irregular coloured masses.

Both painters evoke the visual movement of push–pull effects, but in Kandinsky it is based on the illusion of process, while in Mondrian it is suggested by the geometric relations of line, and coloured planes. In both, there is depth – a pictorial space of three-dimensional forms and relations rather than exclusively two-dimensional patterns.

Between these two stylistic extremes there is scope for a mas-sive range of optical illusion, and allusive visual possibilities consequent on these. And it is here that the real significance of abstract art is to be found. Hofmann describes the basic picto-rial factors involved, but does not explain the relation between abstract art and reality in any detail.

However, an important clue is provided by Merleau-Ponty's notion of the *invisible*. In his words,

The invisible is

(1) what is not actually visible but could be (hidden or inactual aspects of the thing-hidden things, situated 'elsewhere' – 'Here' and 'elsewhere');
(2) what, relative to the visible, could nevertheless not be seen as a thing (the existentials of the visible, its dimensions, its non-figurative inner framework);
(3) what exists only as tactile or kinaesthetically, etc.;
(4) . . . the Cogito.[21]

In these remarks, Merleau-Ponty is directing us to the fact that our perception of discrete visible material bodies and states of affairs is a vast network of visual relations and textural details that are organized into the recognizable things and states of affairs through the body's positioning, and through 'back-ground' knowledge. This background is composed of beliefs, associations, and expectations based on what is not immedi-ately accessible to visual perception.

That these features are not immediately accessible to perception is a condition of there being any such thing as perception, at all. In order to negotiate the contents of space, the embodied subject has to be highly selective in terms of the features it concentrates on. If it were not, cognition would be overwhelmed by the plethora of visual and other details and relations in which it is immersed.

The phenomenal field, in other words, is composed of the immediately perceptible together with factors that are 'invisible' in the sense of not being presently attended to, or not being available to perception under normal circumstances. These are just as much a dimension of the real as our familiar perspectives on the visible's accessible aspects.

Significantly, Merleau-Ponty sees the disclosure of the invisible as central to painting. In this respect, we are told that,

> Light, lighting, shadows, reflections, colour, all the objects of his quest are not altogether real objects; like ghosts, they have only virtual existence. In fact, they exist only at the threshold of profane vision; they are not seen by everyone.
>
> The painter's gaze asks them what they do to suddenly cause something to be and to be this thing, what they do to compose this worldly talisman and to make us see the visible.[22]

On these terms, then, painting discloses that texture and tapestry of visual relations which are constitutive of how a particular item or state of affairs appears to us, but which are generally overlooked – are 'invisible' – by virtue of our preoccupation with practical interests.

Merleau-Ponty's choice of the term 'invisible' to describe this, is somewhat unfortunate. This is because many of the factors involved can become visible under the right conditions, or can be given visual expression through imagining what they might be like. The term *transperceptual*, accordingly, seems a rather better term than the 'invisible' in describing these latent visible features. For they at once cross perception (even if they are not noticed

explicitly) or, in other cases, they can be made visible by changing our bodily orientation, or by extending what is perceptible
by imaginatively projecting how specific latent factors might be
visualized.

We now reach a crucial transition. It is clear that the transperceptual factors addressed by figurative painting comprises a
relation between the artist's style, and the appearance of some
specific kind of three-dimensional object seen under a definite
aspect (or multiple aspects, in the case of early futurism). The
figurative artist addresses a specific visual appearance of his or
her subject matter, and renders a stylized selection of features
that are involved in its visual fabric.

In such cases, we are dealing with details and features that
are invisible, primarily, in the sense of not being noticed under
normal circumstances. However, it is clear, also, that there are
many other aspects of the invisible which involve factors much
more visually elusive or complex, and not at all amenable to
figurative presentation.

This more radically transperceptual visual space might be
analysed in terms of five levels. These are as follows:

(i) Spatial items, relations or states of affairs that are not accessible to perception under normal circumstances, or are incom-
pletely available, or (ironically) so taken for granted as not to
be noticed, usually. (Much 'biomorphic' and 'action-painting'
type abstraction operates at this level.) This encompasses such
things as forms on the margin of the immediate visual field, tiny
or microscopic structures or life forms, the visualization of internal states of a body or state of affairs (e.g. seen in a cross-section),
and unusual perceptual perspectives (such as aerial ones). The
level includes, also aspects or details of specific visual appearances viewed separately from the whole of which they are a part.

(ii) Possible visual items, relations, states of affairs, or life
forms as they might appear in perceptual or physical environments radically different from our usual one. This might centre on ordinary environments that have undergone radical

visual transformation (e.g. through the intrusion of evanescent atmospheric effects, or physical catastrophe, or as experienced in dreams), subterranean, sub-aquatic, or imagined extraterrestrial environments, and effects arising from the inhibition or distortion of the normal conditions of visual perception. Again, this is a level that is much developed by abstract expressionist action painting (especially Pollock's after 1945).

(iii) Visual forms that *appear to be* variations upon recognizable kinds of things and/or their relations and spatial contexts, without amounting to actual representations of them. This can involve apparent distortions or fragmentation of the thing or state of affairs, or configurations that suggest something specific without presenting enough familiar aspects to allow its conclusive identification. (This tendency originates – with very different emphases – in some features of hermetic and synthetic cubism, and Kandinsky's work after 1910.)

(iv) Idealized variations on features basic to the structure of visual perception – such as mass, volume, density, shape, positional relations (such as 'in front of' or 'behind'), and colour. These features are presented (individually, or in concert) as purified *foci* of attention in their own right, rather than as factors embedded in the everyday visual world of things and artefacts. (The tendency again originates with aspects of hermetic and synthetic cubism, is given even stronger impetus by Mondrian and Malevich, and is a recurrent factor in geometrical abstraction, especially.)

(v) Visual correlates of states of mind. Specific kinds of shape and colour – and, of course, the relations between them – carry strong emotional connotations. These are a function of natural factors, in part, but, more pervasively, a shared cultural stock of such connotations. It is at this level, that visual meaning approximates most closely to that of music. However, given the presumption of virtuality, it is likely that our perception of abstract works at this level, bring features from the other transperceptual levels into play. Suppose, for example, that one finds a shape threatening. It may seem that we cannot explain why it is threatening, but it is surely the case that with more sustained reflection we would comprehend that its threatening character is because, say, it reminds us of the teeth of some indeterminate predator – with the indeterminateness (the element of the known unknown) making it all the more threatening.

I am suggesting, then, that transperceptual space consists of five levels of visual details, possibilities, or associations, that facilitate but are not usually noticed explicitly in our visual recognition of things and states of affairs. Which transperceptual levels are to the fore in any specific cognitive situation is determined by the kind of thing or state of affairs involved, and the character of our interest in it. More than one level, can be engaged, imaginatively, on the basis of the configuration's specific visual character.

This why Deleuze's insight about the relation between the painter's 'polyvalent' eye and the body without organs is so especially appropriate to abstract art. Art of this kind allows vision to explore and express without being constrained by the eye's normal 'organic' constraints. It engages with the normal invisible structural and relational forces that subtend and help define the character of that which *is* visually accessible.

We now reach the decisive point in terms of abstraction. If the virtual three-dimensional reality evoked by the optical illusion and planarity of pictorial space is *not* that of familiar recognizable things and states of affairs – then it *must* be taken to be that of transperceptual space. When we scrutinize abstract art, we draw, intuitively from our experiences of transperceptual space, seeing the configuration in terms of some pattern of unity that might characterize a possible configuration in that space – made available to vision.

These claims, of course, require that the link between abstract art and transperceptual space is shown to be compelling, rather than a mere matter of interpretative choice. I will formulate such a justification by answering two potential objections to my approach.

Part Five

First, it might be objected that most people (including artists) surely have no concept of transperceptual space – since it is a rather complex philosophical idea, and second, even if they do, there is no reason why the optical illusion of abstract works *must* be read in terms of it. In describing such works, all we need say are things on the lines of 'this spot of colour looks to be in front of that one', or 'this shape seems to be in motion', or 'that volume appears to be heavy', or whatever. Working strictly within the internal resources of the work itself, in other words, we need nothing but these bare descriptive terms. There is no necessity that the illusion so described must be taken as an evocation of transperceptual space.

In response to the first objection, it must be emphasized first that everyone who can perceive has, by virtue of what perception involves, had experience of transperceptual space even though it will not have been explicitly formulated as a concept. In seeing any thing we overlook the multitude of its *parte-extra-parte* details, of its internal states, or how it might appear swathed in mist, etc. If we did not shut out this dimension perception would be swamped.

However, that being said, there are times when we do consider such details, for example, looking at some specific aspect of a thing independently of its place in the whole of which it is a part. And we sometimes do, in the course, of our dealing with visible things, have to open them up to see what they're like inside, or act on the assumption that they have such and such an internal character, even though we cannot perceive it.

And, again, we may often experience familiar visible things from unusual or wholly unexpected standpoints – for example, in heavy shadow, or mist, or through watering eyes or whatever. Even though things appear differently – out of visual synch, as it were – we learn to negotiate them as unities, as things seen under unfamiliar aspects.

This means that we form a sense of transperceptual visual unities as well as more familiar ones. We learn to negotiate these in the course of everyday perception, and especially when we have to investigate beyond the immediately familiar, or have the luxury of changing its form playfully – as in daydreaming. Hence, when we encounter abstract works, it is only natural that we should negotiate their optical content in terms of this habitually acquired capacity for negotiating transperceptual unity, irrespective of whether we have any concept of the transperceptual or not.

These considerations undermine the second objection, also. For in order to appreciate abstract works, bare literal description of their qualities of optical illusion does not suffice. We are concerned, rather, with the specific way in which they cohere – the character of the individual unity that the illusion embodies.

Formalist approaches might, of course, claim that aesthetic unity is the only thing at issue here, and we need not bring either optical illusion or transperceptual space into the picture. The problem is however (as we saw earlier), that if an abstract work looks harmonious and unified or whatever, this counts for nothing unless we can explain *why* this is the case. And this means that we must question what criteria of formal unity actually amount to. What kind of cohesion is involved here?

Formalist approaches assert the primacy of (some version of) significant form but without saying what it is that makes form significant in the first place. It might seem that the problem could be solved by linking significant form to the expression of spiritual reality or emotion, but, even if we did, the link is not a direct one. For in order to express such things there must be an active visual factor in abstract pictorial creation which takes the work beyond mere decorative two-dimensionality. This extra 'something' is optical illusion, which (for reasons discussed at length, already) is intrinsic to abstract art. This means that criteria of three-dimensional unity must be involved, over and above woolly notions of harmonies of lines and colours (which would make abstract work into little more than decoration).

The challenge is, therefore, to find a principle of unity that can engage with this three-dimensional world, but in terms other than those involved in figurative art. As far as I can see, the link with transperceptual space is the only way in which this can be done. And, in doing it, we begin to explain how abstract art and spiritual reality and/or emotional states, can be linked in more than superficial and rhetorical terms. This is because recognitions of transperceptual unity have, as it were, a special 'spiritual' charge, through employing sophisticated cognitive competences that are usually taken for granted (and thence not noticed) in our mundane practical engagements with the world. Abstract works demand these competences as the *direct* basis of our perceptual engagement with the artwork.

And what is especially expressive about this is that reference is based on *allusion* rather than mere visual resemblance between the pictorial work and what it represents. In this respect, we might consider Agnes Martin's *White Flower* of 1960 (Guggenheim Museum, New York). This work consists of a square canvas covered in repeated sequences of tiny uniformly sized rectangles (and rectangles within rectangles). These forms are distributed across the canvas in exact vertical columns, with further horizontal columns that intersect the verticals at exact intervals (from the top to the bottom of the work).

There is a boundary area (forming a square also) where the basic, uniformly sized rectangles contain no smaller units within themselves. The lessening of visual density, here, creates a plane within the work overall, which appears to stand out from the background.

Superficially, the work suggests a detail from some larger piece of woven fabric; or even a cross-section through some network of lattices (e.g. those formed by the internal girders in a building, or by a network of circuitry). In these respects, it engages with different possibilities from level (i) of transperceptual space.

At the same time, however, the work is, in literal descriptive terms an exploration of how shape creates density in visual appearance – level (iv) of transperceptual space. And to explore this relation highlights an interesting optical gestalt – wherein attending to the density of the rectangles' distribution leads us to focus not only on them, but also on the spaces between them.

Instead of perceiving rectangles we see the less distinct black trellises created through the gaps, and, in this way, the central relief plane now appears as a kind of curtain, with the suggestion of an indeterminate, but living something-or-other showing through it.

Now if this work had indeed been a part of some woven fabric, we would not have noticed any of the effects just described. It would have simply been a factor that enabled us to recognize the whole per se. The fact that the work is a self-contained painting, means that its optical structures are to the fore, and engage different levels of transperceptual space, simultaneously. And it is this allusive complexity which explains abstract art's distinctive expressive power.

This can be elucidated through a further – very different example, namely Jackson Pollock's *Number 1*, 1950 (*Lavender Mist*) (National Gallery of Art, Washington, D.C.). In this 'all-over' painting, Pollock indeed distributes forms all over the canvas – albeit with a slight concentration of black elements around the edges. This concentration creates a dominant – but frayed – frontal plane, whose optical dynamics of fraying invest the work with considerable animation.

The great power of this lies in the complex way in which the animation suggests organic or physical *process*. Of course, it does so allusively, rather than in straightforwardly representational terms. Specifically it plays across the first three levels of transperceptual space with equal insistency.

On the one hand, it may be presenting a highly magnified close-up of some imagined vegetal formation; on the other hand it could be a perspective on an entirely alternative perceptual or physical environment to our own; or yet again, it could be a subtle variation on, deconstruction of, some familiar example of so simple a thing as entwining foliage. It may even be that the work suggests a detail of stone – such as granite, viewed close-up, but with a kind of higher level (and magical) optical reversal taking place – insofar as the 'mineral' ingredients are disposed in ways suggestive of some organic presence growing in, or fossilized within the stone.

The very hovering between these (and, indeed, other possibilities from the three relevant levels) give the viewer a sense of being present at the birth of the visually specific, or at the moment of its transformation.

In a nutshell, figuration explores the significance of immediately recognizable three-dimensional things or states of affairs, whereas abstraction hovers at the point where such things and states of affairs take on form. At this level, the abstract configuration is one which can, as it were, crystallize into one kind of thing or into another, or even hover between what could be different aspects of the same thing. All pictorial art allows the artist to create and transform visual reality, but abstraction allows the transformatory power to be expressed in more explicit terms.

Conclusion

I have completed Hans Hofmann's theory of art by offering a philosophical explanation of how the optical illusion that he sees as central to the very concept of pictorial representation – and modern art, in particular – becomes representationally significant in the specific case of abstract art.

This theory of meaning for abstraction is built on the interface between optical illusion, triplexity, and the levels of trans-perceptual space. As far as I can see there is simply no other possible contender for making the 'content' of abstract art intelligible. Formalist and spiritual reality-type approaches presuppose it, otherwise we would have no grounds for explaining why form can become aesthetically or spiritually expressive.

However, it might be asked as to whether we even want such a theory. Artists such as Mondrian and Malevich, for example, created their work with large-scale metaphysical intentions of a kind that I have not considered here. Such intentions, it might be argued are necessary to understanding their work.

The approach I have taken, in contrast, might be dismissed as one based on generalities and which is a distortion of abstract art. This is because such works can only be understood historically – by reference to the specific circumstances under which they were produced, and the specific conditions of their reception, and subsequent historical transmissions.

It might be argued that my approach, in contrast, ignores the historically specific. However, this accusation is not well founded, and is based on an authoritarian, exclusionist, social history of art. Indeed, the 'social history of art' type approach – if pursued as the only legitimate one – actually *reduces* what is historically (as well as conceptually) significant about abstract art. For, as I have shown, it extends the scope of art to a new and coherent dimension of vision. It is a historical transformation that creates a new paradigm of artistic creation.

It should be noted, also, that many of the individual theories and intentions that inform the making of abstract art are obscure, sometimes contradictory, and sometimes simply no longer historically accessible. But my approach provides an *entrée* to them. For if an artist wants to make art that is about the fourth or nine dimension, or which escapes from being tainted by nature, he or she has to start from forms which have specific features of optical illusion and planarity.

To put it another way, the more specific – but 'difficult' – intentions that guide the making of an abstract work, have to take account of the illusion–triplexity relation by definition, and, in so doing, this means that they are engaging with levels of transperceptual space whether they have an explicit idea of such space or not. In effect, such space is used as a vehicle for personally and historically specific intentions and ideas but it has a more universal meaning that exceeds them in its scope.

And this is exactly what we should expect on commonsense grounds. Abstract art continues to find an audience – mostly of people who have little understanding of the artists' specific intentions and ideas. But the audience still finds their work meaningful despite this. It may have been thought that the only way of explaining this was by reference to variations of 'significant form' or 'spiritual reality' based on intuitive and ineffable meaning.

I have shown that this is not the case. It is not so precisely because what makes form significant or 'spiritual' in abstract art is far more than the understanding of it in mere *formalist* or romantic senses.

Abstract art engages actively with the relation between visual appearance and reality at the deepest levels, and does so through the distinctive and irreducible characteristics of pictorial media. Figuration, modern art, and abstraction have a common root in optical illusion and triplexity, but express visual reality in ontologically distinctive ways. And the character of this expression is determined by how the artist's individual style and the more general tendency embodied in it engage with the medium and its ontology.

In this book, then, I have offered a phenomenological investigation of those individuals and tendencies wherein the main stylistic features of modern art are embodied, and, in particular, the way they overlap with, and modify one another in the course of these embodiments. The features in question are (in summary form):

(1) The overcoming or abandonment of traditional academic notions of finish' and skill in terms of the application of paint – aimed (usually) at more direct and authentic idioms of visual communication.

(2) An emphasis on subject matter that is not constrained by traditional criteria of artistic and moral propriety.

(3) The embodiment of new pictorial codes that represent through partially, or entirely, adopting non-figurative means,

and which extend, correspondingly, the kinds of perceptual relation that can be expressed directly through visual art.

(4) An insistently *planar* emphasis (with a correlated diminution or elimination of perspectival accents).

I have tried, also, to show the limitations of alternative Kantian approaches.

Now, one result of the investigation is striking. Phenomenological description of these different features as they are exemplified in modern art, shows that they are very differently inflected by the individual artists and tendencies involved.

This means that further levels of philosophical significance are opened up by individual engagement with the general stylistic traits. It is hoped that these levels of significance can be explored by other scholars, on the basis of more detailed studies of the individual artists or tendencies in question.

Notes

Introduction

¹ See, for example, Dominic Lopes, *Understanding Pictures*, Clarendon Press, Oxford, 1996; Robert Hopkins, *Picture, Image and Experience: A Philosophical Inquiry*, Cambridge University Press, Cambridge, 1998. Arthur Danto is a curious variant on the tendency, insofar as his discussion of modern art is very much geared towards the construction of a historical 'grand narrative' concerning the end of art. See his *The Transfiguration of the Commonplace: A Philosophy of Art*, Harvard University Press, Cambridge, MA, 1981. Jonathan Gilmore has offered what is, as far as I know, the only sustained analytic philosophy of collective stylistic tendency in his *The Life of a Style: Beginnings and Endings in the Narrative History of Art*, Cornell University Press, Ithaca, NY, 2000. His admirable study ranges over a wide range of styles, and is concerned, mainly, with their morphological potency, that is, scope for development – a scope that is, according to Gilmore, determined by the style's own intrinsic character, and conditions bound up with the artist's personality and broader social context. My orientation in this work is towards determining the meaning of style *qua* world-disclosure, rather than morphological issues. One other relevant work should be mentioned, namely Jason Gaiger's, *Aesthetics and Painting*, Continuum, London and New York, 2008. This fine analysis is, in one respect, introductory, but it goes far beyond this through linking important developments in analytic philosophy of picturing to some of the most important art historical theorists. His criteria of representational painting and abstract art might offer an alternative (in outline terms) to some of the major points proposed in the present work. However, Gaiger's book does not, of course, address the nature of modern art as its main theme, and, like the analytic philosophers, he is better on formal and historical criteria of referential meaning in painting than on *stylistic* criteria of artistic status.

² See Richard Wollheim, *Painting as an Art*, Thames and Hudson, London and New York, 1987. Sustained criticisms of his position will be offered in a work in progress entitled *Phenomenologies of Art and Vision: A Post-Analytic Turn.*

³ See Jacques Ranciere, *The Future of the Image*, trans. Gregory Elliott, Verso, London and New York, 2007; Jean-Luc Nancy, *The Ground of the Image*, trans. Jeff Fort, Fordham University Press, New York, 2005; Jean-Francois Lyotard, *The Inhuman*, trans. Geoff Bennington and Rachel Bowlby, Polity Press, Cambridge, 1991; Gilles Deleuze, *Francis Bacon: The Logic of Sensation*, trans. Daniel W. Smith, Continuum, London and New York, 2003.

⁴ See his essay 'The Origin of the Work of Art' included in *Poetry, Language, Thought*, trans. Albert Hofstadter, Harper and Row, New York, 1975, pp. 15–17. I will discuss Heidgger's work at length in the work in progress entitled *Phenomenologies of Art and Vision: A Post-Analytic Turn.*

⁵ Michel Henry, *Seeing the Invisible: On Kandinsky*, trans. Scott Davidson, Continuum, London and New York, 2009.

⁶ Jean-Luc Marion, *The Crossing of the Invisible*, trans. James K. A. Smith, Stanford University Press, Stanford, 2004. Marion rather misunderstands the scope of the notion of the 'invisible' by linking it far too closely to the notion of 'perspective'. In so doing he misunderstands both. The invisible dimension of the visible – insofar as it applies to visual art – centres on virtual space and the suggestion of it, as such. Virtual space does not have to be perspectival, but can involve simple strategies of foreshortening, or even merely optical illusion. Again, Marion equates perspectival structure in perception with binocular vision. Actually, in formal terms, perspective involves a rigidly *monocular* viewpoint.

⁷ See, for example, the critical remarks on Merleau-Ponty's theory of painting in Giles Deleuze and Felix Guattari, *What is Philosophy?* trans. Graham Burchell and Hugh Tomlinson, Verso, London and New York, 1994, pp. 178–83.

⁸ See, for example, *Deleuze and Contemporary Art*, ed. Stephen Zepke and Simon O'Sullivan, Edinburgh University Press, Edinburgh, 2010; and O'Sullivan's individual monograph, *Art Encounters Deleuze and Guattari: Thought Beyond Representation*, Palgrave Macmillan, London, 2007.

⁹ Quoted from Galen A. Johnson (ed.), *The Merleau-Ponty Aesthetics Reader: Philosophy and Painting*, Northwestern University Press, Evanston, IL, 1993, p. 139.

¹⁰ Most recently in *The Kantian Aesthetic: From Knowledge to the Avant-Garde*, Oxford University Press, Oxford, 2010.

[11] There are, of course, many interesting general approaches to modern art that do not have a systematic philosophical orientation. Perhaps the most insightful of these is T. J. Clark, *Farewell to an Idea: Episodes from a History of Modernism*, Yale University Press, London and New Haven, 1999. Clark's method – such as it is – is a kind of piecemeal dialectical investigation, where the piecemeal aspect is a virtue rather than a vice. It allows Clark to undertake phenomenological descriptions of modern works and their contexts of production, that evokes a sense of *meaning as historically emergent*. My major worry about this approach is that it places an emphasis on spectatorial responses that does not do justice to the way in which the *making* of modern painting intervenes *ontologically* on what it represents, and transforms it. Clark, in other words, evokes the fact and context of transformation without showing how it cashes out in concrete aesthetic/artistic terms.

Chapter One

[1] See, for example, Gilles Deleuze, *Francis Bacon: The Logic of Sensation*, trans. Daniel W. Smith, Verso, London and New York, 2003, p. 178. The approach to painting taken in *Francis Bacon*, is continued in a consistent way to encompass music, and (especially) literature in Gilles Deleuze and Felix Guattari, *What is Philosophy?* trans. Graham Burchell and Hugh Tomlinson, Verso, Cambridge, 1994. The major difference between the two works is that the terms 'percept and affect' are major players in the later work (see pp. 163–99, especially), in a way that they are not in the earlier book. Percept and affect are the artist's perceptions and affective states as embodied in the artwork. They are experienced as 'sensations' by the work's audience. 'Sensation' is a term which is equally fundamental to both books. As I shall argue later in this chapter, there is significant tension between the notions of percept and affect, and that of sensation.

[2] Deleuze, *Francis Bacon*, p. 56.

[3] Ibid., p. ix.

[4] Ibid., pp. xi–xii.

[5] Ibid., p. xiv.

[6] See ibid., p. 2.

[7] Deleuze, *Francis Bacon*, p. 8.

[8] Ibid., pp. 18–19.

[9] See Deleuze, *Francis Bacon*, p. 57.

[10] Deleuze, *Francis Bacon*, p. 59.

[11] Ibid., p. 15.

[12] The body without organs, for example, features in much of Deleuze's work – but tends to alter its meaning according to the context in which he is using it. In *The Logic of Sense*, trans. Mark Lester with Charles Stivale, Minnesota University Press, Minneapolis, 1990, for example, he discusses it as a Kleinian psychoanalytic concept (pp. 188–9), in ways that – as far as I can see – have no immediate relevance to how it applies in painting.

[13] Deleuze, *Francis Bacon*, pp. 44–5.

[14] Ibid., p. 48.

[15] Ibid., p. 45.

[16] Ibid., p. 48.

[17] Ibid., p. 52.

[18] See Ibid., p. 52.

[19] Deleuze, *Francis Bacon*, p. 48.

[20] See Ibid., p. 58.

[21] In Deleuze, *Francis Bacon*, p. 116, this is described as a 'limitation' to photography, but there is a strong case for arguing that it is the source of a very distinctive form of visual meaning in its own right. This is explored throughout Roland Barthes, *Camera Lucida: Reflections on Photography*, trans. Richard Howard, Jonathan Cape, London, 1982; and in chapter 8 ('The Phenomenology of Photography') in my *Phenomenology of the Visual Arts (even the frame)*, Stanford University Press, Stanford, 2010.

[22] Deleuze, *Francis Bacon*, p. 115.

[23] Ibid., pp. 115–16.

[24] Ibid., p. 118.

[25] Ibid., p. 101.

[26] Ibid., p. 102.

[27] Ibid., p. 102. Deleuze describes this further as a 'properly pictorial experience'.

[28] Deleuze, *Francis Bacon*, pp. 97–8.

[29] See Ibid., p. 45.

[30] See Ibid., pp. 54–5.

[31] Deleuze, *Francis Bacon*, p. 157.

[32] Ibid., p. 135.

[33] Ibid., p. 123.

[34] Ibid., p. 124.

[35] Ibid., p. 125.

[36] Ibid., p. 126.

[37] Ibid., p. 133.

38 Ibid., p. 135.
39 Ibid., p. 139.
40 Ibid., p. 135.
41 The primacy of sensation in Deleuze's philosophy in general is due, probably, to the influence of Raymond Ruyer, *Neo-Finalisme*, PUF, Paris, 1952. In the Translators' Introduction to Gilles Deleuze and Felix Guattari, *What is Philosophy?* we are told in relation to Ruyer that the subjective sensation of the visual field,

> tempts us to imagine the 'I' as a kind of invisible center outside, and situated in a supplementary dimension perpendicular to, the whole of the visual field that it surveys from a distance. However, this is an error. The immediate survey of the visual field made up of many visual details takes place within the dimension of the visual sensation itself; it is a kind of self-enjoyment that does not involve any supplementary dimension. (pp. ix–x)

Deleuze is clearly influenced by Ruyer. He tends to treat the relation between sensation and cognition as one in which the former is immanent to, and drives the latter. This is a major error. The relationship between sensation and cognition in human beings is one of reciprocal dependence. Deleuze's hierarchical privileging of sensation has unfortunate consequences – as we shall see in Part Four of this chapter.
42 Deleuze, *Francis Bacon*, p. 34.
43 Ibid., pp. 34–5.
44 Ibid., p. 37.
45 Ibid., p. 39.
46 Ibid., p. 41.
47 Ibid., pp. 41–2.
48 Ibid., p. 42.
49 Ibid., p. 42.
50 Ibid., pp. 80–1.
51 See Ibid., p. 81.
52 See Immanuel Kant, *The Critique of Pure Reason*, trans. Paul Guyer and Allen Wood, Cambridge University Press, Cambridge, 1998, pp. 290–5.
53 Deleuze, *Francis Bacon*, pp. 81–2.
54 See Ibid., p. 82.
55 Ibid., p. 52.
56 Deleuze, *Francis Bacon*, p. 35.
57 Ibid., pp. 144–5.

58 Ibid., p. 153.
59 Ibid., p. 97. It is interesting how the art critic Tom Lubbock inter-
    preted Bacon in terms of this factor. Like Deleuze he plays down the
    symbolic (existential anxiety) dimension. However, he takes a very
    different approach to the relation between figuration and Figure:

> Everyone, on their first encounter with Bacon's art, gets an impres-
> sion of car crash, bomb damage, burns, meltdown, slaughter-
> house. The red paint and the open mouths, of course, encourage
> this response. But they shouldn't distract you from the amazing
> performance that's going on before your very eyes. Bacon is a
> magician, a quick-change artist. He brings off the most sudden dis-
> appearing and reappearing acts, fusions and transformations. The
> flesh slips, slurps, smears, flares, blurs, fades, evaporates, abruptly
> dematerialises. Legerdemain: you just can't see how it's done, how
> it moves from solid to film to spook to gleam to void and back. (*The
> Independent* online edition, Tuesday, 11 January 2011)

    Deleuze would be – doubtless – aghast, at the suggestion of theatri-
    cality in Bacon. I would suggest that, even if we admit such a dimen-
    sion, it adds to the symbolic dimension of anxiety, precisely because
    not being able to 'see how it's done' inflames the general sense of
    unease that has been generated, already, by the extreme torsions of
    Bacon's presentations of the body.
60 Deleuze, *Francis Bacon*, p. 22.
61 Ibid., p. 23.
62 Ibid., p. 118.
63 Ibid., p. 161.
64 Ibid., p. 37.
65 Ibid., pp. 34–5.
66 Ibid., p. 139.
67 The quotation from Gasquet on Cezanne runs 'When the colour is
    at its richest, the form is at its fullest. Contrast and relationship of
    colours – that's the secret of drawing and modelling.' See Joachim
    Gasquet, *Cezanne: A Memoir with Conversations*, trans. Christopher
    Pemberton, Thames and Hudson, New York and London, 1991,
    p. 221.
68 Deleuze, *Francis Bacon*, pp. 35–6.
69 Ibid., p. 72.
70 Ibid., p. 50. The term 'style' is used in a more positive way, but with-
    out its meaning being explained in Deleuze and Guattari, *What is
    Philosophy?* pp. 170, 177.

[71] In Deleuze and Guattari, *What is Philosophy?* p. 231, we are told that 'Mikel Dufrenne . . . produced a kind of analytic of perceptual and affective a priori, which founded sensation as a relation of body and world'. This may be true, but Dufrenne's position involves much more complex considerations that range beyond what can be considered in this book.

[72] Mikel Dufrenne, *The Phenomenology of Aesthetic Experience*, trans. Edward S. Casey, Northwestern University Press, Evanston, IL, 1973, pp. 277–8.

[73] Dufrenne, *The Phenomenology of Aesthetic Experience*, p. 290.

[74] Ibid., p. 292.

[75] It is extraordinary that in Deleuze and Guattari, *What is Philosophy?* p. 191, we are told that 'Composition, composition is the sole definition of art, and what is not composed is not a work of art'. However, as in the Bacon book, this notion of 'composition' is analysed purely in terms of colour modulation and the relation between planes. But, whatever role such features have in composition, drawing is surely equi-fundamental insofar as it determines how figures are placed in or in relation to virtual three-dimensional space.

Chapter Two

[1] For a useful discussion of some of the historical and conceptual issues involved here see J. T. Harskamp, 'Contemporaneity, Modernism, Avant-Garde', *British Journal of Aesthetics*, Vol. 20, No. 3, 1980, pp. 204–14. A useful survey collection of essays can be found in Paul Wood (ed.), *The Challenge of the Avant-Garde*, Yale University Press, New Haven and London, 1999. An influential discussion of more specific themes can be found in Rosalind Krauss, *The Originality of the Avant-Garde and Other Modernist Myths*, MIT Press, Cambridge, MA, 1985; and also in Clement Greenberg's celebrated essay on 'Avant-garde and Kitsch', included in his *Art and Culture: Critical Essays*, Beacon Press, Boston, 1961. Greenberg's notion of the avant-garde rightly links it to a search for absolute values, but sees this as amounting to, in effect, 'the imitation of imitation' (p. 7). Such an interpretation shows the limitations of Greenberg's developing formalist sensibility. This is because it excludes the possibility that the avant-garde attempts to reorientate artistic practice towards new criteria and conventions of visual reference based on transformed phenomenological awareness. It is this possibility which forms the central theme of the present chapter.

² Charles Taylor, *Sources of the Self: The Making of the Modern Identity*, Cambridge University Press, Cambridge, 1990, p. 202.

³ Edmond Duranty, 'The New Painting: Concerning the Group of Artists Exhibiting at the Durand-Ruel Galleries', included in *Impressionism and Post Impressionism 1874–1904; Sources and Documents*, ed. and trans. Linda Nochlin, Prentice Hall, New Jersey, 1966, pp. 3–7. This reference, p. 6.

⁴ Ibid., p.7.

⁵ T. J. Clark, *The Painting of Modern Life: Paris in the Art of Manet and his Followers*, Thames and Hudson, London, 1984, p. 17.

⁶ Clark, ibid., p. 17.

⁷ For further discussion of the significance of ontological reciprocity in this context, see my book, *The Language of Twentieth Century Art: A Conceptual History*, Yale University Press, New Haven and London, 1997. For a different approach to the significance of philosophical factors in the development of avant-garde art see Mark Cheetham, *The Rhetoric of Purity: Foundational Theory and the Advent of Abstract Painting*, Cambridge University Press, Cambridge, 1998. Cheetham assigns a particular importance to Neoplatonist philosophy and operates primarily at the level of the artists' iconographic relation to these and other ideas. My own emphasis, in contrast, is on how changes of general phenomenological standpoints bring about a general artistic reorientation which is far more than the effect of specific philosophical influences. John Golding, *Path to the Absolute; Mondrian, Malevich, Kandinsky, Pollock, Rothko, Newman, and Still*, Thames and Hudson, London, 2002, offers a detailed analysis of the phenomenological depth of his selected avant-garde artists. As I read him, however, he does not negotiate effectively the tension between the artists' craving for the absolute, and the constraints which this puts on their stylistic development. Hopefully this issue is dealt with in the present chapter, and in *The Language of Twentieth-Century Art*.

⁸ The significance of these changes can, of course, be hotly disputed. For a very different and highly critical reading of the artists just mentioned, see chapter 4 of Carol Duncan, *The Aesthetics of Power*, Cambridge University Press, Cambridge, 1993. Duncan's analysis, it should be emphasized, focuses on how women are presented in the relevant art; my emphasis is on the phenomenological transformations implicated in the *means* of such representation.

⁹ The main study of Bergson's relation to avant-garde visual art is Mark Antliff, *Inventing Bergson: Culturing Politics and the Parisian Avant-Garde*, Princeton University Press, Princeton, 1993. Given the

well-known links between Bergson and Italian futurism, Antliff's French emphasis is curious. This is rendered more so by the fact that the main links which Antliff establishes are between Bergson and lesser figures rather than with the likes, say, of Braque and Picasso.

[10] Umberto Boccioni, 'Futurist Painting and Sculpture', cited in *Futurist Manifestoes,* ed. Umberto Apollonio, Thames and Hudson, 1973, p. 178.

[11] These are to be found in *The New Art – The New Life: The Collected Writings of Piet Mondrian,* ed. and trans. H. Holzmann and M. James, Thames and Hudson, London, 1987. The theoretical implications of Mondrian's work are given detailed analysis in Cheetham op. cit. An interesting discussion based on an individual work by Mondrian is Yves-Alain Bois' 'Piet Mondrian. *New York City*' included in *Painting as Model,* MIT Press, Cambridge, MA. and London, 1993, pp. 157–83.

[12] André Breton, *Manifestoes of Surrealism,* trans. Richard Seaver and Helen Lane, University of Michigan Press, Ann Arbor, 1969, p. 259.

[13] Breton, ibid., p. 141.

[14] In this respect, it is significant that the title of Malevich's most substantial theoretical text – *The World as Non-Objectivity* seems to deliberately allude to that of Schopenhauer's magnum opus *The World as Will and Representation.*

Chapter Three

[1] Friedrich Nietzsche, *The Will to Power,* trans. W. Kaufmann and R. Hollingdale, Random House, London, 1967. Aphorism no. 853, p. 451. Some scholars refuse to admit this text as part of Nietzsche's *oeuvre,* on the grounds that he neither sanctioned its publication, nor (more significantly) had any decisive part in the selection and arrangement of the notes which constitute it. Despite this, however, the work *was* published, and became extremely influential. Indeed, while *Also Sprach Zarathustra* was the more important text for expressionist painters, *The Will to Power* contains some of Nietzsche's finest and most sustained writing on art, and other topics (such as the doctrine of eternal recurrence). It is significant, surely, that he kept these notes. Indeed, he may well have intended to develop them for use in a future work. This, in itself, is justification for using them. It should be emphasized, also, that in this chapter, I am *not* attempting

some detailed study of Nietzsche's official position on aesthetics per se, but only to show how his ideas can illuminate the character of the expressionisms. I take this as further justification for focussing on *The Will to Power*. For interesting approaches to Nietzsche which bypass *The Will to Power* and address the development of his official theory of art, see Julian Young, *Nietzsche's Philosophy of Art*, Cambridge University Press, Cambridge, 1995, and Aaron Ridley, *Nietzsche on Art*, Routledge, London and New York, 2007. For a more comprehensive study of Nietzsche's aesthetics which situates him in a broader philosophical and cultural context see Matthew Rampley, *Nietzsche, Aesthetics and Modernity*, Cambridge University Press, Cambridge, 1999.

2 Nietzsche, *The Gay Science*, trans. Walter Kaufmann, Vinatage Books, New York, 1974, Aphorism 299, p. 239.

3 Ibid., no. 802, p. 402.

4 Ibid., no. 805, p. 425.

5 Ibid., no. 811, pp. 428–9.

6 Ibid., no. 1050, p. 539.

7 Ibid., no. 846, p. 446.

8 Ibid., no. 846, p. 446.

9 The availability of Nietzsche's ideas is effectively discussed at length in part one of Donald E. Gordon's excellent *Expressionism: Art and Idea*, Yale University Press, New Haven and London, 1987. See also Ivo Frenzel's essay 'Prophet, Pioneer, Seducer: Friedrich Nietzsche's Influence on Art, Literature, and Philosophy in Germany' included in *German Art of the Twentieth-Century: Painting and Sculpture 1905–1985*, Prestel Verlag, Munich, 1985. A relevant collection of artistic and critical writings can be found in Rose Washton Long's *German Expressionism: Documents from the End of the Wilhelmine Empire to the Rise of National Socialism*, University of California Press, Berkeley, 1995.

10 Nietzsche, op. cit, no. 837, p. 437.

11 Friedrich Nietzsche, *The Gay Science*, Aphorism no. 47, p. 112.

12 See Mark Rothko, *The Artist's Reality: Philosophy of Art*, Yale University Press, New Haven and London, 2004, p. 36.

13 As we saw in chapter 1, in *Francis Bacon: The Logic of Sensation*, trans. Daniel W. Smith, Continuum, London and New York, 2003, Gilles Deleuze puts a good case for taking Bacon to rise above identification with expressionism (or any other 'ism). Deleuze shows, indeed, that what is at issue in Bacon involves a re-thinking of some fundamentals of pictorial structure. However, this being said, in terms of common cultural stock, Bacon's paintings appear grotesque, and

are psychologically disturbing. They are a part of the expressionist tradition, even if there is much about them which, does indeed, go far beyond it.

14 See for example, his *Simulations*, trans. Brian Foss and Paul Patton, Semiotext(e)/Foreign Agents, Cambridge, MA, 1983.

Chapter Four

1 Much Merleau-Ponty scholarship is content to simply run with his ideas rather than take a constructive critical distance from them. One exception is the late Martin J. Dillon's exemplary study, *Merleau-Ponty's Ontology*, Northwestern University Press, Evanston, IL, 1998. A more complex case is presented by Galen A. Johnson (ed.), *The Merleau-Ponty Aesthetics Reader: Philosophy and Painting*, Northwestern University Press, Evanston, IL, 1993. This has an excellent selection of texts by Merleau-Ponty, and useful outline introductions to them by Johnson himself. However, the accompanying critical essays, as far as I can see, do little to focus the ellipticality of Merleau-Ponty's theory or to develop it further, in substantial terms. The one exception is the late Linda Singer's essay which takes a real critical stance. It should be emphasized that the interpretative approach I am criticizing here can have positive results also. Johnson's more recent monograph, *The Retrieval of the Beautiful: Thinking Through Merleau-Ponty's Aesthetics*, Northwestern University Press, Evanston, IL, 2010, is a case in point. For while, I do not think that it 'thinks through' Merleau-Ponty's aesthetics in any systematic sense, it certainly deploys his ideas in a fascinating and insightful clarification of beauty.

2 Merleau-Ponty, 'Film and the New Psychology', in *Sense and Nonsense*, trans. Hubert and Patricia Dreyfus, Northwestern University Press, Evanston, IL, 1964, p. 48.

3 Johnson, *The Merleau-Ponty Aesthetics Reader*, p. 140.

4 Ibid., p. 127.

5 See ibid., p. 91.

6 Ibid., p. 125–6.

7 See ibid., pp. 91–2.

8 Ibid., pp. 106–7.

9 Ibid., p. 147.

10 Ibid., p. 141.

11 Ibid., p. 128.

12 Ibid., p. 141.

¹³ For more on this see Merleau-Ponty, *The World of Perception*, trans. Oliver Davis, Routledge, London and New York, 2004, p. 96.

¹⁴ Johnson, *The Merleau-Ponty Aesthetics Reader*, p. 139.

¹⁵ Ibid., pp. 61–2.

¹⁶ Ibid., p. 62.

¹⁷ Ibid., p. 65.

¹⁸ Ibid., p. 65

¹⁹ Ibid., p. 65.

²⁰ Ibid., p. 66. Surprisingly, the origin of this idea is in a thinker other than Merleau-Ponty. It derives from the art historian Fritz Novotny whose description of Cezanne's paintings as 'those of a pre-world in which as yet no men existed' is quoted by Merleau-Ponty in the *Phenomenology of Perception*, trans. Colin Smith with additions by Forrest Williams, Routledge Kegan-Paul, London, 1974, p. 322. A fairly substantial English translation of extracts from another book by Novotny on Cezanne (and which culminates in remarks akin to the point quoted by Merleau-Ponty) can be found in Judith Wechsler's extremely useful compendium of writings about Cezanne, *Cezanne in Perspective*, Prentice-Hall, Englewood Cliffs, NJ, 1975, pp. 96–107.

²¹ Johnson, *The Merleau-Ponty Aesthetics Reader*, p. 141.

²² The importance of hyper-reflection for philosophical method is set out most fully by Merleau-Ponty, in *The Visible and the Invisible*, trans. Alphons Lingis, Northwestern University Press, Evanston, IL, 1964, pp. 38–9.

²³ Johnson, *The Merleau-Ponty Aesthetics Reader*, p. 141.

²⁴ These issue are discussed at more length in chapter 2 of my *Phenomenology of the Visual Arts*.

²⁵ See, for example, *Hans Hofmann*, ed. James Yohe, Rizzoli, New York, 2002, p. 49.

²⁶ Johnson, *The Merleau-Ponty Aesthetics Reader*, p. 145.

²⁷ Gilles Deleuze and Felix Guattari, *What is Philosophy?* trans. Graham Burchell and Hugh Tomlinson, Verso, Cambridge, 1994, p. 179. Their discussion of Merleau-Ponty's 'Fleshism' – 'this final avatar of phenomenology' (p. 178), is marked, also, by a curious restrictiveness. Rather than follow the link with 'total visibility' – which is the basis of Merleau-Ponty's main link between painting and Flesh, they understand it in terms of only one aspect of reversibility – the 'feeling and felt'. What is equally odd, is that they mention only *The Visible and Invisible* book – making no reference to the 'Eye and Mind' essay which is the main focus of Merleau-Ponty's theory of painting.

28   Deleuze and Guattari, *What is Philosophy?* p. 179.

29   I discuss the relation between individual artistic style and canonic-ity at length in chapter 6 of *The Kantian Aesthetic: From Knowledge to the Avant-Garde*, Oxford University Press, Oxford, 2010.

30   This fusion of subject and medium is a major thematic in chapters 2 and 4 of my book, *The Language of Twentieth-Century Art: A Conceptual History*, Yale University Press, London and New Haven, 1997.

Chapter Five

1   It is worth noting that a link between Husserlian phenomenology and cubism has been outlined by Jaako Hintikka in, 'Concept as Vision: On the Problem of Representation in Modern Art and in Modern Philosophy', in *The Intentions of Intentionality and Other New Models for Modalities*, Reidel Publishing, Boston, 1975. Hintikka makes use of the Kantian theorists whom I will criticize in this chapter. His approach is interesting but does nothing to address the interpretative problems that I will raise in relation to them. The very considerable historical and conceptual problematics of Hintikka's own position are dealt with effectively by Meirlys Lewis in, 'Hintikka on Cubism', *British Journal of Aesthetics*, Vol.20, No.1, 1980, pp. 44–53. I am indebted to Professor Christina Lodder, Peter Suchin, and Dr. Louise Durning for their comments on early drafts of Part Two of this chapter.

2   Edward Fry, *Cubism*, McGraw Hill, New York, 1966. Fry's compen-dium is still widely accessible, so my references are to his book. However, another anthology is now available, also – *A Cubism Reader: Documents and Criticism, 1906–1914*, ed. Mark Antliff and Patricia Leighten, Chicago University Press, Chicago, 2008. There are, of course, many individual works that interpret cubism, art-historically. In this discussion, however, the burden of discussion is specifically on the limitations of the neo-Kantian dimension. Of the more art-historical approaches, I find John Golding's *Cubism: An Analysis and History, 1907–1914*, Faber and Faber, London, 1988, to be especially useful, and also David Cottington's *Cubism and its Histories*, Manchester University Press, Manchester, 2004. Chapter 4 ('Cubism and Collectivity') of T. J. Clark's *Farewell to an Idea: Episodes from a History of Modernism*, Yale University Press, London and New Haven, 1999, is, perhaps, the most thought-provoking art-histori-cal analysis of cubism. However, so many thoughts are provoked that Clark ends up presenting it as a kind of *intrinsically enigmatic*

pictorial phenomenon. There is no doubt that it has something of this character in terms of specific visual details, but Clark's account fails to negotiate – in adequate terms – the role of *painting as a planar medium*. This is a clear strategy of pictorial intervention that, in cubism, adapts three-dimensional subject matter to its demands, to a level that is qualitatively different from the demands operative in other pictorial idioms (even modern ones).

[3] Lynn Gamwell, *Cubist Criticism*, UMI Press, 1980, p. 103.
[4] This is at least true of Kant in the first edition *The Critique of Pure Reason*. By the time of the second edition, however, he had wholly dispensed with the 'synthesis of apprehension'.
[5] Kant, op. cit., p. 48.
[6] John Nash, 'The Nature of Cubism: A Study Conflicting Interpretations', *Art History*, Vol. 3, No. 4, December 1980, pp. 435–47. Nash's refutation of the Kantian approach is nowhere near as comprehensive as the arguments offered in this chapter.
[7] J. Riviere, 'Present Tendencies in Painting', 1912 included in Fry, *Cubism*, op. cit., p. 76.
[8] Roger Allard, 'At the Paris Salon d'Automme', 1910, included in Fry, ibid., p. 62.
[9] Leon Werth, 'Picasso', 1910, included in Fry, ibid., p. 57.
[10] Apollinaire, 'Modern Painting', 1913, included in Fry, ibid., p. 112.
[11] Immanuel Kant, *The Critique of Pure Reason*, trans. Norman Kemp-Smith, London, Macmillan, 1973, p. 48.
[12] Olivier-Hourcade, 'The Tendency of Contemporary Painting', 1912, included in Fry, op. cit., p. 74.
[13] John Locke, *Essay on the Understanding*, Vol. 1, London, Dent and Sons, 1974, p. 104.
[14] Kahnweiler, 'The Rise of Cubism', included in Fry, op. cit., p. 159. Far and away the best discussion of Kahnweiler's writing is 'Kahnweiler's Lesson' in Yves-Alain Bois' *Painting as Model*, MIT Press, Cambridge, MA and London, 1993, pp. 65–97.
[15] Kahnweiler, in Fry, ibid., p. 159.
[16] Quoted in Dore Ashton, *Picasso on Art*, London, Thames and Hudson, 1972, pp. 59–60.
[17] Kant, op. cit., p. 111.
[18] Maurice Raynal, 'What is Cubism', 1913, included in Fry, op. cit., p. 130.
[19] Christopher Green, 'Synthesis and the "Synthetic Process" in the paintings of Juan Gris 1915–19', *Art History*, Vol. 5, No. 1, March 1982, p. 87.
[20] 'Present Tendencies in Painting' included in Fry, op. cit.

21 Dora Vallier conversations with the artist, included in Irina Fortunescu, *Braque*, trans. Richard Hillard, London, Abbey Library, 1977, p. 12. I have slightly amended the translation.

22 For more details of this interpretation see chapter 2 of my book *The Language of Twentieth-Century Art: A Conceptual History*, Yale University Press, New Haven and London, 1997.

23 In *The Language of Twentieth-Century Art*, chapter 1.

24 Mark Cheetham, *Kant, Art, and Art History: Moments of Discipline*, Cambridge University Press, 2001, p. 85.

25 Ibid., p. 82.

26 Ibid., p. 85.

27 Ibid., p. 87.

28 An example of this is Gauguin's remark on the meaning of his model's facial expression in the work *Manao Tupapau – The Spirit of the Dead*, discussed in Griselda Pollock's *Avant-Garde Gambits 1888–1893*, Thames and Hudson, London, 1992, pp. 25–6. Gauguin writes that the model is looking fearful, but, in terms of how the picture itself appears, the model's expression is much more ambiguous for the third-party viewer. (Pollock, it should be noted, emphasizes Gauguin's written description rather than the visual evidence of the work itself).

29 Cheetham, op. cit, p. 87.

30 Ibid., p. 81.

31 Ibid., p. 83.

32 Ibid., p. 84.

33 Ibid., p. 83.

Chapter Six

1 Gilles Deleuze and Felix Guattari, *What is Philosophy?* trans. Graham Burchell and Hugh Tomlinson, Verso, Cambridge, 1994, p. 198.

2 Thierry de Duve, *Kant after Duchamp*, MIT Press, Cambridge, MA and London, 1996.

3 This section is based on my review of de Duve's book, originally published in the *British Journal of Aesthetics*, Vol. 37, No. 4, October 1997, pp. 411–13. I have modified it, in accordance with the character of the present work.

4 de Duve, op. cit. p. 164.

5 Ibid., p. 164.

6 Ibid., p. 179.

7 Ibid., p. 275.

8 Ibid., p. 312.

[9] The work can be found at http://www.slashseconds.org/issues/ 002/002/articles/pesuchin/index.php

Chapter Seven

[1] Clement Greenberg, 'Review of *Piero della Francesca* and *The Arch of Constantine*, both by Bernard Berenson', included in *The Collected Essays and Criticism, Volume 3: Affirmations and Refusals, 1950–1956*, ed. John O'Brian, University of Chicago Press, London, 1993, pp. 247–53. This reference p. 249.

[2] David Carrier, 'Greenberg, Fried, and Philosophy: American-Type Formalism', included in *Aesthetics: A Critical Anthology*, ed. George Dickie and Richard Sclafani, St Martins Press, New York, 1978, pp. 461–3. This reference p. 461.

[3] Clement Greenberg, 'Complaints of an Art Critic', included in O'Brian, ed. Vol.3, pp. 265–72. This reference p. 265.

[4] For example, in the aesthetic judgement Kant holds that we '. . . immediately connect with a perception a feeling of pleasure . . . and a delight attending the representation of the Object and serving it instead of a predicate' – *Critique of Judgement*, trans. J. C. Meredith, Oxford University Press, London, 1937, p. 144.

[5] Clement Greenberg, 'Necessity of "Formalism"', *Art International*, October 1972, pp. 105–6. This reference, p. 106.

[6] In Clement Greenberg, 'After Abstract Expressionism', included in O'Brian, ed. *The Collected Criticism and Essays Volume 4: Modernism with a Vengeance, 1957–1969*, University of Chicago Press, 1993, Vol. 4, pp. 121–34. See especially p. 132.

[7] See, for example, Kant's *Critique of Judgement*, pp. 42–50.

[8] Clement Greenberg, 'Avant Garde and Kitsch', included in O'Brian, ed. *The Collected Criticism and Essays Volume, Vol. 1, Perceptions and Judgments, 1939–1944*, University of Chicago Press, 1986, pp. 5–23. This reference p. 16.

[9] Clement Greenberg, 'Modernist Painting', included in O'Brien, ed. Vol. 4, pp. 85–94. This reference p. 85.

[10] 'Modernist Painting', O'Brian, Vol. 4, p. 86.

[11] A term used by Greenberg in 'After Abstract Expressionism', in O'Brian, Vol. 4, p. 131.

[12] Deane W. Curtin, 'Varieties of Aesthetic Formalism', *Journal of Aesthetics and Art Criticism*, Vol. XL, No. 3, Spring 1982,

pp. 315–26. This reference pp. 319–20. Curtin generally takes a different approach to mine and construes the fundamental tension in Greenberg's theory, in terms of a contradictory desire to affirm that the aesthetic judgement is both corrigible and incorrigible. The way Curtin articulates and traces the development of this conflict is, however, rather confused and leads to a misinterpretation of both Kant's and Greenberg's attitude towards the artwork's artefactuality. This is brought about to some degree by Curtin's emphasis of isolated points made in Greenberg's early reviews; and his relative neglect of the systematic arguments broached in the longer and more recent articles. Indeed, the crucial 'After Abstract Expressionism' (see above) seems not to have been consulted at all. A more viable comparison and contrast of Kant and Greenberg's relation to the aesthetic (but which does not negotiate the issue of Kantian 'infra-logic') is Jason Gaiger's 'Constraints and Conventions: Kant and Greenberg on Aesthetic Judgement', *British Journal of Aesthetics*, Vol.39, No.4, 1999, pp. 376–91.

[13] Greenberg, 'Necessity of "Formalism"', p. 105.

[14] Ibid., p. 105.

[15] 'Modernist Painting', O'Brian, Vol. 4, p. 87.

[16] 'After Abstract Expressionism', O'Brian, Vol. 4, pp. 123–4.

[17] Clement Greenberg, 'Abstract and Representational', included in O'Brian, Vol. 3, pp. 186–93. This reference, p. 191.

[18] Robert Rosenblum, 'The Abstract Sublime', *Art News*, February 1961, pp. 38–41, 56–7.

[19] 'After Abstract Expressionism', O'Brian, Vol. 4, p. 132.

[20] See, for example, Robert Goldwater quoted in Irving Sandler, *The Triumph of American Painting: A History of Abstract Expressionism*, Harper and Row, New York, 1970, p. 274.

[21] 'Modernist Painting', O'Brian, Vol. 4, p. 91.

[22] Ibid.

[23] See, for example, Clement Greenberg, 'Post Painterly Abstraction', included in O'Brian, Vol. 4, pp. 192–7.

[24] 'After Abstract Expressionism', O'Brian, Vol. 4, p. 132.

[25] Quoted in Robert Rosenblum, *The Northern Tradition of Romantic Painting: From Friedrich to Rothko*, Thames and Hudson, London, 1975, p. 215.

[26] Quoted in Michael Fried, *Morris Louis 1912–1962*, Museum of Fine Arts, Boston, 1967, p. 82.

Chapter Eight

[1] Giles Deleuze, *Francis Bacon: The Logic of Sensation*, trans. Daniel W. Smith, Continuum, London and New York, 2003, p. 103.

[2] Deleuze, *Francis Bacon*, p. 103.

[3] Ibid., p. 34.

[4] See also, for example, Deleuze, *Francis Bacon*, p. 53.

[5] See Deleuze, *Francis Bacon*, p. 117.

[6] Deleuze, *Francis Bacon*, p. 154.

[7] Ibid., p. 104.

[8] See Deleuze, *Francis Bacon*, p. 103.

[9] Deleuze, *Francis Bacon*, p. 117.

[10] This search is especially manifest in the extensive theoretical writings by Mondrian and Kandinsky. The fullest presentations of these are, for Mondrian, *The New Art, the New Life: The Collected Writings of Piet Mondrian*, ed. and trans. Harry Holzmann and Martin S. James, Thames and Hudson, London and New York, 1987; and, for Kandinsky, *Kandinsky: Complete Writings on Art*, ed. and trans. Kenneth C. Lindsay and Peter Vergo, Faber and Faber, London, 1982. Michel Henry has offered the most sustained philosophical analysis of Kandinsky in his book, *Seeing the Invisible: On Kandinsky*, trans. Scott Davidson, Continuum, London and New York, 2009. Henry's approach mainly, however, explores and expands Kandinsky's *theory of art*, without subjecting it to any sustained critical scrutiny, or testing it in relation to close and extended analyses of specific paintings.

[11] Deleuze, *Francis Bacon*, p. 109.

[12] Ibid., p. 104.

[13] Ibid., p. 105.

[14] Ibid., p. 105.

[15] Ibid., p. 106.

[16] Ibid., p. 106.

[17] Ibid., p. 106.

[18] See Deleuze, *Francis Bacon*, p. 107.

[19] Deleuze, *Francis Bacon*, p. 110.

[20] Ibid., p. 110.

[21] Ibid., p. 110.

[22] This is, of course, allowing, for the sake of argument, that there is such a thing as a legitimate distinction between a painting that appeals to the brain, and one which impacts on the nervous system directly. The considerations explored in Chapter 1, suggest that the distinction is not, in fact, worthwhile.

[23] Deleuze, *Francis Bacon*, p. 52.

Chapter Nine

1   The most accessible comprehensive selection of Hofmann's writings
    is found in *Hans Hoffman*, ed. James Yohe, Rizzoli, New York, 2002.
    This includes the key essays such as 'Plastic Creation' and 'The
    Search for the Real in Visual Arts'. My account of Hofmann's gen-
    eral position is a synthesis of the main ideas in both these papers.
    It should be emphasized that Hofmann's theories in these papers
    (and in other essays and documents) offer a wealth of insights wor-
    thy of much more detailed analysis than I am able to offer here.

2   One exception to this is Richard Wollheim. At various points in his
    writings, Hofmann's notion of the push–pull effect is used to make
    important points about the nature of pictorial art. See, for example,
    his *Art and its Objects (Second Edition)*, Cambridge University Press,
    Cambridge, 1980, p. 15.

3   I have taken a similar approach in relation to other artists in my
    book *The Language of Twentieth-Century Art: A Conceptual History*, Yale
    University Press, London and New Haven, 1997.

4   *Hans Hofmann*, ed. Yohe, p. 45.

5   Ibid., p. 41.

6   Ibid., p. 42.

7   Maurice Merleau-Ponty, *Phenomenology of Perception*, trans. Colin
    Smith with additions by Forrest Williams, Routledge & Kegan-Paul,
    London, 1974, p. 333.

8   *Hans Hofmann*, ed. Yohe, p. 49.

9   Ibid., p. 42.

10 Ibid., p. 43.

11 Ibid., p. 44.

12 Ibid., p. 43. At this point, there is an especially close affinity between
    Hofmann's theory and Merleau-Ponty's conception of line in paint-
    ing. Merleau-Ponty claims, for example, that in visual art – be it
    representational or non-representational – the line is no longer a
    thing, or a mere imitation of a thing. Rather,

    > It is a certain disequilibrium contrived within the indifference
    > of the white paper; it is a certain hollow opened up within the
    > in-itself, a certain constitutive emptiness – an emptiness which as
    > Moore's statues show decisively, sustains the supposed positivity
    > of things. The line is no longer the apparition of an entity upon
    > a vacant background, as it was in classical geometry. It is . . . the
    > restriction, segregation, or modulation of a pre-given spatiality.
    > (Quotation from 'Eye and Mind' included in *The Merleau-Ponty*

Aesthetics Reader: Philosophy and Painting, edited and introduced by Galen A. Johnson, Northwestern University Press, Evanston, IL, 1993, p. 144.

This being said, however, Merleau-Ponty does not – as Hofmann does – offer a phenomenology of the line. In the absence of this, he cannot even begin to understand the significance of planarity for pictorial art.

[13] *Hans Hofmann,* ed. Yohe, p. 43.

[14] Ibid., p. 46.

[15] Ibid., p. 47.

[16] This is the position taken by Dominic Lopes in his book *Understanding Pictures,* Oxford University Press, Oxford, 1996. I have criticized the position in chapter 2 of my *Phenomenology of the Visual Arts (even the frame),* Stanford University Press, Stanford, 2009. There, I explain the key importance of planarity as a focus of meaning in *figurative* pictorial art.

[17] Hofmann is clearly inheriting a tradition in German art theory which also assigns the greatest significance to the plane. See, for example, Adolf Hildebrand, 'The Problem of Form in the Fine Arts', included in *Empathy, Form, and Space: Problems in German Aesthetics, 1873–1893,* ed. Harry Francis Mallgrave and Eleftherios Ikonomou, Getty Center Publications Programs, Santa Monica, 1994; Heinrich Wolfflin, *The Principles of Art History,* trans. M. D. Hottinger, Dover Publications, New York, 1950; Alois Riegl, *Historical Grammar of the Visual Arts,* trans. Jacqueline E. Jung, Zone Books, New York, 2004. Comparative and critical analyses of the treatment of the plane in these thinkers is long overdue.

[18] *Hans Hofmann,* ed. Yohe, pp. 49–50.

[19] Ibid., p. 43.

[20] The concept is discussed, at length, from a different viewpoint in chapter 6 of my *Phenomenology of the Visual Arts.*

[21] These remarks are from the 'Working Notes' to Merleau-Ponty's posthumous work *The Visible and the Invisible,* trans. Alphons Lingis, Northwestern University Press, Evanston, IL, 1968, p. 257.

[22] Merleau-Ponty, 'Eye and Mind', included in *The Merleau-Ponty Aesthetics Reader,* p. 128.

Bibliography

Allard, R. (1910), 'At the Paris Salon d'Automme', incl. in Fry (1966), p. 62.

Antliff, M. (1993), *Inventing Bergson: Culturing Politics and the Parisian Avant-Garde*, Princeton: Princeton University Press.

Antliff, M. and Leighten, P. (eds) (2008), *A Cubism Reader: Documents and Criticism, 1906–1914*, Chicago: Chicago University Press.

Apollinaire, G. (1913), 'Modern Painting', incl. in Fry (1966), p. 112.

Ashton, D. (1972), *Picasso on Art*, London: Thames and Hudson.

Barthes, R. (1982), *Camera Lucida: Reflections on Photography*, trans. R. Howard, London: Jonathan Cape.

Baudrillard, J. (1983), *Simulations*, trans B. Foss and P. Patton, Cambridge, MA: Semiotext(e)/Foreign Agents.

Boccioni, U. (1973), 'Futurist Painting and Sculpture', cited in *Futurist Manifestoes*, ed. U. Apollonio, London: Thames and Hudson, p. 178.

Bois, Y.-A. (1993), *Painting as Model*, Cambridge, MA and London: MIT Press.

Breton, A. (1969), *Manifestoes of Surrealism*, trans. R. Seaver and H. Lane, Ann Arbor: University of Michigan Press.

Carrier, D. (1978), 'Greenberg, Fried, and Philosophy: American-Type Formalism', incl. in *Aesthetics: A Critical Anthology*, ed. G. Dickie and R. Sclafani, New York: St Martin's Press.

Cheetham, M. (1998), *The Rhetoric of Purity: Foundational Theory and the Advent of Abstract Painting*, Cambridge: Cambridge University Press.

—(2001), *Kant, Art, and Art History: Moments of Discipline*, Cambridge: Cambridge University Press.

Clark, T. J. (1984), *The Painting of Modern Life: Paris in the Art of Manet and his Followers*, London: Thames and Hudson.

—(1999), *Farewell to an Idea: Episodes from a History of Modernism*, London and New Haven: Yale University Press.

Cottington, D. (2004), *Cubism and its Histories*, Manchester: Manchester University Press.

Crowther, P. (1997), *The Language of Twentieth Century Art: A Conceptual History*, New Haven and London: Yale University Press.

—(2010), *The Kantian Aesthetic: From Knowledge to the Avant-Garde*, Oxford: Oxford University Press.

—(2010), *Phenomenology of the Visual Arts (even the frame)*, Stanford: Stanford University Press.

Curtin, D. W. (1982), 'Varieties of Aesthetic Formalism', *Journal of Aesthetics and Art Criticism*, Vol. XL, No. 3 (Spring Issue), pp. 315–26.

Danto, A. (1981), *The Transfiguration of the Commonplace: A Philosophy of Art*, Cambridge, MA: Harvard University Press.

Deleuze, G. (1990), *The Logic of Sense*, trans. M. Lester with C. Stivale, Minneapolis, MN: Minnesota University Press.

—(2003), *Francis Bacon: The Logic of Sensation*, trans. D. W. Smith, London and New York: Continuum.

Deleuze, G. and Guattari, F. (1994), *What is Philosophy?*, trans. G. Burchell and H. Tomlinson, Cambridge: Verso.

Dillon, M. J. (1998), *Merleau-Ponty's Ontology*, Evanston, IL: Northwestern University Press.

Dufrenne, M. (1973), *The Phenomenology of Aesthetic Experience*, trans. E. S. Casey, Evanston, IL: Northwestern University Press.

Duncan, C. (1993), *The Aesthetics of Power*, Cambridge: Cambridge University Press.

Duranty, E. (1966), 'The New Painting: Concerning the Group of Artists Exhibiting at the Durand Ruel Galleries', incl. in *Impressionism and Post Impressionism 1874–1904; Sources and Documents*, ed. and trans. L. Nochlin, New Jersey: Prentice Hall, pp. 3–7.

Duve, T. de (1996), *Kant After Duchamp*, Massachusetts and London: MIT Press, Cambridge.

Fortunescu, I. (1977), *Braque*, trans. R. Hillard, London: Abbey Library.

Frenzel, I. (1985), 'Prophet, Pioneer, Seducer: Friedrich Nietzsche's Influence on Art, Literature, and Philosophy in Germany', incl. in *German Art of the Twentieth-Century: Painting and Sculpture 1905–1985*, Munich: Prestel Verlag.

Fried, M. (1967), *Morris Louis 1912–1962*, Boston: Museum of Fine Arts.

Fry, E. (1966), *Cubism*, New York: McGraw Hill.

Gaiger, J. (1999), 'Constraints and Conventions: Kant and Greenberg on Aesthetic Judgement,' *British Journal of Aesthetics*, Vol. 39, No. 4, pp. 376–91.

—(2008), *Aesthetics and Painting*, London and New York: Continuum.

Gamwell, L. (1980), *Cubist Criticism*, Ann Arbor, MI: UMI Research Press.

Gasquet, J. (1991), *Cezanne: A Memoir with Conversations*, trans. C. Pemberton, New York and London: Thames and Hudson.

Gilmore, J. (2000), *The Life of a Style: Beginnings and Endings in the Narrative History of Art*, Ithaca, NY: Cornell University Press.

Golding, J. (1988), *Cubism: An Analysis and History, 1907–14*, London: Faber and Faber.

—(2002), *Path to the Absolute; Mondrian, Malevich, Kandinsky, Pollock, Rothko, Newman, and Still*, London: Thames and Hudson.

Gordon, D. E. (1987), *Expressionism: Art and Idea*, New Haven and London: Yale University Press.

Green, C. (1982), 'Synthesis and the "Synthetic Process" in the Paintings of Juan Gris 1915–19', *Art History*, Vol. 5, No. 1, March, p. 87.

Greenberg, C. (1939), 'Avant-Garde and Kitsch', incl. in his *Art and Culture: Critical Essays*, Boston: Beacon Press, 1961, and incl. in O'Brian, ed. (1986), *The Collected Criticism and Essays Volume 1: Perceptions and Judgments, 1939–1944*, Chicago: University of Chicago Press, pp. 5–23.

—(1954), 'Abstract and Representational', incl. in O'Brian, ed. (1993), *Volume 4: Modernism with a Vengeance, 1957–1969*, Chicago: University of Chicago Press, pp. 186–93.

—(1955), 'Review *of Piero della Francesca* and *The Arch of Constantine*, both by Bernard Berenson', incl. in O'Brian, ed. (1993), *The Collected Essays and Criticism, Volume 3: Affirmations and Refusals, 1950–1956*, pp. 247–53.

—(1960a), 'Modernist Painting', incl. in O'Brien, ed., Vol. 4, pp. 85–94.

—(1962a), 'After Abstract Expressionism', incl. in O'Brian, ed., Vol. 4, pp. 121–34.

—(1964), 'Post Painterly Abstraction', incl. in O'Brian, Vol. 4, pp. 192–7.

—(1967), 'Complaints of an Art Critic', incl. in O'Brian, ed., Vol. 3, pp. 265–72.

—(1972), 'Necessity of "Formalism"', *Art International*, October, pp. 105–6.

Harskamp, J. T. (1980), 'Contemporaneity, Modernism, Avant-Garde', in the *British Journal of Aesthetics*, Vol. 20, No. 3, pp. 204–14.

Heidegger, M. (1975), 'The Origin of the Work of Art', incl. in *Poetry, Language, Thought*, trans. A. Hofstadter, New York: Harper and Row, pp. 15–87.

Henry, M. (2009), *Seeing the Invisible: On Kandinsky*, trans. S. Davidson, London and New York: Continuum.

Hildebrand, A. (1994), 'The Problem of Form in the Fine Arts', incl. in *Empathy, Form, and Space: Problems in German Aesthetics, 1873–1893*, ed. H. F. Mallgrave and E. Ikonomou, Santa Monica: Getty Center Publications Programs.

Hintikka, J. (1975), 'Concept as Vision: On the Problem of Representation in Modern Art and in Modern Philosophy', in *The Intentions of Intentionality and Other New Models for Modalities*, Boston: Reidel Publishing Company.

Hopkins, R. (1998), *Picture, Image and Experience: A Philosophical Inquiry*, Cambridge: Cambridge University Press.

Hourcade, O. (1912), 'The Tendency of Contemporary Painting', incl. in Fry (1966), p. 74.

Johnson, G. (ed.) (1993), *The Merleau-Ponty Aesthetics Reader: Philosophy and Painting*, Evanston, IL: Northwestern University Press.

—(2010), *The Retrieval of the Beautiful: Thinking Through Merleau-Ponty's Aesthetics*, Evanston, IL: Northwestern University Press.

Kahnweiler, D.-H. (1920), 'The Rise of Cubism', incl. in Fry (1966), p. 159.

Kant, I. (1998), *The Critique of Pure Reason*, trans. P. Guyer and A. Wood, Cambridge: Cambridge University Press.

Krauss, K. (1985), *The Originality of the Avant-Garde and Other Modernist Myths*, Cambridge, MA: MIT Press.

Lewis, M. (1980), 'Hintikka on Cubism', *British Journal of Aesthetics*, Vol. 20, No. 1, pp. 44–53.

Lindsay, K. C. and Vergo, P. (eds and trans.) (1982), *Kandinsky: Complete Writings on Art*, London: Faber and Faber.

Locke, J. (1974), *Essay on the Understanding*, Vol. 1, London: Dent and Sons.

Long, R. W. (1995), *German Expressionism: Documents from the End of the Wilhelmine Empire to the Rise of National Socialism*, Berkeley: University of California Press.

Lopes, D. (1996), *Understanding Pictures*, Oxford: Clarendon Press.

Lyotard, J.-F. (1991), *The Inhuman*, trans. G. Bennington and R. Bowlby, Cambridge: Polity Press.

Marion, J.-L. (2004), *The Crossing of the Invisible*, trans. J. K. A. Smith, Stanford: Stanford University Press.

Merleau-Ponty, M. (1964), 'Film and the New Psychology', in *Sense and Non-Sense*, trans. H. Dreyfus and P. Dreyfus, Evanston, IL: Northwestern University Press.

—(1964), *The Visible and the Invisible*, trans. A. Lingis, Evanston, IL: Northwestern University Press.

—(1974), *Phenomenology of Perception*, trans. C. Smith with additions by F. Williams, London: Routledge & Kegan-Paul.

—(1993), *The Merleau-Ponty Aesthetics Reader: Philosophy and Painting*, Johnson, G. (ed.), Evanston, IL: Northwestern University Press.

—(2004), *The World of Perception*, trans. O. Davis, London and New York: Routledge.

Mondrian, P. (1987), *The New Art, The New Life: The Collected Writings of Piet Mondrian*, ed. Holzmann, H. and James, M. S., London and New York: Thames and Hudson.

Nancy, J.-L. (2005), *The Ground of the Image*, trans. J. Fort, New York: Fordham University Press.

Nash, J. (1980), 'The Nature of Cubism: A Study of Conflicting Interpretations', *Art History*, Vol. 3, No. 4, December, pp. 435–47.

Nietzsche, F. (1967), *The Will to Power*, trans. W. Kaufmann and R. Hollingdale, London: Random House.

—(1974), *The Gay Science*, trans. W. Kaufmann, New York: Vinatage Books.

O'Sullivan, S. (2007), *Art Encounters Deleuze and Guattari: Thought Beyond Representation*, London: Palgrave Macmillan.

Rampley, M. (1999), *Nietzsche, Aesthetics and Modernity*, Cambridge: Cambridge University Press.

Ranciere, J. (2007), *The Future of the Image*, trans. G. Elliott, London and New York: Verso.

Raynal, M. (1913), 'What is Cubism', incl. in Fry (1966), p. 130.

Ridley, A. (2007), *Nietzsche on Art*, London and New York: Routledge.

Riegl, A. (2004), *Historical Grammar of the Visual Arts*, trans. J. E. Jung, New York: Zone Books.

Riviere, J. (1912), 'Present Tendencies in Painting', incl. in Fry (1966), p. 76.

Rosenblum, R. (1961), 'The Abstract Sublime', *Art News*, February, pp. 38–41, 56–7.

—(1975), *The Northern Tradition of Romantic Painting: From Friedrich to Rothko*, London: Thames and Hudson.

Rothko, M. (2004), *The Artist's Reality: Philosophy of Art*, New Haven and London: Yale University Press.

Ruyer, R. (1952), *Neo-Finalisme*, Paris: PUF.

Sandler, I. (1970), *The Triumph of American Painting: A History of Abstract Expressionism*, New York: Harper and Row.

Taylor, C. (1990), *Sources of the Self: The Making of the Modern Identity*, Cambridge: Cambridge University Press.

Wechsler, J. (1975), *Cezanne in Perspective*, Englewood Cliffs, NJ: Prentice-Hall.

Werth, L. (1910), 'Picasso', incl. in Fry (1966), p. 57.

Wölfflin, H. (1950), *The Principles of Art History*, trans. M. D. Hottinger, New York: Dover Publications.

Wollheim, R. (1980), *Art and its Objects* (*2nd edn*), Cambridge: Cambridge University Press.

—(1987), *Painting as an Art*, London and New York: Thames and Hudson.

Wood, P. (ed.) (1999), *The Challenge of the Avant-Garde*, New Haven and London: Yale University Press.

Yohe, J. (ed.) (2002), *Hans Hofmann*, New York: Rizzoli.

Young, J. (1995), *Nietzsche's Philosophy of Art*, Cambridge: Cambridge University Press.

Zepke, S. and O'Sullivan, S. (eds) (2010), *Deleuze and Contemporary Art*, Edinburgh: Edinburgh University Press.

Index